HUNTER-KILLER
SQUADRON

HUNTER-KILLER SQUADRON

Aero-Weapons • Aero-Scouts • Aero-Rifles
Vietnam 1965–1972

Matthew Brennan
Editor

PRESIDIO

Published by Presidio Press
31 Pamaron Way, Novato CA 94949

Library of Congress Cataloging-in-Publication Data

Hunter-killer squadron : aero-weapons, aero-scouts, aero-rifles,
   Vietnam 1965–1972 / edited by Matthew Brennan.
        p.   cm.
   ISBN 0–89141–394–4
     1. Vietnamese Conflict, 1961–1975—Personal narratives, American.
   2. Vietnamese Conflict, 1961–1975—Regimental histories—United
States.   3. United States. Army. Cavalry, 9th. Squadron, 1st.—
History.   I. Brennan, Matthew, 1946–
DS559.5.H86   1990
959.704'342—dc20   90–7649
                                                                CIP

Printed in the United States of America

To two Air Cavalry troop commanders: Major George Burrow for his unassuming bravery, and Major Frank Stewart for his compassion. They are men.

CONTENTS

ACKNOWLEDGMENTS

This book ends my efforts to add my squadron's significant contributions to the history of the Vietnam War. It would not have been possible without the assistance of a few very special people. John Hazelwood (a squadron pilot) gave me much needed encouragement and provided addresses of 9th Cav helicopter pilots. Colonel Robert Litle, executive director of the First Cavalry Division Association, supported me throughout this effort.

My wife, Sally Oliver, endured another enforced period of widowhood and assisted greatly in proofing each story and rewriting my awkward sentences. Adele Horwitz, editor-in-chief of Presidio Press, never failed to provide encouragement and sound technical advice.

They will always be remembered and deeply appreciated.

INTRODUCTION

"Hunter-Killer" says it all. Especially in the later years of the Vietnam War, these teams of one LOH (Light Observation Helicopter) down low and one Cobra as high bird scoured the countryside on missions called "search and destroy." There are few stronger images of that war than an LOH skimming over the treetops with a gunner's machine gun blasting a long tongue of tracers from the rear compartment, or a Cobra nosing over to dump rockets on a target. We called them Pink Teams, but other units called them hunter-killer teams. The reason is apparent from their method of operation and the staggering toll they took on the enemy. This book isn't just about helicopter attack teams, but they were the essence of the way we fought the Viet Cong and NVA. The title fits the teams and the Air Cavalry troops that first spawned them as such devastating instruments of destruction.

Every combat veteran comes home from the war with the great war novel hidden somewhere in his diary, or etched deeply in his memory. I am one of the lucky ones. It took twelve years, and a lot of rejections, before my story was published.

After it was, I began thinking about the other men from the 9th Cavalry who still had their stories to tell. We were a special unit. Any small group of men who kill more than one-half of all the enemy soldiers claimed by a war's premiere fire brigade (the 1st Air Cavalry Division), and start all of its major contacts, have a lot of history to share. The first twenty-eight stories appeared in *Headhunters* over three years ago.

I thought that was the end of it, although many important battles weren't covered there, and very few pilots had contributed. But the stories kept arriving, in writing or on tapes, and I realized just how

1

much had been missed. Here are more stories from all ranks and all years, and this time, they include many pilots. Most importantly, the veterans from the last years are now ready to talk.

These two books provide the most complete history of a single combat unit in Vietnam, from a soldier's point of view. They are important because of this, their time span, and because they tell the story of the first, and most famous, assault helicopter squadron in the history of warfare.

I covered the organization and operations of the squadron in detail in the introduction to *Headhunters*. Here I will provide only a short overview. A Blue Platoon was the infantry platoon of an Air Cavalry troop. It was used for ground recon missions and the rescue of downed air crews. A White Platoon was the scout unit in a troop. It had ten OH-13 helicopters, or later in the war, ten LOHs. The scouts did what their name suggests, flying low and slow and scouting for signs of the enemy. A Red Platoon was the gunship unit in an Air Cavalry troop. It consisted of ten Huey helicopters, or later in the war, ten Cobra helicopters. The Huey gunships, with their two door gunners, also flew low and slow in the early years. When the Cobras assumed the gunship role, they became awesome fire support platforms with their 40mm grenade launchers, miniguns and seventy-six rockets.

White ships first flew in pairs called "White Teams." Gunships first flew in pairs called "Red Teams." Later in the war, a White ship was combined with a Red ship to make the famous "Pink Team." In addition to the three Air Cavalry troops (Alpha, Bravo and Charlie), there was a ground recon troop (Delta Troop). It had three "Rat Patrol" platoons that used jeeps mounting machine guns and recoilless rifles, and small trucks carrying a mortar squad and an infantry squad.

It was my personal experience that the majority of people who served with the 9th Cav came home dead or wounded. A full tour was the exception, not the rule. It couldn't have been otherwise, considering the dangerous missions that the squadron routinely conducted. We often operated in areas that other units, even other 1st Air Cav units, went out of their way to avoid. This doesn't take away from them in any way. It was just the nature of our "work."

This is my last writing on the war, and I am satisfied that the effort was worth it. Here are some powerful stories about combat in Vietnam and its neighboring countries. As always with the 9th Cav, they tell about the beginnings of major battles. The squadron's mission was to start battles. Most importantly, they give you a firsthand view of helicopter warfare by the men who fought it with such uncommon day-to-day heroism. Read, understand, enjoy, and always keep a place in your hearts, America, for your Vietnam veterans. They were a generation's bravest sons.

1. THE HOSPITAL BATTLE

(Infantryman, Bravo Troop, 1965)
*Specialist **Steve Yarnell** only had a few months left in the army when he went over to Vietnam with the Cav. Here he tells about early operations and the ground battle that started the Ia Drang Valley campaign.*

In February 1963, I left Loogootee, Indiana, to join the army. My training took me to Fort Knox for Basic, and eventually to Fort Benning for jump school. From there I was assigned to the 101st Airborne Division at Fort Campbell, Kentucky. I was with the 101st for about fourteen months and didn't like the unit. I was happy when my request for a transfer came through and I was assigned to another airborne unit at Fort Benning. When I arrived at the fort, I explained to a first sergeant that I just wasn't happy being Airborne anymore, and he arranged a transfer to the 11th Air Assault Division that same afternoon. They needed people, and it sounded new and exciting.

The relaxed atmosphere in 11th Air Assault surprised me. I was relieved to see people with hair on their heads, instead of the shaven heads of the Airborne. Officers actually talked with enlisted men, something that just didn't happen at Fort Campbell. The commander of my new unit was Col. John B. Stockton, a colorful person to say the least. He strutted around in a cavalry hat with the crossed sabers. He even had his own charger and that damned mule named Maggie.

One day, Colonel Stockton decided that he wanted a drum and bugle corps, and when no one volunteered, a major picked about seven volunteers. Unfortunately, I was chosen and ordered to learn to play the drums. The soldier standing next to me was told that he would learn to play the trumpet. He said that he had no idea what a trumpet looked like, and the major said, "That's all right. You're going to learn." It was a real fiasco, but the drum and bugle corps did function after a few weeks of practice.

We played reveille every morning and retreat in the evenings, and people hated us because we sounded so awful. We were laughed at, heckled, jeered and threatened. The harassment suddenly stopped when it was announced that the drum and bugle corps would no longer have to pull guard duty, and we were off after Retreat on Friday evenings, until Monday morning. After that, people who had once insulted me began asking if there was any way that they could take my place. The answer was, "No way." It was one of the happiest days of my life when they disbanded the damned thing. A rifleman shouldn't be made to play drums, not even for a colonel.

We trained hard every day and I really enjoyed being in the army for the first time. We did a lot of rappelling out of helicopters.

In August, we boarded the troop ship *William S. Darby* for the long trip through the Panama Canal and across the Pacific Ocean. It was a sickening, overcrowded mess. We slept in narrow hammocks stacked four or five high, and it seemed like the guy above you always had his hind end stuck in your face, and you had your hind end stuck in somebody else's face. It was unbelievably hot below decks, and the smell would just knock you down. MPs patrolled the decks at night to keep us down in the hold.

When we arrived off the coast of Vietnam, the local people came out to us on boats. We were told that we weren't going to need our plastic shower shoes anymore, so we tossed those, and other useless things, overboard. There were hundreds of pairs of shower shoes floating on the water, and the Vietnamese were collecting everything as quickly as they could get to it. If I remember right, General Westmoreland was there that day on the beach.

Planes flew us to An Khe. It was a muddy place with brush-clearing crews and pup tents all over the place. The first night, another soldier and I dug a hole and tried to keep dry. I had guard duty that night and I have never been so frightened. It seemed like every bush out there was moving. We had jeeps lined up at intervals to provide illumination if we were attacked. I was lying right next to a jeep and didn't think that was such a great idea, because the lights would give our positions away.

I'll never forget how cool and calm First Sergeant Morrison was in those first days. He was like a father figure to all of us and made us feel a lot safer. Sergeant Ortez, a veteran of the Korean War, was our platoon sergeant. Leading us was a man whom I admired tremendously, Capt. Jack Oliver. He was a stocky fellow of average height and I made an effort to stay as close to him as I could. He was a talented, stern, no-nonsense soldier who cared about his men. When we were on patrols, he was constantly reminding us to be careful, to watch out for explosive or crossbow booby traps, and not take chances.

I got more than my share of warnings and they made me feel good. Every time he got on my ass, it showed that he was watching and really cared about my safety. He watched over all of us, and we all looked up to him. Captain Oliver was always careful to know exactly where we were. It seemed like he had a map in his hands all the time.

We started the patrols in September 1965. I was fascinated by the gorgeous scenery, by the beautiful mountain streams and by those giant trees whose thin roots rose out of the ground and reached above our heads. They were spooky looking trees, like something out of a fairy tale or a horror story. Those patrols were like walking through an enchanted forest.

The Vietnamese in the mountains were different from those in the town of An Khe. The city people were merchants and vendors. They sold, among other things, hot Cokes and luggage made out of cut beer cans. I remember in particular a "Black Label" suitcase. The people in the mountain hamlets were impoverished and timid. Most of the villages had only old men, women and those beautiful little children you just wanted to reach down and hug. We knew that these people were farmers by day and Viet Cong by night, but I was impressed by their curiosity and genuine politeness.

It seemed like we walked continuously, every day, seven days a week. It rained like hell every night and we stayed wet through the whole month of October. Once they tried to resupply us with C-rations by helicopter and couldn't even find us under the canopy. I realized then how much trouble we would be in if we were attacked and needed some quick help. We wore stateside fatigues and leather combat boots, and my boots literally rotted off my feet. I took a strap off a Claymore mine, put the mine inside my shirt, cut notches in my heel and tied it to the boot. Our feet stayed so wet for so long that anyone in the platoon could reach down and scrape away the flesh from their toes. The meat on our feet would come away in strips. Mosquitoes and leeches were another problem. It was a depressing and exciting month, in spite of the fact that I was terrified.

One vivid memory from that month was of sitting in the helicopters as they orbited at 2,000 feet, waiting for the Air Force to blow the hell out of one of those villages. It was great to watch each jet make a run and then do a victory roll at the end of it. When they came in with bombs and rockets, the sound was deafening. I still hear that thunderous roar. It was a beautiful sound and a frightening one. Every time I hear a jet at low level, I remember that scene.

Our first major contact came to be known as the "Hospital Battle." Word reached us in the helicopters that the NVA had been sighted and we were going down and going in. We jumped from the choppers as quick as we could, and could already hear a lot of sniper fire. Spec-4 Don Perrichon and myself were on point with Captain Oliver behind us, to our right. The fire got heavier as we got deeper into the woods. Then Captain Oliver tapped me on the shoulder and pointed to a man in black shorts. He was trying to camouflage himself with two large banana leaves, one in each hand, as he moved farther into the woods.

I knew what the captain wanted me to do, but I pulled the M-16 to my shoulder and shot over the man's head. Captain Oliver gave me a long stare for about three seconds. It seemed a hell of a lot longer. I come from a big family and had never hunted back home, and I just didn't have it in me at that moment to kill an unarmed man. The captain motioned for me to keep moving forward.

About twenty to thirty NVA were killed in the first contact. They say the creek, I called it the ditch, ran red with blood that day, and it did. It was one of the most eerie sights that I have ever seen. At that point, we laid out the dead in rows of four. I remember one NVA that another soldier and myself had picked up. His left foot came off and the blood was still pumping over my hand. I thought that he was dead, but he was staring at me. We had taken some prisoners who were very sick from malaria or wounds. They were all very young, except for one older man who looked Chinese to me. I was put in charge of nine of them.

After the first round, we picked up a lot of weapons and supplies. I collected two 7.62mm pistols for myself. I was picking up surgical instruments and drugs when we came under serious fire and scattered for cover. Everyone was caught with his pants down. I wanted to get back to the safety of the ditch, but the fire was so intense that I couldn't move, so I laid where I was with the left side of my face in the dirt. I kept hearing this zinging, buzzing, popping sound by my right ear, and then noticed that the ground was being dug up about eight inches in front of me, and bushes and weeds were being snapped off. I was in the middle of a cross fire. Some of the bullets were coming from behind me. I shouted for our guys to stop firing. They couldn't move, either. Just a few feet in front of me, I could hear the North Vietnamese talking to each other and shouting orders. I began raising my rifle above my head and firing short bursts in that direction, without raising my face out of the dirt.

Someone to my right shouted that we needed a grenade in there. I liked grenades and figured it might as well be me. I pulled the pin on one, and then it dawned on me that I would have to get up on one knee to throw it. I began thinking about my brothers, especially my brother Keith, who was wounded in Korea. If only he was there to tell me what to do. It just wasn't going to be my day. I tried to put the pin back in the grenade, but my hands were shaking so bad that I couldn't do it. Finally, I said, "Goddammit! Here it goes!" I popped up and threw the hand grenade as far as it would go, just missing some tree branches that would have sprung it back on me. It took forever to go off, and when it finally did explode, the blast almost tore my head off. That stopped the talking and I began to crawl toward the ditch. At that point, it dawned on me that this had now become a fair battle. I had a gun, they had a gun, and I would have to fight to survive.

The ditch was only about twenty-five feet away, but it seemed to take a lifetime to get there. I tumbled in and crawled down it like a snake. I saw McTyre from Bravo Troop, sitting on an ammo can in the creekbed under a big tree. A machine gun was chewing up the tree, and bullets were dancing down the trunk, blowing off chunks of bark and wood. I shouted to warn him and he looked up at the tree, raised his butt off the can, moved it over about three feet and sat back down again. I said to him, "What the hell are you doing, Mac?"

He said, "There's nothing you can do. You can't stick your head over the top of this ditch without getting it blown off."

He was right. Bullets were just riddling the front bank of the ditch. All we could do was raise our rifles over the edge of the ditch and fire quick bursts. I crawled down the ditch to the left about twenty-five yards past McTyre, and came to the body of a dead North Vietnamese soldier in full uniform. He had been shot and fallen in. I shot him again to be sure that he was dead. I came to a point where I thought it would be safe to stick my head up over the bank and saw a very tall NVA a few meters in front of me. He was mad, and was standing next to a tree, screaming at other people that I could not see. I pulled up my rifle without even aiming and shot him in the right side of the chest. I could hear the bullet hit him. He dropped like a rock. As soon as that happened, I jumped back down into the ditch and crawled toward Mac, because I knew they were going to come after me and kill me for what I had just done.

I couldn't find Captain Oliver, and that was like having my umbilical cord cut. I finally found Staff Sergeant Johnson. He told me that we were under fire from all directions and there was nothing to do, except stay in the ditch and fight back. He said, "Just fight until you can't fight anymore." That sounded depressing as hell.

It seemed that they were moving in on us and the fire was getting closer, so I headed in a direction that I thought might be safe, toward where we had been stacking the captured equipment before. I crawled on my stomach as fast and as quietly as I could until I was staring down the barrel of an M-16 held by Spec-4 Ramon Charles. He was as confused as I was.

We moved off together until we came to a Specialist-4 Diamond from Delta Troop who was wounded in the face and couldn't see. We pulled him along with us. Next we heard loud cursing and screaming in English, and came to a soldier from Delta Troop who had been shot through the shoulder. He was pissed, talking about what the army could do. He was also giving our position away. I finally told him to shut up and get down. It was a pitiful scene.

Charles saw an enemy soldier to our right that I couldn't see, so I started crawling in that direction. I was so exhausted by this time that I don't know how far I crawled. I leaned up against a small sapling to rest. The next moment, there was a crashing through the trees above me and a big wooden crate of ammo smashed down about two feet away and made a hell of a noise as it dug into the ground. It figured. First I was getting shot at by the enemy, and now almost killed by our own ammo resupply. I crawled back over to Charles and the wounded man, and we kept on moving in search of somebody else, anybody else. I looked down at the souvenir pistols in my web gear and threw them as far as I could throw them. I did the same thing with a wallet full of ID papers from the prisoners that I had been guarding earlier. I didn't want them on me in case I was taken prisoner. I wish that I had known the outcome of the battle, because I would like to have those pistols now.

We finally reached Sergeant Ortez, who was standing beside a tree with a miserable look on his face. He asked me who was dead and I told him I didn't know. He was saying, "Oh, my God! My boys! My boys!"

I walked on by him and came to Colonel Stockton. He was screaming on the radio at the pilots to land and start evacuating the wounded. He was pissed, and was using some pretty heavy language.

A silence suddenly fell over the jungle. I hadn't noticed before, but the 2/12th Cav had air assaulted in and attacked the NVA. I worked my way back to where I had come from. Sniper fire was starting up again. I found Captain Oliver in the ditch. In front of him were a lot of dead and wounded North Vietnamese. One of the badly wounded jumped up to run and I shot him. I crossed another creek and came to an NVA who looked like a bullet had taken off the top of his head. As I approached him, Captain Oliver screamed, "Yarnell! Yarnell! Watch that son of a bitch! He's not dead!"

I said, "I believe he is, sir!"

I had a fixed bayonet and Oliver told me to stick him to be sure. I poked him in the shirt without penetrating the skin. The man rolled away. He had a potato masher grenade in his hand, but was probably too weak to use it. I kicked it away from him and started pulling him by the shoulder, and he went into one of those Vietnamese bowing routines. I searched him for papers and took him prisoner. He surely had the strength to pull the trigger, if he had wanted to do so. The captain had saved my ass again.

They pulled us back for extraction. There was a scramble in the PZ to be the first one on the helicopter and out of there. It was a great feeling to hear the *"Whop-whop-whop!"* of those chopper blades as they pulled us out. I finally felt that I could let my guard down a little bit. First Sergeant Morrison came out to greet us with a sad look on his face, but he gave us words of encouragement and pats on the shoulders. It was good to see him again. We talked about my good friend Jimmy Hoover from Delta Troop, who had been killed out there. Within a half hour, we were out on guard duty, and I was one paranoid son of a bitch.

I was evacuated with malaria a few days later. By the time I was well enough to go back to Vietnam, my time in the service was over and they sent me on home. Being back in the snow-covered winter of Indiana was a shock to me, and I felt bad about being there. I often thought about Captain Oliver and my friends in the troop, but never mustered the courage to go back. There have been many times when I wish that I had gone back into the army and returned to Vietnam. I never thought that anything could make me feel as good as the day I first got my jump wings at Fort Benning, but that was before I became one of the original members of Bravo Blues. I have accomplished a few other things in my life, like going through college and having a wonderful family, but being in the Bravo Blues is my proudest memory.

2. MY PRISONER

(Scout Pilot, Bravo Troop, 1965–66)
David Bray was a scout pilot in the days when H-13s went on missions in pairs. The Cav ran head-on into the 3d NVA Division in the early days of 1966, and the enemy troops fragmented to escape. After hunting little groups of soldiers for a while, Bray got tired of all the killing and decided to take a prisoner.

Early in February 1966, B Troop, 1/9th Cav, received orders to move into the Bong Son area and support Operation Masher, which was then under way. Charlie Troop had preceded us by three weeks and had already suffered more than its share of casualties. As our formation of H-13s, flying at 2,000 feet, neared Bong Son we could see several downed aircraft burning or being rigged for sling-loading back to An Khe. Artillery strikes were pounding targets along a coastal valley, and air strikes were taking place north of our final destination, the village of De Duc, which was code-named LZ (Landing Zone) Dog.

Squadron elements were set up on the edge of De Duc. A dirt airstrip had been carved out between two Buddhist temples. The Cav was well represented by lift companies, medevac units and infantry battalions. The "pod" modular operating room that was carried by a flying crane was there, too. The fighting would be bloody, and it would be needed.

Our infantry platoon had arrived ahead of us, so our gear was waiting when we landed. As soon as we touched down, a team of scouts was needed to move out north to screen for ground units that were engaging elements of the People's Army of Vietnam (PAVN). Capt. Jerry Leadabrand (my section leader) and I took the mission. His observer was Spec-5

Paul Bechburger, the son of a Marine general and the best chopper gunner in our squadron. Spec-4 Melvus Hall volunteered to accompany me. Hall shared the irreverent sense of humor of Flip Wilson, as well as his looks, but when he was not clowning around he was a good man in a firefight. It didn't take long to learn that there would be no humor on this flight.

We took off and climbed to our fighting altitude of five to ten feet off the deck, and immediately began to receive fire from hidden NVA and VC positions. As close as we were to the ground, they never got a second shot at us as we flew ahead to our assigned area. Near the southern edge of the battle area, which was a large scattering of villages, a Huey was burning and artillery fire was exploding. We circled to avoid flying through the artillery fire, but could see immediately that our mission was pointless. Our job was to locate the enemy and maintain visual contact "at all costs," which we usually did by placing fire on the enemy to make them dig in until we could call infantry, artillery or air strikes on them. But up here, the enemy was standing and fighting toe-to-toe with our troops.

There were so many NVA below us, most in khaki uniforms, but many in black pajamas, that it was impossible and senseless to attempt to give a spot report. All we could do was draw their fire and duck. I felt like a deer on the first day of hunting season. Every place we turned we were under fire. As long as we were over a village thick with palm trees we were all right. They couldn't get a clear shot at us. Dashing between villages was something else again. Without cover, we could only cross rice paddies, zigzagging and praying, while Paul and Melvus emptied magazine after magazine of 5.56mm from their M-16s in the direction of the enemy. Passing over one village, I could see several NVA crouching in the midst of a herd of cows and shooting at us. Making a fast 180-degree turn, I fired two rockets at them and kept going without waiting to see if I had hit anyone.

Leadabrand and Bechburger were having things pretty much the same way. We were generally flying together, but in no sense were we in formation. That would have been too dangerous for the second chopper and one of us would have gone down for sure. Passing over one coconut palm, I could have sworn I saw a man look into my eyes from less than twenty feet away. I thought for a moment that I was hallucinating, but Jerry and Paul had seen him, too. They made a fast pass, and Paul blew him and his AK-47 out of his treetop and into lullaby land.

About eight small villages were arranged around a large central rice paddy, and the paths between them crossed like spokes on a wheel. It was several hundred yards across this hub, and as we crossed it, I pointed my rockets toward any spot where I thought machine guns would likely be hidden. There were gun emplacements bordering the hub on all sides, but as low as Jerry and I were, firing at us would place machine-gun fire into the neighboring villages, so they held off with the heavy stuff. We only had to face sniper fire as we crossed back and forth.

Off to our left we could see a couple of downed Hueys inside the paddy. Strangely, just as I reached the center of the hub, I noticed an old lady, standing almost dead center and casually planting rice. Still zigzagging, I looked back over my shoulder at her and tried to figure out what she was doing. Was she crazy or just determined not to let the war interfere with her schedule? Glancing again at the burning Hueys, it dawned on me what she was doing out there. I turned back.

"Shoot that woman, Hall!" I yelled. Hall had been busy on his own side of the chopper and hadn't seen her before. He looked at me as if I had gone crazy. So we passed her without firing and I zigzagged around the paddies, dodging sniper bullets, while I filled him in. "She has a 360-degree view over the trees around the villages, Hall!" I yelled, "The machine gunners are watching her and when she sees Hueys coming, she faces them and they concentrate their fire over that spot. That's why so many are down around here. She's a goddamned weather vane for them! Shoot her!"

Hall gave me a thumbs up and I turned to make another pass, but Jerry and Paul had caught on to her and had already put her down. For some reason, as I again passed our burning Hueys, I couldn't feel anything but relief at the old woman's death.

As we approached the edge of the village ring, I saw a machine gun nest just ahead of us. "Get the coordinates, Hall," I shouted, but as he reached for the map, I made an uncoordinated pedal turn to avoid fire and the wind sucked the map out of his hands. At first, knowing that our map had many positions marked on it, we felt that we should try to retrieve it, but an attempt at landing near the machine gun nest to get it back nearly got us killed. We decided that they knew where we were anyway and got the hell out of there.

About this time, I got the H-13 over the trees of a village, to relative safety. A violent shaking reaction took hold of my body, and the chopper must have been a blur as my hands and feet shook on the controls.

Since it was my practice to weave back and forth over treelines to keep myself as poor a target as possible, this added shaking could only have made us harder to hit.

Jerry radioed me that it was time for us to get the heck out of there, and I went to join him west of the village. He cut cross-country in a straight line, but I would have none of the straight-line flying. I weaved back and forth over the treeline that bordered our right side, and using my peripheral vision to fly with, watched the ground below. Under one tree, as if it were a Sunday afternoon, casually stood a young man wearing Italian-style shoes (they were very popular with Vietnamese teens), wraparound sunglasses, neatly creased wash-and-wear slacks and a sport shirt. His hair was in a ducktail and his left hand was against the palm tree. He was looking down, as if the helicopter only twenty feet over his head was no concern of his.

He sported the cool young punk look that movies used to portray during the 50s, only this guy had a problem that concerned me. Like a crutch, he held a rifle muzzle down under his right arm, and as I darted away still looking back over my shoulder, I watched him prop it against the tree and attempt to get a bead on me. I was counting the distance, and as soon as I was 300 feet from him, the point at which a rocket would arm itself, I made a violent left pedal turn with the chopper, stabilized it for just a second, and squeezed off a rocket. I don't know if I hit the well-dressed young sniper or not, but the tree he was leaning against snapped forward and fell when the rocket hit it at ground level.

We arrived back at our refueling point at De Duc and there I ran into CWO Eddy Scott, a friend and classmate of mine from flight school. He was flying a scout ship for Charlie Troop. They had taken a lot of hits. He told Jerry and me to stay at altitude in the De Duc area, since there were so many NVA that our mission was pointless, anyway. As shaken up as the four of us from Bravo Troop were, we could not have agreed with him more.

Back at our bivouac area, we parked our H-13s and shut them down. As I started toward the place where I would set up my pup tent, I looked back and saw Paul Bechburger lean back against the bubble of his chopper and have a violent case of the shakes, just as I had earlier while airborne. I was thankful that my shakes had come where no one could see me.

After a few days of toe-to-toe slugging it out with the Cav's various elements, the NVA melted away into the hills. Groups of two, three and four would endeavor on their own to hide wherever they could, until the time came for them to reassemble elsewhere. It was at this time, in my opinion, that the 1/9th scouts did their best work. As the NVA broke up and headed for the hills, Col. John Hemphill's 2/12th Cav, "Wild Joker," went in pursuit. We were often sent to support this crack infantry unit on one of its missions. We began flying real search missions again, not just the "Let's see how many people can shoot at us today" type stuff we had experienced the first day.

We would slip up and down the hillsides, always moving horizontally along the face of the mountain. This kept us from being targets on most flights, and we began to be very efficient executioners, a role we took no real pride in. I had mixed feelings about this, but as bad as it was, it was better than leaving NVA alive to attack American troops somewhere else. Often, our orders for the day would be: Find NVA in this or that area for the Blues to pick up for interrogation. We would drift along the hillsides, following trails and literally looking under big rocks until we could find several NVA huddled on the ground, trying to hide. We would then radio back to headquarters as we backed off far enough to arm our rockets.

Orders would be, "Wait, we'll check it out." Then the bad news would come. "Wrong area, Fixer. Are they making any signs of surrender?"

We would reply, "Negative."

They would come back with, "Kill them if you can."

"For God's sake, can't you send someone out to take them prisoner?"

"There is no one available. Shoot them."

"Roger," we'd reply, and then we'd cut loose. Sometimes they would understand and take off running for cover, but usually, they would just crouch in their holes until our rockets hit. Common sense told me that the senior officers were right. It was foolish to send a platoon after every little band of three or four armed men, but it took all the rationalization I could muster before I could accept what I was doing.

Dealing death as we were, I found myself wondering about an afterlife and religion as I had never wondered before. I never did come up with answers, just more questions. Distasteful as it was, looking back, I can see that what we did was the only way to counter the NVA tactic of breaking into such small units that there was no effective way to go after them. It was as if a deer hunter took aim at a nice fat buck and the animal was able to turn itself into molecules of gas, disperse, and reassemble again elsewhere.

During this period, known as Operation Masher, I landed at Colonel Hemphill's CP (command post) to see what sector he wanted me to concentrate on. One of our crew chiefs, a young fellow from New England, was flying observer for me. Colonel Hemphill greeted me with his usual, "How are you today, Mr. Bray?" and held out his hand. I'd always salute before shaking his hand and did so today. A second lieutenant stood nearby while the S-3 briefed me on the area they wanted checked out. I paid the lieutenant no mind, until the colonel came over and introduced him to me. "Mr. Bray, this is Mike Durkin. He just got out here to the field with us today and would like to see some action. Would you mind letting him fly a mission with you?"

I didn't even look at him as I nodded my head—I was making notes on my map—but I told the colonel that as long as my observer didn't mind sitting one out I'd be glad to take him along, providing he could read a map. As we took off, I told Mike what we had been finding and advised him to watch rocks and bushes as we passed them. As I spoke, we covered perhaps a mile. Now, on my left, I saw a stack of immense boulders, larger than houses, that formed a natural cave. In the cave's mouth, peacefully watching the fighting in the valley below, sat an NVA next to his black rubber-tire sandals. I almost dumped the chopper bringing it to a hover, and at that moment had an inspiration.

"There's one now, Lieutenant. Want to take a prisoner?"

Startled by my sudden maneuver, Mike could only stammer, "Uh, oh, yeah, sure." The NVA ran inside the cave.

Leadabrand and Tex Helms were several hundred yards ahead of us and I transmitted, "We have a North Vietnamese cornered and we're going to land and pick him up." Then I turned off the radio before Jerry could order me to stay airborne.

We found a small, terraced rice paddy a couple of hundred feet downhill, and I made a quick circle to make sure we weren't landing in the midst of a bunch of Charlies. Confident that I had one of Hemphill's well-trained infantry officers along to protect me from my poor marksmanship, I handed Durkin my M-16 and pulled my .45. He was carrying no weapon and my observer had taken his with him. I felt more confident with the .45 (on which I had barely qualified) than I did with an M-16, which I had only fired one-handed from my door hinge, where it was mounted. After all, Hemphill's troops were the best I'd worked with, outside of our own Blues.

Before starting up the hill, I took one M-34 WP (white phosphorous) grenade from the case between the seats and placed it in the pocket of my flak vest. We looked for a trail leading up to the cave, and as I tried one, the grenade slipped down between two large rocks. Not about to stand on my head trying to get it back, I went to join Mike as he yelled that he had found a trail. As we started up the trail, I noticed Mike studying the M-16.

"What are you doing?" I asked.

"How do you work this damned thing?" he replied.

"What do you mean, 'How do you work that thing?' For God's sake, you're an infantry officer, aren't you?"

"Negative, Chief. I'm a frigging medic." He flipped up his collar so I could see the insignia, and for the first time, I really looked at him. Above his big, wise-ass grin sat a pair of Coke-bottle glasses that projected his eyeballs to the front of his face. He continued, "I've never even held one of these things."

Still, I felt committed. I showed Mike how to work the safety, and had him set it on semi as I prayed to myself that this dumb stunt wasn't going to get us killed. I was tired of shooting people, and besides, Fred Carll and Sergeant Butt had taken a prisoner the day before. They were both small. When they saw an NVA waving at them with a rifle pointed down over his shoulder and a safe conduct pass in his hand, they landed, sat him on Butt's lap and flew him in. This would give me a chance to play catch-up, if it worked. As Mike and I headed up the twisted trail, Jerry and Tex kept passing back and forth overhead, which is probably what saved us from getting our butts shot off. I acknowledged their presence with a casual wave, but would not look directly at them, because I knew Jerry would be waving me back toward my chopper.

We reached the cave entrance and Mike covered me as I went inside. We jumped from one boulder to another as we went down successive levels. When we'd reach a corner, the lead man would cover while the second man would move to the front and proceed. Just as Mike passed me for the second time, I saw our quarry slip beneath a rock at Mike's feet. I yelled, and Mike, who had balls even if he didn't know how to shoot an M-16, reached down and dragged the NVA out by his ankles. He was a pitiful figure, this "warrior from the north." He had a two-day growth of beard and could not have been over five feet tall, yet it was obvious that he was several years older than either of us.

We looked around the well-lit comfort of the shelter. From where we were now, we could see another trail leading out of the cave, which was open in back. Our man obviously had friends nearby. There were three hammocks that had been fashioned out of parachute flare material. Near them was a bundle of khaki uniforms, a large leather saddlebag, a gunnysack half-full of potatoes, and about a dozen rolls of cooked rice. I thought that we might have hit the jackpot. The division commander had recently announced that anyone capturing a battalion commander or higher would receive a two-week R&R in Japan. Still, looking over at this little man crying his eyes out, I realized that we had no great leader here. Mike grinned at the guy and made as if he was going to shoot him, and he cried even louder. I told Mike to knock it off, and handed him some sack cord and had him tie the man's hands behind his back.

Through the spaces between the overhead rocks, I could see Jerry and Tex passing back and forth over us. Below the place where we were tying up the POW, there was a natural square hole, about eight feet across, that opened to the dirt below. Around the perimeter of this hole, below us and between the rocks, were several shelves. I was certain that the man's friends and his weapons were hidden there, but I was not about to go down after them. I looked at the prisoner, pointed down in the hold and fired my .45 into the dirt below. "VC! VC!" I shouted, but all the poor man did was nod and cry louder. I told Mike to start loading up with their stuff, and motioned for my prisoner to sit while I did the same.

Looping the rice rolls over our shoulders, just as the VC carried them, we picked up the saddlebags, potatoes and uniforms. I shredded the hammocks with my bayonet, then Mike and I began the trek out of the cave. I was not used to carrying heavy packs and not used to the humidity. I found it a real effort to pick up the POW, lift him up four feet to the next higher rock, and then pick up the other stuff and climb up after him. Mike had his hands full, since he was carrying most of the supplies out of the cave. At one point, the POW tried to indicate an easier way, but I was having none of that and we kept working our way out. Once we exited the cave, I saw a very relieved Jerry Leadabrand giving me a big smile as he passed overhead.

I was bushed. We'd walk a few steps and I'd grunt loud and the POW would stop in his tracks and wait while my chest heaved, and sweat poured off me. Arriving back at our paddy, where the H-13 was still running, we made our POW lie face down while Mike covered him and I went to radio Jerry for a Huey to pick him up. Jerry told me that one was already on the way, and suggested that I move our chopper so it would have more room to land. I moved the chopper, then Mike and I sat down to wait for the arrival of the Huey.

As it touched down, two troopers ran over and picked up the POW and placed him aboard. Another trooper grabbed the supplies we had brought out with him. As this was happening, a very gung ho major, wearing a steel pot and pack suspenders, came running out of the Huey and shouted at Mike and me, "I saw another one over here as we landed! Charge!" He took off down the trail at a dead run. I looked at Mike. "Do you think we ought to follow that silly son of a bitch?" Mike gave me that wise-ass grin once more. "Not me. I'm a frigging medic."

Note: This story first appeared in *Soldier of Fortune* magazine. Reprinted here with permission of David Bray.

3. CHU PONG LANDING

(Lift Pilot, Alpha Troop, 1965–66)
*Warrant Officer **Joe Salamone** watched this day begin like any other in an air assault troop. It didn't end that way. This is a wrenching story of A Troop's disastrous landing at the Chu Pong Massif. The colonel mentioned in the story was not a 9th Cav officer.*

Dawn did not come to the jungle in a rosy pink glow, but was announced by a few shrieking birds perched high enough in the trees actually to see first light. The men who had been in various stages of rest, or in some cases, anxious lonely terror, began to stir in the cool grey light, and raise harsh morning noises that blended into a single, unharmonious symphony. First, there was coughing and spitting, followed by belching and the sound of noses being blown. There was the splatter of water striking the ground amid drowsy mutterings and low oaths, the rattle of steel against steel, and the slapping and flapping of clothing being shaken out. The noise of crew chiefs pre-flighting their helicopters blended with the whining of a jet engine with its ignitors clicking away, as a Huey left early to scout the landing zone. The sounds of an air assault troop rising to greet the day are like no other sounds in the world.

Once again we were operating out of a Special Forces camp when our scouts returned with information that they had seen an enemy force estimated at two battalions near the landing zone. As usual, our mission was to search and destroy, or at least start a firefight and then call reinforcements in to help out.

But this day would be different, for better or worse. The colonel called together all the platoon leaders and requested that we take our

21

only three squads of riflemen, land in the area, take a prisoner and return. I remember objections being made that we should wait until our whole squadron was there, because even the scout ships admitted that you couldn't begin to see the total enemy force under the thick cover. The colonel insisted, since time was of the essence, so we made plans to depart with the promise that an air strike would be made.

Our scouts marked the area with smoke, but unfortunately, the Air Force bombers missed the target by a mile. We were already airborne near the area, and it was too late to turn back. Skip Blanton and I always took turns on making the approach and landings, and the first today was mine. I was leading the formation, and made the approach and landing in an area large enough to accommodate our four choppers. The area seemed secure. The rifle squads jumped out with no immediate contact, as was sometimes the case.

I lifted off and as I was clearing the trees in front of me, I saw countless VC within the treeline, moving in and out like the fangs of a dark, ferocious animal. The sight was unbelievable. "We should be dead," I thought. "Why didn't they shoot while we were on the ground? As vulnerable as we are, why aren't they shooting now?"

Those thoughts kept going through our minds. Skip radioed down to the riflemen about the extremely dangerous position they were in. Insanely, they radioed back that they had a prisoner and had not encountered any large resistance.

Then it happened. For the riflemen on the ground, making their way back to the LZ where we had dropped them off was only a trip of a hundred yards, but under fire it probably seemed like a hundred miles. The infantry RTO (Radio-Telephone Operator) called us on his PRC-25 and requested immediate extraction. During his transmission, I could hear the explosions and rifles cracking over the radio, then his voice faded. He was dead. I turned the formation back and landed in the midst of the firefight. Bullets were flying everywhere; concussions from mortars rocked us. In the middle of all this, I could see riflemen pinned down by automatic fire and unable to make it to the choppers. My crew chief "Mac" (Jerry McNinch) was firing away with his sidemount M-60 at VC. They moved along the treeline in slow motion, as if they were on opium.

Gunships overhead were rolling in and out of daisy chains. I heard some of the ships running out of ammo and using pistols. The gunship platoon leader was actually throwing C-ration cans at the enemy. Skip

Blanton and I couldn't figure out why we weren't being targeted when the ships on either side of us were taking hits. Were they saving us for last? There was nothing we could do at this time, so we lifted off, made a sweeping two-mile turn, and returned to the LZ with hopes that the surviving infantry would be closer and still able to get on board.

Skip was flying this time and he said to me, "Joe, one of us is going to die today. Be ready and take the controls if it's me. I don't want to die in this LZ. Just get me out of here." Those were the last words he ever spoke.

Coming closer to the ground, I wanted him to land closer to the edge, closer to the infantry. I was directing him when I observed a few stumps below us. I stuck my head out the window and motioned him down with my left hand when I felt the strange, unusual attitude of the chopper. I turned to look inside the cockpit and saw Skip slammed back against his seat, slumped down, with his left leg straightening out and pushing full left pedal. His hands were off the controls. Within seconds, the chopper began to roll over and backward to its left side.

I grabbed the controls. The only way to recover was to pull full pitch, disregarding engine limitations. It was an automatic instinct with no thought process involved. The only thought was to get my friend out, and not roll into the chopper beside us and kill us all. I remained clear, then realized that this machine of mine was being heavily hit. The adrenaline was flowing and my mind was in a fog. I could hear the *"Tick-tick!"* of rounds punching through sheet metal, and watched holes appearing in the windshield, and the circuit breaker panel being blown out. I thought that I was hit, but then it didn't matter. Then my thought process changed. I had to get the infantry out also.

Instinctively, I hovered back over to the trees. Riflemen were huddled behind fallen tree trunks. They made their break and came on a run. Meanwhile Mac was trying to remove Skip from the front seat to help me fly out. I told him to give the infantry cover fire first, then take care of Skip with the help of the few riflemen. In front of me, the dark shadows of the treeline opened up like a Christmas tree full of lights. The riflemen were on board and everyone was firing full auto. The smell of gunpowder was intense.

I used everything I had and made a maximum performance take-off. The VC below us were pointing rifles straight up, and their fire was poking holes all through us. Skip slumped again on the controls, and I yelled to Mac to move him out of the seat, or at least hold him upright.

Still noises of *"tick-tick!"* were coming through, then the windshield turned red. I thought that I was hit in the face or eyes, but found out that one of the riflemen had been hit in the neck with a .50 caliber bullet. His blood was being sucked up between the seats and sprayed on the windshield. We could barely fly at a fast hover over the trees. Priority was to keep flying and not crash into the VC regiment below us.

We made it back to the Special Forces camp with a running landing, hydraulics shot out, and skidded to a stop and shut the engine down. Then the realization set in that someone had tried to kill us. While it's happening, you don't think about it. You don't have the time. But now I was consumed by a deep, yet controlled rage; an anger so fierce that I probably could not have expressed it in words, even if I had tried.

4. OPERATION MASHER

(Gunship Door Gunner, Charlie Troop, 1965–66)

Mike Kelley was trained as a helicopter mechanic and didn't know much about Vietnam until he got orders to go there. He was soon flying at treetop level over the mountains of the Central Highlands with veterans of the Ia Drang, and trying to prove to them that he had what it took to be a door gunner.

I joined the army in August 1964, about two months after graduating from high school. I wanted a little excitement in my life, and the army didn't let me down. After basic training, I was sent to Fort Rucker to attend three different helicopter mechanics' schools, and there I met many soldiers from the 11th Air Assault Division who were retraining in aviation specialties. The 11th Air Assault would later become the 1st Air Cavalry. One of my extra duties at Fort Rucker was KP, and I served in a mess hall for the warrant officer candidates who were undergoing a grueling flight training schedule. Seeing what they were going through made me glad to be an enlisted man. I would later serve with some of those same men when they were pilots in Vietnam. After my training was completed, I was assigned to the 3rd Helicopter Company at Fort Belvoir, Virginia. The company flew CH-21 cargo aircraft and made VIP passenger flights for the Pentagon. In addition to those duties, I was also a crew chief on an OH-13 training helicopter.

In November 1965 I received orders for the 1st Cavalry Division in Vietnam. I arrived in Vietnam the following month, as one of the first replacements to be assigned to the 1st Cav after the Ia Drang Valley campaign. We were quickly processed at the Camp Alpha replacement depot, and the next morning, a C-130 cargo aircraft took us to the Central Highlands, a short flight away to the north.

The C-130 landed at An Khe on a rainy, overcast day. About twenty replacements stood in the rain for about an hour, until a beat-up truck arrived to transport us to the Cav base camp. As we left the airstrip, we passed a bunch of foxholes full of weary, dirty infantrymen. They had poncho canopies over their holes with M-16 rifles and M-60 machine guns protruding out from under them. It didn't look very comfortable. I looked at them and they stared back, and I wondered what they thought of us in our shiny new uniforms.

We followed Highway 19 through the Central Highlands shanty town of An Khe. Beside the highway was a river with a lot of army trucks parked in the shallow water. The Vietnamese kids had a business enterprise where they washed the trucks with small gasoline-powered pumps while the soldiers lounged around and sipped soft drinks. None of the soldiers had weapons, and that struck me as unusual in the middle of a war. We took a right turn off the main road and entered Camp Radcliff.

It was still raining, and we had missed the last meal of the day, so they gave us pup tents and blankets and we pitched a little camp in an open field behind the replacement center tent. Our clothes and the contents of our duffle bags were soaked through, but we tried to get comfortable as we watched flares swinging down over the perimeter and listened to outgoing artillery rounds. It was the scariest night I spent during my entire tour. We just didn't know what to expect.

The next morning, we ate and were given assignments, and then a truck took us along the perimeter road and dropped us off at our units. The truck stopped at the headquarters of the 1/9th Cav, and the driver told PFC John Youst and me to get off. I had no idea what kind of outfit it was, but figured it was some kind of maintenance unit.

We reported to the squadron orderly room and were assigned to Charlie Troop. The troop first sergeant gave us a brief introduction and then took us to meet the troop commander, Capt. Billy Nave. The captain told us what the troop had already accomplished in Vietnam, and said that they were shorthanded in the weapons platoon. We were going to be gunship crew chiefs.

We slept in a large squad tent. Most of the other men there were gunship crewmen who liked to brag about their adventures in the Ia Drang. I'm sure they were trying to impress us that they were combat veterans, and that we would have to prove ourselves before being accepted.

I remember two of them very well. One was Spec-4 Clark, who had received a Bronze Star in the Ia Drang Valley. He used to sit on his cot with a knife and a sharpening stone. He would spit on the stone and tell us war stories. We were in awe of him and his exploits. Clark was a totally fearless man, and I never did figure out whether he was the ultimate professional soldier or just completely crazy.

The other soldier was "Chief," a big Indian kid. He would come over to John and me and threaten to kick our asses the first time we screwed up in combat. Not only did we have to worry about being shot at, but here was a six-foot Indian who was waiting for the chance to kick our asses.

Chief had a mortal fear of being shot in the butt. Ironically, that's what happened to him later on. It must have been a painful wound, but his departure made us new guys breathe easier.

The first couple of days were spent at the "Golf Course" helipad, learning what was required of Huey crew chiefs and door gunners, especially the maintenance and repair of gunship weapons systems and the M-60 door guns. It was during this time that I got my introduction to hard labor, 1st Cav style. We would go down in the evening as a group and clear the perimeter of the Golf Course, using axes, picks and shovels, cutting trees and brush and moving rocks. After I had been there about a week, we prepared for a 3d Brigade operation called "Clean House." This was the last major 1st Cav operation in 1965, and took place in the Soui Ca Mountains east of An Khe and north of Highway 19.

We flew along Highway 19, down the An Khe (Gia Mang) Pass toward the coast, and passed over rugged terrain and the wreckage of several aircraft strewn over the mountainsides. I particularly remember the silver wreckage of an A1E Skyraider that glittered in the sunlight as we flew over. This was my first flight in a Huey gunship with its open doors, flying along at eighty knots at treetop level. The wind was blowing in my face, I had a machine gun across my lap and ammunition piled all around, and I was exhilarated. It was hard to believe that it was happening to me. I had envisioned working in the rear echelon, and now this.

The brigade had set up its operations base south of the highway, and our troop parked its choppers there and awaited developments. As we waited at the brigade laager, a large firefight broke out a few kilometers north of us and the noise echoed across the valley floor. A few minutes later, a large "eagle flight" of about fifty Hueys filled the sky. They crossed the valley and descended toward the place where the firefight had been. We left the brigade CP and flew the short distance to the Advanced CP on the edge of the battle. While the pilots were being briefed, a couple of us decided to have a look around.

Soldiers were stacking piles of captured enemy equipment: AK-47s, old French rifles, RPGs, rice sacks filled with loose ammunition, and all sorts of other military gear. When we tried to move in closer to get a better look, they told us to stay away. The firefight started up again in the distance, and we were pretty close to where the action was happening. About twenty-five meters from us was a group of about ten or twelve VC suspects with their hands tied behind them. They had no shirts or sandals, were tied to each other by ropes around their necks, and they were frightened. The infantry guards were tired, wet and dirty and they looked like they meant business. It was easy to see why the prisoners were so afraid.

The pilots returned from their briefing and we lifted off to join the battle. I was flying with Tichnell, a combat-experienced crew chief, and the idea was to give me on-the-job training as a crew chief/door gunner. A short distance from where we had been, there were young infantry guys about my age, sprawled out on the ground. They must have just arrived on the eagle flight, and most of them looked scared. Unlike me, they would soon be locked in close-up combat with the enemy. I leaned out the door and gave them the "thumbs up" sign. Some of them returned it, but others just stared at us.

Mine was the lead gunship as we flew recon over a village and saw people running under the palm trees below us. My ship was carrying quad-60 machine guns and small rocket pods, while our back-up ship was a "hog" with forty-eight rockets. We had orders not to fire unless we could confirm enemy contact, so we dropped down to treetop level.

We flew over peaceful village scenery for a while, then went north along old railroad tracks through a picture postcard kind of region with lush green foliage, palm trees, and mountains in the distance that gave off a bluish haze. It looked like Hawaii, like the kind of place you'd want to build a high-rise condominium.

When we ran low on fuel, the pilots decided to turn back south so we could refuel. We were about twenty-five feet above the treetops, flying parallel to the railroad tracks, when I heard a loud *"crack"* toward the back of the ship. The copilot began shouting that we had taken a hit, and banked the aircraft so that my side was facing the ground. My stomach felt like it was somewhere in my chest, and my heart pounded with excitement and fear. Palm trees were flashing by my open door like pickets on a fence. Everyone was yelling at the same time—both my pilots, the crew chief, and the two pilots on the other ship.

The gunship rapidly climbed into an attack position for a rocket run as the pilot shouted to the crew chief, "Do you see them? Do you see them?"

Tichnell pointed out the door to a cloud of white smoke rising through the palm trees next to the railroad tracks. He had dropped a grenade at the instant we took fire. He yelled to the pilots, "Right there! Right there! You see them little bastards? Get closer so I can rake the shit out of them!"

We went into a turning, diving motion and came up parallel to the target. I turned in my seat and watched the crew chief spring into action. He opened up with his machine gun, and the sound was deafening. Hot brass flew everywhere in the cabin and it stung when it hit. I watched the line of tracers chewing up the dirt, crossing the tracks, moving through some bushes and then striking around a small white hut under the palm trees.

One VC appeared to be in charge, and he was passing out rifles from a box or a hole in the ground. Tichnell walked the tracers from the head VC and along a line of men who were waiting beside the hut. He mowed them down like a carnival sharpshooter, and they toppled over, one by one. The inside of the aircraft was now full of spent brass and gun smoke. We pulled up so our chase ship could go in with door guns.

As we climbed away, the copilot told me to provide covering fire with my M-60. I stuck the machine gun out the door and squeezed the trigger. It fired about eight rounds, then jammed. As I frantically tried to unjam the gun, we got ready to make our rocket run. The copilot was pretty well pissed off at me, and began shouting, "Goddammit! Goddammit! Get your head out of your ass!" I was shaking with fear, and felt like a real loser.

Underneath the palm trees beside the hut was a slit trench where some of the Viet Cong were hiding and firing at us, so Tichnell grabbed some Willy Peter grenades. He dropped the grenades as we flew over the trench. They hit the palm trees and exploded into white, flowery air bursts. The Viet Cong soldiers took some hard casualties from that run.

When we landed back at the base, the copilot jumped out of his seat and really tore into me. He accused me of freezing up on him, then he stormed off with the other pilots. One of the old-timers, a crew chief named George Gavaria, came over and put his arm around me. He told me not to worry about it, that it had happened to all of them. It wasn't the first time it had happened and it wouldn't be the last.

He wanted to check the weapon to see if he could fix whatever had caused it to jam. He pointed the machine gun muzzle up and set it down on the floor of the cabin, and, *"Bang!"* Everybody jumped through their shirts. The round went through the roof of the cabin. The pilots ran back, led by the copilot, who proceeded to tear into me again. The older crew chief explained that he had caused the gun to fire, but the copilot kept shouting at me. Finally he left me in my embarrassed state. I was trying to prove myself to those veterans, and I felt that I had failed them.

A short time later, we flew another mission in the same area. We came to an open field and saw a guy stand up. The pilots flew back for a closer look to determine if this was an innocent farmer, and the Vietnamese opened up with an automatic weapon. I was looking past the other crew chief at the guy blasting away at us. The crew chief opened up and walked his tracers across the field toward the VC. Both of them were firing at each other point blank and missing.

I heard this muffled popping noise, our machine gun stopped firing, and I heard some yelling and moaning. The crew chief was leaning against the bulkhead with his machine gun dangling in front of him. The gun had an assault pack on it that held one hundred rounds, and a bullet had hit the pack and exploded the ammunition inside into the crew chief's face and body. There was blood everywhere.

The copilot began yelling for me to get the first aid kit. I just sat there, frozen in panic. The copilot unbuckled himself, crawled back over his seat, pulled the kit from the bulkhead and gave the man first aid, cursing me all the while. Bloody gauze was unraveling and blowing out the door of the gunship.

It took only a few minutes to fly back to an aid station at the brigade base. The pilot came barreling in and flared about twenty feet from the tent. The rotor wash blew dirt and debris everywhere and almost knocked the tent down.

A couple of medical men ran out. One was a captain, and he ran up to the left side of the helicopter and started screaming at the pilot that this was a restricted area. Everything was sterile there, and the dirt was going to cause them a lot of problems. The pilot was a major. He sat there and took it, and apologized to the doctor over and over again. The doctor told him there were a lot of men with open wounds there, and to get "that God-damned helicopter out of here at once."

The major hovered the aircraft back to the C Troop area. I felt pretty good about seeing someone else get chewed out. As soon as we landed, the copilot was on me again, calling me a Number One screw up. He called me everything in the book before he finally left. I felt that I had completely, miserably failed, but the major came over and said, "Son, don't worry about it. You've got plenty of time to learn and you will be a good crew chief. Do the best you can, and eventually you'll fit in."

It didn't do much to boost my self-confidence, but as the days went on and turned into weeks, I began to learn the job. With the older crew chief gone, I was on my own. My training was over and I was given a new door gunner who was as green as me. Each time we took fire, each time we made a rocket or machine-gun run, we got better, but my heart always pounded, and I was always afraid that we would be shot down. The story went that Charlie Troop had a gunship crew shot down, hung in trees and skinned by the NVA in the Ia Drang. I didn't want that to happen to us.

Flying at treetop level in a gunship, feeling the wind in my face and watching the rockets leave their tubes was exciting, but there was danger everywhere we flew. After the missions, the veterans from the Ia Drang would joke and laugh about what had gone on. I would lie on my cot and relive the events of the day.

I knew that the next day would just be a repeat, and I wondered how many times we could go out and do those things before something happened. I didn't want to end up like the door gunner on my first missions.

There were times when I prayed for a light flesh wound to get me out of that horrible, nightmarish world. They were out there, trying to kill me, and it was only a matter of time before I caught a bullet. The question I could never answer was if I would live or die.

I was now a combat veteran. After Operation Clean House, the troop headed back to An Khe. We pulled routine maintenance on the aircraft and got ready for the next operation. On New Year's Eve, we had quite a fireworks display. Everyone in the camp opened up with rifles and machine guns and fired into the air. Two days later, on 2 January

1966, there were more fireworks when the VC hit An Khe with mortars and a sapper attack.

The next day, we began flying cover for convoys moving west through the Mang Yang Pass for operations around Pleiku. It was during this time that a CH-54 Sky Crane crashed just east of the pass near An Khe. Mine was the first aircraft on the scene, and we found no survivors. We saw only one body in the smoldering wreckage.

We were slated to relieve Alpha Troop at Pleiku on 24 January, but in typical military fashion, we were sent in the opposite direction toward the coast. On 25 January, we flew down the An Khe pass once again and set up camp in an open, sandy area near Phu Cat along coastal Highway One. The 3rd Brigade was kicking off a big Army-Marine-ROK operation, "Masher-White Wing," that eventually involved the entire division.

There was an air strip near where we were located, and all day long, C-123 cargo planes would deliver supplies and troops. This was the main staging area for a hell of a large operation. We flew a lot of missions around Phu Cat, but didn't stir up much action. We took some ground fire in areas that were so rugged that it was impossible to insert the Blues. Our missions were more diversionary as the brigade prepared for the big push north to the Bong Son Plains.

On 28 January, a drizzly, rainy morning, we flew recon missions north along Highway One into the Binh Dinh Province, a very dangerous place, as veterans of the battles there well know. The weather there was another danger. It varied across the region and was always a hazard, especially in the mountains. Visibility was no more than three miles, and often only a hundred feet. The cloud level was low in the mornings and usually lifted by afternoon. Fog and mist hung over the mountaintops and in the valleys and made assisting the heavily engaged infantry forces a risky undertaking. There were times when we just couldn't help them.

On the first morning, we arrived over the village of Bong Son and flew low-level over the palm trees and the marketplace. Women were washing clothes and taking baths in the Bong Son River, and the pilots came back around to take a look at the naked women. It was one of the high points of the entire Bong Son campaign, at least for those of us who were on that helicopter. We headed farther north toward the new landing zone at LZ Dog, and passed a French railroad trestle bridge before setting down.

Dog was on a plateau area, surrounded by woods on the lower slopes.

The wreckage of aircraft was scattered through the trees. There was one Vietnamese farmhouse, and the farmer and his family were packing their belongings for evacuation from the plateau. The little man was waving his arms and yelling, trying to tell the American infantry that this was his home and he didn't want to leave. Soon they were gone and some infantrymen ransacked his hut. I still think about that farmer, and how he must have hated us after losing his precious home.

There was a Vietnamese graveyard at Dog, and a lot of helicopters taking off and landing. I went over to inspect the graveyard, and found an old, rusty piece of a French artillery shell sticking out of the ground. I kicked around in the dirt some more and came up with a fragment from a World War II pineapple grenade. We decided that there must have been some sort of big battle there. Before Masher was over, we would scatter a good deal of our own ordnance around the area for some future historian to find.

It started to rain, so we climbed inside the gunship. Out of the rain came a scout helicopter crew who climbed in and told us about the mission where they had just been shot down, then rescued by the infantry unit that they had been scouting for. We didn't have to fly that evening, but there was a big battle going on while we sat inside our gunship. Parts of three infantry battalions had air assaulted onto the Bong Son Plains and were locked in heavy combat with the Third NVA, Yellow Star Division. We flew a lot of missions the next day.

The first one I can remember was when an Air Force spotter plane accompanied us out to a valley to look for enemy troops. We had just returned from that flight and had settled down to relax when the pilots ran up the side of the hill and shouted that we had a special mission.

We slid the barrels of the quad-60s into their breeches, checked our door guns and buckled up. The pilots pulled pitch and headed south toward the Kim Son Valley. Near the bend in a big river was a village that was supposed to be enemy controlled. We did a low-level recon and received no ground fire, so it was decided to pick up a couple of people in the rice fields for questioning. This was called "Operation Snatch."

A helicopter swooped down and the crew grabbed two villagers, but just as they prepared to take off, the Viet Cong opened up with heavy fire from a treeline. We hit the trees with rockets and machine-gun fire. The Blues were inserted into the village and the VC withdrew from the area for a few days.

Later on, the village became hot again, and ground fire became quite common. One day we were told to take a division photographer over the area for an aerial surveillance mission. We made a couple of passes at about seven hundred feet while he took pictures. The thing that struck me was that the boxes of Polaroid film came from my home town, Cambridge, Massachusetts. Here we were, in the middle of nowhere, and there were boxes with my home town printed on them.

Then the local VC decided to take us under fire. The pilots banked the aircraft so that I was looking down at the river, and I pumped about two hundred rounds into the same old treeline. The photographer had never witnessed a firefight, and it really excited him. It reminded me of how I had felt on my first mission. He must have told quite a story when he got back to his unit.

Another significant flight was a rescue mission in the An Lao Valley. A couple of Special Forces Delta Teams had been inserted into the valley and made contact very quickly. The Cav was supposed to send in supporting infantry units, but most of the brigade was engaged in that big battle along the coast. The pilots came scrambling up to the helicopter, shouting that we had a red alert. Two gunships were soon airborne.

The valley was socked in with low-level clouds, and the pilots wondered how we were going to get in. Then one of them spotted a gap in the clouds, which allowed us to dive through and skim along the top of a mountain, almost dragging our skids in the treetops. We flew down the side of a mountain into the valley, and began to pick up the Delta Team transmissions. They weren't the standard military banter. A soldier was begging for help. "Please! You've got to help us! They're all around us! We're wounded and running low on ammunition! Please get us out of here!" He said it over and over again, and his fear gripped all of us.

The pilots circled around and around in the clouds while trying to keep from crashing into the trees. We finally saw smoke coming up from the mountainside and made a rocket run where the Green Beret told us to attack. After two more passes with rockets and door guns, the Green Beret told us to stop the machine-gun fire.

The bullets were hitting rocks and ricocheting back through his position. Our fire was able to momentarily stop the enemy.

An Air Force spotter plane arrived about that time, and we began a dangerous aerial ballet with two gunships and the spotter plane flying in the clouds over the treetops. We were relieved by another team of gunships, and just as we were ready to leave the valley, a flight of slicks arrived with a load of infantrymen.

We left the same way we had come—climbing up the side of a mountain and ascending through a gap in the clouds. The infantry landed at the base of the mountain and moved up to relieve the Delta Team. Only two Special Forces men survived that attack. The rest were left behind in the valley and listed as missing in action. The officer in charge of that operation was Major Charles Beckwith, later Colonel Beckwith of the ill-fated Iranian rescue operation.

We were all busy and involved in different missions, so even though John Youst and I were in the same platoon, we didn't get to see much of each other. There were so many routine things to keep us busy when we weren't flying. During the operation, my helicopter would pick up a bad vibration at any speed over eighty knots. I explained the problem to some of the experienced crew chiefs, and one of them, a tall, black fellow, got a roll of masking tape. We dropped the end of the rotor blade and he wrapped about an eighth of an inch of it around the leading edge. He told me that it would put the blades back into balance. I was skeptical, but it worked. Whenever the tape tore itself apart in the wind, we wrapped some more tape around the blade. The gunship flew that way for the rest of the Masher campaign.

We also had problems with mechanical failure. Once, we had just cleared the wire of Dog when the RPMs dropped off, the helicopter started to shudder, and we dropped toward the trees. The young copilot began to yell that we were going to crash. I braced myself for the crash as the branches began slapping against the skids. The copilot froze on the controls, and the pilot, an older warrant officer, had to give him a judo chop on the wrist to get him to release them.

Instead of dropping straight down, he tilted the helicopter so that the aircraft fell forward on its nose to gain forward movement and airspeed. We sort of slid down the hill, using the treetops as our slide. The aircraft stopped shuddering and regained its power, and we continued on with the mission.

It had been a compressor leak. The helicopters required a lot of mainte-nance and were supposed to have an inspection after every twenty-five hours. We didn't have the time for that, so we ran inspections every time we were on the ground. By the time we were finished with one round of inspections, it was time to start over again. It was almost like a dog chasing its tail. We were a team, and the pilots often pitched in to help with even the dirtiest maintenance jobs.

At one point in the operation, we were sent north on recons of some coastal villages. We found nothing, but saw medevac helicopters evacuating infantry casualties below us. It was in the same area that Captain Nave's helicopter was shot down and the crew evacuated as the chopper burned up. A number of helicopters were shot down or crashed in that coastal area, including a CH-47 Chinook, but we were lucky.

On another mission near the coast, we were sent to recon an area where one of the first B-52 missions of the campaign had hit. I remember the mission so well, because it had been hot at Dog and I was wearing only a T-shirt when we took off. We climbed to 1,500 feet over the area and just circled, and I nearly froze my ass off in the sudden cold. I bit my lips and tongue and prayed that any minute now we would drop down close to the ground. I always felt that it was safer over the trees anyway.

We finally descended to cover a Blue patrol through the B-52 strike zone. The NVA had been holed up in caves, in some sort of way station along the infiltration routes. They had all been killed by concussion from the 500-pound bombs, so the Blues collected a lot of souvenirs and intelligence items.

Back at LZ Dog, the Blues brought over some of their booty, like NVA star belts and rifles. There was a white rice bag with the clasped hands emblem of U.S. aid, and a message that said something like, "A gift from the people of America." The bag was filled with ammunition.

When I first arrived in Charlie Troop, the aircraft had yellow circles painted on the doors to show they belonged to the troop, but there was very little in the way of "nose art." The Blue Lift ships later had a set of aviation wings and the motto "Bushmasters," and some of them had a snake's head on the nose that looked something like a skull. A couple of the early gunships had a caricature of the Pink Panther holding a submachine gun.

After Captain Nave had one gunship shot up, he rigged up a D Model Huey lift ship as his personal gunship. He wanted me to paint something for him on the nose, but I put it off until the day he asked me if I would like to make PFC again. When I said, "No," he told me he wanted that painting.

I quickly painted a logo to his design. It was an egg-shaped circle with a light green background. A black magnet horseshoe emitted yellow rays that were drawing hot rounds up from the ground. The good captain had taken a lot of ground fire and quite a few hits in his day, so the logo sort of reflected his style. About a month later, he was killed in a mid-air collision at Tuy Hoa.

One night at LZ Dog, a small-scale firefight broke out in a mountain range over toward the An Lao Valley. A blacked-out, twin-engine plane flew over Dog and headed for the fight. This was a CH-47 minigun ship, known as "Puff the Magic Dragon." Long red tongues of tracers came out of the sky in thousand-round bursts, hit the ground and ricocheted off in all directions, like red splashes of Fourth of July fireworks.

It was an awesome sight that I witnessed several times while at Dog. When we heard the distant rumbling of the CH-47, all of us went outside to see the show. On another morning at Dog, I watched B-57 Canberra bombers hitting the same mountains with napalm canisters. The Canberras would release the bombs and then climb straight up into the sky, either for show or to avoid enemy fire.

It was a sight to see the napalm sliding along the ground and bursting into a bright orange flame that enveloped the jungle and the mountainsides. This would be followed by a cloud of dense black smoke. On still another morning, A1E Skyraiders made rocket runs against the mountains. The sound of the propellers reminded me of World War II movies.

The last mission of significance was in the Kim Son Valley, called the Crow's Foot. We had flown several missions during the day, back and forth over mountains with dense jungle, and didn't see a thing. Toward evening, there was a red alert.

The Blues had been dropped on top of a mountain and were sweeping down its slopes, trying to push any VC who were there toward a blocking force. The Blues had stopped about halfway down the mountain and decided to set up an ambush position and wait until morning to continue the sweep. They were soon under attack.

Every available 9th Cav gunship at Bong Son was alerted and sent out as part of the relief operation. We joined up with Huey hogs from the aerial rocket artillery, and I have never seen so many gunships in the air at one time—thirty to forty of them. We formed a huge daisy chain—an enormous aerial circle. First, we almost had a mid-air collision as we tried to fit into the daisy chain. Then enemy heavy machine guns opened up at us from the mountainsides.

We were there to take out the gun positions and deliver some heavy suppressive fire on the enemy, who had surrounded the Blues. As each helicopter came to a point in a saddle between two mountains, it would dive down and make a run with rockets and machine guns. Each gunship did this a couple of times. The tracers from the enemy antiaircraft guns were like long, flickering fingers of death.

It was the heaviest and most exciting mission that I was ever on. When we reached the point in the daisy chain where we began our diving runs into the saddle, a mountaintop was so close that you could almost reach down and touch the trees. If they had placed a machine gun there, or even a couple of AKs, we would have been sitting ducks. As we dived into the saddle, they were actually firing down on us from two sides. We took hits, but somehow didn't lose any aircraft. The intensity of the antiaircraft fire made me wonder how it was possible. We eventually returned to Bong Son, and the Blues held their positions throughout the night under intense attack. Two infantry companies were landed at first light. This was the beginning of a large operation in the Kim Son Valley.

These are my memories of the First Bong Son campaign. I continued flying with the gunships until I was assigned to the Aero-Scout Platoon. I finished my tour in December 1966, and was one of the lucky ones who went home.

5. IMAGES OF WAR

(Combat Photographer, 1966–67)
*Specialist **Robert Hillerby**'s "noncombat" training eventually led him to the Bravo Troop Blue Platoon. His experiences there constituted a rite of manhood that he has never forgotten.*

I was trained as a "Still Photographer," known in army terminology as MOS 84B20. The training never really emphasized the combat aspect of photography. At least, if it did, our class was largely unaware of it. Most of us in the Photo School at Fort Monmouth, New Jersey, thought of the job as a way to avoid the infantry. In 1966, staying far away from the infantry was of utmost importance, because large numbers of infantrymen were being kept very busy in Vietnam. In fact, my class had two Spec-4s who had been stationed with the 8th Infantry Division in Germany, and had decided that the prudent thing to do would be to re-enlist and get transferred to another branch. I guess we thought that the army would send everyone to Europe. Orders to report to Vietnam came as a surprise to most of us.

When I arrived at Oakland Army Terminal, one thing was immediately obvious—there was definitely something special about personnel assigned to the 1st Cavalry Division. They were immediately segregated from everyone else and sent on their way. I noticed the same thing when I arrived "in-country." Personnel assigned to the 5th SFG (Special Forces Group) or the 1st Cavalry were called out from the rest of the formation and processed immediately.

In late 1966, the 1st Cav was already a well-known unit, although I had no idea how elite this division really was. Furthermore, I had no conception of what the 9th Cavalry was really all about. When I arrived at "LZ Two Bits" for the first time, I didn't know that I was to become an adopted part of one of the most efficient fighting units in U.S. Army history. By that time, I had been along on several operations with regular infantry units. Some of these were major operations that involved multiple units and task forces.

The differences between the 1/9th and any other unit were more than significant, to say the least. I arrived at HQ B Troop, 1st Squadron, 9th Cavalry, with no particular expectations. It was just another assignment to me. After carefully scrutinizing me, most of the Blues decided I was not totally green, although I didn't know the first thing about air cav operations. They broke me in right. We made eight landings the first day.

The big difference in being on a combat photography team was that we were observing and recording the events as they occurred and trying to remain totally detached from them at the same time. For example, during an intense firefight, or when coming into a "hot" LZ, my primary concern was to position myself so that I could get the most photos with the least possible unnecessary movement.

The cavalrymen were a little apprehensive about accepting outsiders. This applied particularly to photographers, because many of the civilian correspondents would ask for a slick to carry them out at the first sign of danger. We were accepted because we shared the hardships and dangers of the Blues, and never asked for any special treatment. They knew that we had volunteered for this duty and they respected us for it. Later, I would become as suspicious of outsiders as they were.

My photo team consisted of myself and an eighteen-year-old from Cincinnati. Bob was new in-country and trusted me implicitly, mainly because I had already been on several operations prior to arriving at Photo Detachment A in An Khe. I told Bob that I preferred to stay in the field as much as possible, since we weren't hassled by the lifers so much out there. He was not excited by the prospect of spending much time in the field, but didn't argue the matter. We became close friends and learned to work together as a team. I would later save his life, and he would save mine, acts for which we only got a "thank you" from each other, but events that would change our definition of trust and friendship forever. We both had easygoing personalities and made friends easily, which was an asset in our job.

Our arrival at Two Bits was uneventful and went unnoticed by several Blues who were resting on cots and hammocks in the shade. We reported to the CO, our usual practice upon arrival in a new unit, and were told to get with one of the squad leaders and be integrated into the troop. As attached personnel, we were often allowed a great deal more freedom than those actually assigned to the unit.

We met all of the squad leaders, the medic and the interpreter (a Vietnamese soldier assigned to the troop). In most units, there is a handful of men who seem to have a pretty good idea of what is going on most of the time. These were the men you needed to know to get along, and we had just met them. When the squad leaders briefed us on the mission and how they operated, I knew at that moment that my life would never again be the same. Bob knew it, too—that at the tender age of eighteen, he had entered his passage into manhood.

Our missions were often reconnaissance-oriented, and that usually meant "hot" LZs (enemy fire). For some reason, Bob and I often ended up flying with the first bird, and the lead helicopter usually took the most ground fire. After landing, we would hook up with one of the squads and start shooting pictures. If we captured any enemy personnel, weapons, equipment or documents, we would begin photographing and writing caption sheets to go with the photos. The Blues were always understrength, so we usually ended up helping round up any indigenous personnel and then going back with them to help with questioning and/ or guarding prisoners. If we stayed in an area at night, we *always* helped by volunteering for a shift on guard.

One night after a shift on guard, I was exhausted and found a place to lie down next to a small pen where the local dinks shoveled all of their animal dung. There was a wall that was sort of U-shaped, and I decided to sleep beside it. Bob had already pulled his turn and was asleep, so I tried not to disturb him and others as I settled down for what was left of the night.

At about two in the morning, all hell broke loose. The night sky was bright with the explosive light, and the noise was deafening. I saw the location from which Charlie was throwing grenades, and watched tracers from the squad machine gun being fired up the hill. The gunner was one of the squad leaders, and he was screaming for me to get him more ammo. I thought that this was all a bad dream, rolled over and went back to sleep. The next morning, the only way any of the others could make me believe that we had been attacked was by showing me the pieces of poncho liners that had been blown high into the treetops above us. Fortunately, we took no casualties that night, due to quick reaction by those on duty and the fact that Charlie was outgunned and outmanned.

We regularly had to go back to An Khe to turn in film and resupply ourselves for return to the troop. The trips back out to the troop were always hard for me, because that was when we would find out about the most recent casualties. I remember that once we had brought back whiskey and the latest *Playboy* magazines for the Blues, and learned that the platoon sergeant had been killed while we were away. He had been in Korea and had served with the Cav on a previous tour in 'Nam.

He had gone up to check on a point man who was down, and caught an AK round between the eyes. The thing was, he is said to have fallen forward and hit the ground in a firing position. Sarge was well liked and respected by his men, and he died the same week that he was going home. It seemed like such a waste. Events such as these reminded us that even though we were only photographers, we were neither immune nor invulnerable to the indiscriminate death around us.

The primary mission of the photo team was always to record photographs for news releases, but we often received specific requests from the Department of the Army. It was the news coverage, though, that was our real bread and butter. There have been many times over the years that I have been browsing in a bookstore, only to see a photograph that I had taken a score of years earlier. There is one very famous photograph of a team of Blues jumping onto a rocky hilltop in the An Lao. I was crouched next to the photographer credited with that picture, and took one at the same time. To this day, I don't know if it is my picture or his.

Bob and I made it a practice to get as many "people" pictures as possible. I never met an infantryman who didn't make a big deal out of getting his picture taken. They would always ask, "You gonna put me in the news back home?" My answer, of course, was always, "Sure, man. As pretty as you are, you deserve to be on the front page!"

I can't give any explanations about the war, the soldiers, the aftermath or the problems it caused. However, I can bear witness that the 1/9th changed my life forever. I will never forget the men that I met there. I never knew the names of many of them very well, but I will never forget the faces, especially of those who died. I don't look at the pictures much anymore, but there are hundreds, maybe a thousand of them!

As I write this, I am looking at a photo that Bob took from behind me of a bird flaring into the PZ. The other Blues and I are anxiously awaiting the final moment when we can clamber aboard and feel the air buffeting our bodies as we lift into the peaceful calm above us.

6. NVOC NGOT BAY

(Grenadier, Alpha Troop, 1966–67)
John Wiegert writes about a Blue Platoon landing that started a major battle. He killed the crew of a heavy machine gun and won a Silver Star that day, and somehow manages not to mention those facts. Following his personal story is an amazing document—a summary of the troop's after action report.

October 2, 1966 is a day that many of the members of Alpha Troop, 1/9th Cav, will never forget. It had an impact on many lives. For some of us, it was the first taste of combat. For others, it was a test of their skills as soldiers. For still others, it provided career enhancement, not necessarily by choice. For some, it was the end of life. Those who died that day will never be forgotten. This story is one grunt's view of a given squad, on a given day, in battle at a place called Nvoc Ngot Bay.

We were assigned to Bong Son at the time. I was a grenadier in the infantry platoon, and carried an M-79 grenade launcher, a bag of 40mm grenades, four fragmentation grenades and a .45 caliber automatic. The job of the infantry platoon was to recon or scout an area. If there were signs to indicate large Viet Cong or North Vietnamese activity, we would be extracted from a landing zone and much larger units would be sent in.

Shortly after breakfast on 2 October, the shout to "saddle up!" came from the deep voice of P/Sgt. James Petergal. This meant it was time to put on combat gear, grab your weapon, and prepare to board a Huey helicopter for some sort of mission. Being a PFC and a nineteen-year-old draftee, I never knew where we were going, why, or for how long. That morning we were sent to recon Nvoc Ngot Bay, which is twenty miles north of Qui Nhon.

Our role as a recon patrol quickly changed when we got there. From the moment our helicopters landed in the LZ, we began hearing and seeing gunfire from gunships, scout ships, our platoon and the North Vietnamese. The firefight continued, and when we were later extracted we were still under fire. My squad leader, Sgt. Otis Davis, directed us into a series of large hedgerows.

I was staying close to Sergeant Davis and Spec-4 Ronald Mis, because they had been in previous engagements with the NVA and Viet Cong. Almost immediately, the enemy started shooting at us. I watched Mis fire into a foxhole and kill an NVA soldier. Being a grenadier, I could not fire at close range for fear of hitting some of our own men.

As soon as we tried to advance through the hedgerows, there was intense enemy machine gun and AK-47 fire. My whole squad hit the ground. I only remember seeing Sergeant Davis. Ron Mis was at least one hedgerow ahead of us, and the rest of the squad was somewhere behind us.

I was both scared and concerned about Mis. I used the grenade launcher to shoot over the hedgerows by jumping up, firing, and then hitting the sand and crawling closer to Mis. Within a short time, I had used up almost all my 40mm grenades and most of my hand grenades, with my fire directed by Sergeant Davis. I crawled to Mis and found him face-down in the sand.

I yelled to Sergeant Davis, ''Ron is dead!''

The sergeant tried to instill confidence in us by saying Ron Mis wasn't dead. He instructed another squad member and me to carry Mis back to him, which we did. We were still receiving fire and couldn't retreat, even with support from the gunships. Knowing that I was running out of ammo, I fired into an NVA bunker, reached in and grabbed an AK-47. I began throwing grenades into NVA positions and hoping for the best. Afterwards, I exchanged fire with enemy soldiers with my captured AK.

Sergeant Davis told me that we were leaving. We started to pull back with the support of a gunship firing furiously overhead. I soon found out that Ronald Mis and PFC Bobby Bryant were dead, and PFC Elie Medlin, our medic, was wounded.

We finally made it back to the LZ with our casualties, with a lot of help from the gunships. I was the last one from our squad to board the helicopter. I asked Sergeant Davis if there were any casualties in the other squads, and he told me, "Yes." PFC Doug Lueck had been killed. This made a bad day even worse. Doug had been a close friend, always with a smile, and he had made my tour go faster.

The platoon suffered three dead and three wounded. The enemy casualties were not important. We were extracted from a "hot" LZ and returned to Bong Son. The grim faces of the members of our unit who were not involved in the battle told me that they already knew what had happened.

The Battle of Nvoc Ngot Bay could produce many stories from many different angles. It certainly won't be forgotten by the soldiers who were there, or the families of the men who were killed. It was no doubt a revelation for many, and this is one grunt's view of what happened there.

This story is dedicated to all of the men and women who were killed during the Vietnam War, and especially the following servicemen whom I knew: PFC Douglas Lueck (A/1/9, KIA, 10/02/66), Spec-4 Ronald Mis (A/1/9, KIA, 10/02/66), PFC Robert Johnson (D/2/8, KIA, 03/01/67), S/Sgt Walter Dart (USAF, KIA, 06/06/69), and M/Sgt James Petergal (died of a heart attack on 06/30/89).

The above is an understated personal account of the beginning of a major battle. What follows is a condensation of the after action report from the same battle. It is unique, because it puts John Wiegert's story in perspective, and shows the complicated maneuvering associated with so many 9th Cav fights. It is an incredible story.

Operation Irving commenced on 2 October, 1966, in the area twenty miles north of the port city of Qui Nhon. Intelligence had pinpointed an area of NVA operations in the coastal plains between Highway One and the South China Sea. Alpha Troop's mission was to screen the Ngot Bay Area and peninsula, and maintain surveillance along the coastline. The action started at 0720 hours when the troop commander, Apache Six, joined two scout helicopters over the peninsula. At 0725, the scouts spotted three people with packs and weapons who were trying to hide. They opened fire, but the enemy soldiers apparently escaped. Apache Six then flew his gunship to the northern side of the bay, landed and captured a suspected VC who was running across a rice paddy. He was captured at 0730 hours, and was later found to be a Viet Cong sergeant. He told his interrogators that twenty VC normally operated in the area.

Five minutes later, the two scout choppers spotted seven men in green and tan uniforms with weapons and packs. Apache Six flew to the area, was fired on, and returned the fire. Three enemy soldiers were killed. He flew farther north and hovered over some rice paddies at twenty to thirty feet above the ground. Below him were five men in NVA uniforms with packs on their backs. They were crawling down a trench toward a bunker. The troop commander's door gunners opened up, then they marked the area with smoke for firing passes by two more gunships, including "Red," the gunship platoon leader. The gunships made two runs on the target and killed all five NVA.

Aerial reconnaissance had now determined that the enemy force was located in the village of Hung Lac (1) and to the south. At 0745 hours, Apache Six decided to put the infantry platoon on the ground to sweep through the village from east to west, then turn south and establish a blocking position. Elements of an infantry battalion, which had been scheduled to air assault into the area about noon, were alerted to be ready as soon as possible as a quick reaction force. Because of the proximity to possible noncombatants, artillery concentrations were registered with smoke rounds east of the village. A gunship made a machine-gun and rocket attack on the hedgerows close to the landing zone as the lift ships came in. The Blues were on the ground by 0830 hours. The two scout ships screened for the infantry platoon.

Ten minutes later, the 5th Squad on the platoon's left flank made light contact seventy-five meters west of the LZ. They killed one NVA soldier. The squad came under heavier fire as they moved into the hedgerows. In the exchange that followed, they killed four North Vietnamese soldiers and captured two more. Now they were pinned down by about nine automatic weapons and two machine guns. At this point, Apache Six flew back to Hammond to refuel and left Red in charge of the battle. Red and his accompanying gunship soon spotted two groups of NVA who were trying to escape from the area and killed seven of them.

While the 5th Squad was pinned down, the rest of the platoon continued moving into the hedgerows. The 3rd Squad (Wiegert's squad) now made the contact in which Spec-4 Mis was killed. Wiegert first attempted to knock out two .50 caliber positions with 40mm grenades and hand grenades, then he low-crawled to Mis and helped bring him back. He went forward again, and killed the two-man crew of a .50 caliber machine gun with his .45 automatic. Now he grabbed an AK-47 and opened fire on more NVA. Another .50 caliber machine gun, this one covered by a BAR (Browning automatic rifle), opened fire on the platoon.

Apache Six was back on station by this time, and located his ground troops by hovering over them. He discovered that every courtyard and field in and around the village was encircled by two or three deep trenches and hedgerows. Heavily armed squads of NVA were hiding in these positions and firing at the Blues. Others were crawling away to the west in an attempt to escape. Apache Six's door gunners fired machine guns and grenade launchers down into the trenches while he hovered at twenty feet over the top of them. They killed more than thirty NVA and destroyed two machine-gun positions. This relieved some of the pressure on the ground platoon.

Another Blue grenadier, PFC Lynn Gaylord, spotted a .50 caliber machine gun that no one else had seen. He stood up and ran from place to place until the crew opened fire. Gaylord was hit in the shoulder. His squad destroyed the machine gun with hand grenades. Two more bunkers were flanked, and the Blues tossed in tear gas grenades that drove an enemy squad into the open. They were cut down as they tried to run away. By this time, the Blues had confirmed killed about thirty enemy soldiers. Apache Six estimated that they were engaging 200 or 300 men.

Ten NVA were spotted trying to swim across a stream to the west of the village and gunships killed all of them. Two new scout ships arrived on station and began to fire on the enemy soldiers who still had the 5th Squad pinned down. They soon killed six more NVA and destroyed two machine guns. A Blue lift ship evacuated 5th Squad's one dead and two wounded a few minutes later under heavy enemy fire.

Apache Six returned to 3rd Squad (Wiegert's squad) and hovered down between the NVA and the Blues to draw enemy fire. The two new scout ships covered him. The squad had refused to leave its two dead and one wounded man behind, and Six's bravery enabled them to break contact and pull back. None of Apache Six's weapons were working as he hovered over to evacuate the wounded man (Elie Medlin). As the door gunners got out to lift Medlin aboard, the pilot saw one NVA to the rear of the helicopter and hit him with his spinning tail rotor. The helicopter was under heavy enemy fire, and four rounds hit the fuel cell, the hydraulic lines and the transmission, just before they got

Medlin aboard. They flew the aircraft 150 meters east to the LZ. Two .50 caliber holes were later found in the skids. A lift ship evacuated the wounded man a few minutes later.

Apache Six's gunship was unflyable, so he took control of the battle from the ground, until a new helicopter could be flown out to him. An infantry element had landed and was advancing toward the village. They were also under heavy fire, including mortar rounds that were being fired up at the orbiting aircraft. Two Alpha Troop gunships spotted the mortars and destroyed them with several rocket runs.

The two new scout ships spotted two more machine-gun positions that were still pinning down the 5th Squad. One of the scouts (Apache 15) was seriously damaged, but the crew managed to destroy one gun with a hand grenade and mark the other with a smoke grenade. Two gunships destroyed the second machine gun. Meanwhile, Apache 15 flew back east and crash-landed next to Apache Six's downed gunship. At 1050 hours, a gunship (Apache 27) evacuated 3rd Squad's two KIAs. The gunship escaped from the area while drawing heavy fire from two directions.

The Scout Platoon leader, "White," had his aircraft severely damaged a few minutes later. By 1105 hours, all the Blues were in the LZ and the prisoners were being tagged for evacuation. Chinooks extracted the downed helicopters under heavy fire five minutes later, while troop gunships made rocket and machine-gun runs on the village area. All troop elements were back at Hammond by 1230 hours. Apache Six returned to the village later in the day in a lift ship with one door gun to assist a pinned-down infantry platoon. He attacked the enemy with the one machine gun, and when that ammo ran out, with a .38 caliber revolver. The crew marked the target with smoke grenades for gunship runs. The NVA were so close to the friendly troops that no door guns could be used, but two gunships made three firing passes that silenced the enemy fire.

As a result of this action on the first day of Operation Irving, the 7th Battalion, 18th NVA Regiment, was found and attacked. The total body count was 320, and ninety-two of them came from Alpha Troop's actions before the quick reaction force even reached the contact area. PFC Wiegert received a Silver Star for his bravery that day.

7.   CHARLIE-CHARLIE

(Lift Pilot, 229th AHB, 1966–67)

Warrant Officer **Robert Sisk** *flew with the 229th Assault Helicopter Battalion. Here is an excerpt from one chapter of his new book,* Wings for the Valiant, *where he describes an encounter with a 9th Cav scout crew.*

Flying the CC ship was beginning to look more and more unattractive. Owen flew the Charlie-Charlie helicopter the next several days. He was flying twelve to sixteen hours a day. Doug Clyde relieved Owen as aircraft commander. I went to fly as Clyde's copilot a few days later. Clyde's regular copilot was on R&R.

We were orbiting high over a small village located in the northwest corner of the Bong Son Plain, watching the helicopters from our company assault the village.

A scout helicopter from the 1st of the 9th Cavalry had spotted a large number of North Vietnamese regulars infiltrating into the village from the mountains just west of the town.

There was an American artillery firebase about three-quarters of a mile south of the village. The general consensus was that the enemy force was going to launch an attack on the firebase after darkness had set in.

The battalion CO asked us to set down on the small hill where the artillery firebase was located. We landed and shut the helicopter down. The colonel, his sergeant and the battalion artillery officer grabbed their weapons and packs and started down the hill toward the village. We could hear firing between our troops and the enemy.

"Wait here for us. If we're not back by dark, fly back to Bong Son and come back out first thing in the morning," the colonel shouted as he disappeared over the hill. He was going to join with his men on the outskirts of the village and lead the assault on the North Vietnamese himself.

Clyde and I walked out to the highest point on the hill to watch the artillerymen blast the village with 105mm guns.

They had the guns depressed and were firing point-blank into the village. Every once in a while they would get a direct hit on a thatch house. The house would explode into bits and pieces and the burning material would be blown into other houses, setting them on fire.

I was sitting on a large rock watching the action. Clyde was squatting down just to my left puffing on a cigarette. I started hearing noises like a bee zinging by my head. *"Zzz-et, zz-et."*

"Clyde, I think we're getting shot at," I said, not really wanting to believe it.

"Na, I think we're out of range. I think it's just insects or bees or something," he said, still drawing on the cigarette. Just then a bullet smashed into the base of the rock, sending dirt and pieces of gravel flying. I fell backwards off the rock. I landed on the ground and scrambled on all fours for the backside of the hill. Clyde was already there, panting like a dog after a long chase.

It took several minutes to catch my breath. "If those were bees, that son of a bitch just had one helluva collision with that rock," I had to say sarcastically. We wandered back over to our helicopter and kept a low profile.

A half hour later, the 105 howitzers ceased firing. The small arms and automatic weapons firing increased furiously. I chanced another look. I duck-waddled back to the rock and peered cautiously around it.

Our soldiers had risen from behind the small rice paddy dikes and were rushing the village.

Two helicopter gunships had arrived and were patrolling the northwest side of the village to keep the enemy from escaping to the foothills and the mountains.

I could see an OH-13 scout helicopter snooping around the outskirts of the village on the southwest side. The crazy bastard was hovering down below the tree line and trying to cave in the thatch roof of one of the hootches with the skids of the helicopter.

There was a sudden burst of an automatic. Unmistakably the deep, throaty rattle of an AK-47. The scout helicopter did a 180-degree spin over the hootch and began a laborious climb straight up.

As soon as the helicopter cleared the palm trees, it headed straight toward us. It was trailing smoke and I could hear the reciprocating engine cutting in and out. The nose of the ship would yaw from each loss and resurgence of power.

The scout helicopter made a run-on landing just to the left of our parked ship. As the helicopter skidded to a halt, the engine let out a huge bellow, backfired and quit. It was strangely quiet. The only noise was the *"Swish, swish"* of the blades as they wound down and drifted to a halt.

The pilot was already outside the helicopter. He was busy pulling an M-16 out of a rifle scabbard and inserting a clip into the rifle. He seemed totally indifferent to the damage his helicopter had sustained.

"That little rat bastard has been poppin' rounds at us all day," he said, as Clyde and I walked up to the helicopter. He was now busy stuffing hand grenades into the pockets of his jungle shirt. I couldn't believe all the crap they had on the little helicopter. The center seat held a small wooden box crammed full of hand grenades, rifle clips, smoke grenades and several boxes of .45 caliber shells.

"He's got me pissed. I'm gonna go down there and bust his cookies once and for all, now," he continued, as he released the slide on the .45 automatic.

The pilot was a chief warrant officer, a W-2. If he had been wearing a pointed cowboy hat, he would have been the spittin' image of Festus of the old "Gunsmoke" series. It looked like he hadn't shaved in several weeks. Four or five of his upper front teeth were missing. When he wasn't talking, his teeth were clenched shut and his tongue moved in and out through the gap left by the missing teeth. I'm sure he wasn't, but he looked to be fifty years old. Damn, he's ugly, I thought. I wasn't about to tell him, though.

The 1st Air Cavalry wasn't known for its "spit and polish" while in combat but this guy would have made the grimiest guy in the cavalry look like a member of the Honor Guard.

There is no way of preflighting an OH-13 without getting a little greasy. This pilot looked as though he long ago quit using a grease rag and just started using his jungle fatigues to wipe his hands on. His clothes were shiny from the rubbed-in grease and oil. If he would have caught on fire, they would have had to bring in Red Adair to put him out.

The gunner/observer was quietly checking his weapons and stuffing grenades into his pockets, also. He appeared to be about nineteen. His clothes were a lot cleaner and he seemed to be more soldierly.

"You ready, Jimmy? Let's go get the little motherfucker," the warrant officer said, not giving Jimmy time to answer.

By this time some of the artillerymen had ambled over to see what was going on.

"We can put a salvo into that hootch and blow it off the map, Chief," the artillery sergeant said.

"No, I'm going to scratch this Commie bastard myself. I've got him figured out. He's got a tunnel leading from inside that hootch to a spider hole about thirty yards west. When we first saw him, he was firing at us from the doorway of the hootch. While we were trying to punch a hole in the roof with the skids to drop a grenade in, the little slope bastard popped out of the spider hole and riddled us."

"How do you know it's the same dink?"

"He's got a yellow bandanna tied around his neck. Probably one he took from the body of one of our guys."

Without further comment they started down the hill. We watched them for the next half hour moving cautiously across the paddies, sometimes crawling, sometimes running in a low crouch. They reached the edge of the village and disappeared in a clump of bushes.

For lack of anything else to do, Clyde and I attempted to count the bullet holes in the little observation helicopter. We lost track after seventeen. There was no way of telling whether the bullets or fragments had caused the holes in the plastic bubble. It was short of a miracle that neither crewman had been injured. One bullet had hit the M-60 machine gun, putting it out of action. The fact that the gunner was holding the gun and was not injured was a miracle in itself.

The sun had disappeared behind the mountains west of us. It had been several hours since the pilot and the gunner of the OH-13 had left the village. It would be dark soon. We had heard nothing from the battalion commander. Clyde decided we would wait until last light and if the colonel didn't show by then, we would fly back to LZ English.

The battle in the village was still going on. The small arms fire had diminished somewhat but would increase dramatically whenever a helicopter landed in a paddy southeast of the village. Several "Dustoff" medevac helicopters with the big Red Cross painted on the sides had been shuttling in and out, evacuating wounded Americans. Several of our company's helicopters had also made trips in, bringing ammo and supplies.

Just as we were preparing to leave, we heard someone working their way up the hill. We could hear muffled voices. "Must be the colonel," said Clyde.

Five minutes later, the warrant officer topped the hill. His greasy fatigues were now covered with mud and slime from the rice paddies. His breathing came in gasps. He dropped to the ground and leaned back against the skid crosstube on our helicopter. With each gasp for air, his tongue would shoot out through the missing teeth gap. He reminded me of a snake trying to pinpoint its prey. The gunner flopped down beside the pilot.

After a few minutes, his breathing eased somewhat. "Got 'im," he said, not even looking up. "I don't know how far it is to Buddha land but that little son of a bitch should be checkin' in 'bout now. Got a souvenir, too," he added.

Carefully, as if he was about to display the Star of India, he pulled the blood-stained yellow bandanna from the breast pocket of his jungle shirt. Delicately, he began to unfold the bandanna. Inside were two blood-caked human ears. A cocklebur was stuck to the earlobe of one of them.

The pilot looked up grinning, as if seeking approval.

The colonel never showed, so we lifted off for Bong Son. The OH-13 pilot asked us to drop him and his gunner off at Two Bits. On the way, he told us how they had stormed the hootch but didn't find the enemy soldier. The gunner began lobbing grenades into the tunnel hole they had found concealed in the hootch. The pilot had crawled out to the spider hole and waited a few yards away, concealed behind a palm tree. The dust, smoke and concussions had finally driven the enemy soldier out of the tunnel and to the spider hole. When he eased his head out to take a look, the pilot had fired a whole magazine from his M-16. The burst had killed the NVA soldier instantly.

We dropped the two airmen off at Two Bits and departed for LZ

English. "I'm glad to get away from those two guys. They give me the creeps," stated Clyde.

"Be glad of one thing," I said.

"What's that?" Clyde asked.

"Be glad that they're on our side!"

Note: This is an excerpt from *Wings for the Valiant*, by Robert W. Sisk. Published by J. Flores Publications, P.O. Box 163001, Miami, Florida 33116. Reprinted with permission from the publisher.

8. CHERRY PILOT

(Scout and Lift Pilot, Charlie Troop, 1967–68)

*Warrant Officer **Stephen Douglas** flew for a year with C Troop and never admitted to being shot at. This small untruth made him a lucky charm to the enlisted men assigned to fly in his helicopter.*

I have been interested in flying since I was a boy. Other kids built model cars. I built model airplanes. When I was sixteen, I read an army recruiting pamphlet that had been mailed to my older brother. It said that you could be an army pilot with only a high school education, and would fly either fixed wing aircraft or helicopters. I wanted to fly fixed wing, because at the time I knew very little about helicopters.

Shortly before I graduated from high school, I went to see the local recruiter to inquire about the flight program. He sent for further information, but only received the same pamphlet that I had found years before. I eventually got the information that I needed, and applied for the program. I left for basic training at Fort Polk, Louisiana, in late December 1965.

I started flight training at Fort Wolters, Texas, in March 1966, and graduated from the primary helicopter phase, with 125 hours of flight time, in June. I turned down the offer of two weeks' leave, requesting instead to be sent directly to Fort Rucker, Louisiana, to attend advanced flight training. I was eighteen, so I was anxious and impatient to finish the course. I graduated as a warrant officer (WO-1) in December, three months after my nineteenth birthday, with 225 flying hours. I was the youngest graduate in Flight Class WORWOC 66-19, and WO-1 Crawford was the oldest at thirty-one.

I arrived in South Vietnam in January 1967. Virtually all members of Class 66-19 sent to Vietnam at this time were assigned to the 1st Air Cav. Prior to arriving in Vietnam, I had met only one person who had served with the 1st Cav—one of my instructors. He had told us many exciting stories. Once he had been hit by a Russian 12.7mm machine-gun bullet. He survived only because the round was almost spent when it struck his bulletproof vest.

When we found out where we were going, many of my classmates wrote their wills and sent goodbye letters to their wives and sweethearts. When we arrived at An Khe, the 1st Cav Headquarters, they took us into a big tent where blackboards listed all the units and how many pilots they needed.

Warrant Officer Crawford wanted to be a lift pilot, and the 1/9th needed one. Several guys wanted to fly gunships, and they had several slots opening up for them. I found out that the 1/9th flew the OH-13, a two-seat scout helicopter, with a pilot in the left seat and an observer in the right seat. Just like many pilots right out of flight school, I thought that I was a good pilot, and did not want to fly as a copilot, so I joined the 1/9th scout section. My radio call sign would be "Phantom Raider One-Three." The other guys thought I was crazy.

We went through a brief familiarization course that was geared to infantry. In the late afternoon, we were flown out to LZ Hammond, a 1/9th base camp south of the Bong Son Plains. I shared a tent that first night with a pilot who told me to head for the bunker if I heard incoming fire. The first time I heard shelling, he told me that it was friendly fire. The second time I heard shelling, I asked him, "Is that friendly fire, too?" He didn't answer me and I realized that I was alone. I heard several more *"Crump-Crump-Crumps,"* but didn't know for sure what they were and, in any case, didn't know where the bunker was located.

When the pilot returned, he was surprised to discover that I had remained in the tent throughout a mortar attack. It was the only time that I ever allowed myself to be caught so flat-footed during two tours in Vietnam.

I reported officially to C Troop the next morning, and was told, among other things, that I could transfer to the lift or gunship platoons after successfully completing six months of scout flying. What happened when I later requested that transfer is a tale in itself. Anyway, that same morning, before I was sent back to An Khe to get checked out in the OH-13, I was sent out on one flight as a scout observer. This was so that I could learn the observer's responsibilities, and also see what was expected of a 1/9th scout pilot. I did not know where the mess hall was, so I ate half a can of peanuts that I brought with me, and then went on the flight a few minutes later.

The Blues, our infantry, were in contact, chasing three Viet Cong rice collectors: two men and a woman. They were running down a streambed. One of the Vietnamese men ran out onto a dry rice paddy, straight towards a single palm tree. He was trying to place the tree between himself and the Blues. The Blues opened fire on him, and most of the rounds were on target. He must have been hit a hundred times before he fell to the ground. I had never seen anyone killed before. It was like watching something on TV.

The Blues started firing at the other Viet Cong. Bullets were flying all around them, but like in a John Wayne movie, they were not hit. The pilot, CWO Kimmel, saw that the VC did not have any weapons, and told me to tell the Blues to cease fire. However, the radioman was shooting and could not hear my transmissions.

They finally stopped firing and the people were captured. The man was scared, but unharmed. The woman, a tough-looking customer, had been wounded in the upper right arm. When a black trooper began to bandage her arm, she suddenly punched him, knocking him to the ground. He got up, gave her a look like he understood, and finished bandaging her arm. This was my first combat mission. I was still suffering from jet lag and all the excitement on an empty stomach made me airsick on the flight back to LZ Hammond.

My final checkout in the OH-13 was a flight down to the C Troop scout detachment at the small coastal city of Phan Thiet. I had very few flying hours in the aircraft at this time, and couldn't fly it very well. The OH-13 has a manual throttle sort of like a motorcycle handgrip. When you put more pitch in the rotorhead, the throttle is increased. The throttle is decreased with less pitch. This is done automatically in most helicopters, because having to do it manually in combat is a difficult procedure, requiring a fast, highly coordinated left hand. Fortunately, I'm left-handed. Our old scout ships were equipped with throttle compensation systems that were supposed to adjust the throttle, but they didn't work. You really had to be on the ball during combat maneuvers close to the ground to keep the helicopter from falling out of the sky.

The OH-13 is a bubble-topped, piston engine, two-seater helicopter that could fly 60–70 miles per hour overloaded. The scouts worked in two-ship teams called "White Teams." Each team consisted of a lead ship, a scout team leader, who generally flew six feet over the terrain.

The lead ship flew around trees, under trees or between them, rather than over them. This presented the smallest possible target and allowed good observation. The second ship was called the chase ship, and it flew 200 feet above and 500 feet behind the leader. Its job was to keep the lead ship in sight at all times and maintain radio contact with the base camp. If the lead helicopter was shot down, the chase immediately climbed to a high altitude and radioed for help, etc. Only after this had been done would the chase descend to engage the enemy and provide air cover until rescue could arrive.

When I first arrived, the scout ships were armed with an M-60 machine gun on each skid. The observer carried an M-16 rifle, and plenty of extra 20-round magazines. We also carried several dozen fragmentation, white phosphorous, thermite and smoke grenades. Pilots usually carried .38 Smith and Wesson revolvers as sidearms. I carried a Colt .45 automatic. Later on, the ships were armed with a single M-60 machine gun, mounted on the left skid. The observer carried an M-60 in place of an M-16. Shortly before I arrived at Phan Thiet, a single enemy bullet had sheared off the tail rotor drive shaft on CWO Kimmel's OH-13, and he had to crash-land. He and his observer were able to hold off a VC squad with the weapons on board until help arrived.

Various types of armament had been tried on scout ships before I arrived. They had tried eight 2.75-inch rockets in two tubes, one on each skid. They also tried dropping mortar bombs, but there was insufficient velocity to arm them. We would aim the skid machine gun by using a grease pencil mark on the bubble as a "gunsight." My skid gun usually jammed after about 100 rounds had been fired, so I started using the machine-gun ammo as an immediate resupply to the Blues. We used a lot of fragmentation grenades, and I instructed the observer to throw them down as hard as he could, so they would penetrate the treetops and land on target before they exploded.

We wore heavy ceramic and metal honeycomb breastplate armor called chicken plates. Some pilots preferred to wear only a flak jacket, believing that a bullet from behind would go through the body, bounce off the chicken plate and ricochet back through the body. We tried using pieces of APC (armored personnel carrier) armor under our seats. The first to try this was Captain Hardin, the detachment commander.

The day after the armor was installed, he was hit in the seat bottom by two bullets. The bullets literally lifted him up and banged his head on the top of the bubble. He had a black and blue butt from the hits, but the armor saved his life. Captain Hardin "put the heat on," and we soon received flat pieces of ceramic armor to put under the seat cushions.

The fuselage of the OH-13 is not solid as with most helicopters, but has a framework of welded one-inch steel pipe, making it very easy to "flat spin." The VC liked to fire at a helicopter after it had passed overhead. The OH-13's maneuverability let us flat spin, so we could spin the tail around in mid-flight and come face to face with an enemy soldier while still traveling in the same direction backwards. Upon seeing us do this, many of the enemy just dropped their weapons and surrendered on the spot. The big, solid structure of the Huey gunships prevented them from doing maneuvers like "the spin." They could make fast or slow passes, or hover around near the ground.

The gunships, like the scouts, flew in two-ship teams. The scout teams worked closely with the Blues, directing them and flying cover. We would often alternate, with a gunship team replacing a scout team over the Blues, or vice versa. The gunships that replaced us on station would many times "go hunting" away from the infantry, only returning if the Blues got into a firefight. The scouts' philosophy, especially when I was a scout team leader, was to prevent firefights from happening. Later on, when the Huey Cobra replaced the older Hueys, the scout "White" birds and the gunship "Red" birds were combined into two-ship OH-6A scout and Cobra gunship combinations called "Pink" teams.

The city of Phan Thiet was where Ho Chi Minh had been a schoolteacher, which was about the only thing important about the place that anyone could remember. Everything was more relaxed down there than at Hammond. Captain Hardin commanded the detachment at Phan Thiet, and he assigned the most experienced scout observer, a senior sergeant, to train me. Well, I was nineteen, and I thought that I was a great pilot. When I asked the captain what instructions to give the sergeant, he said, "You don't tell him to do anything! He'll tell you what to do! If you follow his instructions, you'll learn how to stay alive, and how to be a good scout pilot." I didn't know it at the time, but new, "green" pilots are very dangerous in combat. After the sergeant had showed me the ropes, he never flew with me again.

Early on, I chose Corporal Dornellis for my observer. He was not popular with the other pilots. He loved to fire his machine gun, but didn't want to work the radio and do the other things that observers were supposed to do. However, he had one redeeming quality that made me want to keep him throughout virtually all my scout flying.

He was an expert shot; a combination of Wild Bill Hickok, Buffalo Bill and Billy the Kid. Firing from the hip, single-shot from a moving helicopter, he could hit anything I told him to, even at a fair distance. We once chased a small dog, and Dornellis consistently shot between the dog's hind legs so that the bullets kicked up dirt against its belly. He stopped shooting after a dozen rounds, without injuring the dog.

If Dornellis didn't want to work the radio, it was okay with me. In my opinion, the most important quality a scout observer should have is to be an expert shot. Dornellis was part of my incredible luck in flying 1,800 combat hours in South Vietnam and never having my helicopter hit by enemy fire.

On my first combat patrol, Captain Paul was flying lead and I was flying chase. We came upon a patrol of nine heavily armed enemy soldiers. One of them was carrying a machine gun. When the captain turned to attack, I called him on the radio and asked him what he wanted me to do. He ordered me to fly to the fork of a river that we had just passed and circle over it. My lack of combat experience made me a liability on that patrol, so I was kept out of harm's way.

Captain Paul continuously attacked the enemy, until the observer was down to one WP grenade, and was firing his .38 revolver. I watched as they chased a VC. The observer shot him in the leg and then tossed the WP grenade, which exploded in a big puff of white smoke. I thought that they should have gotten some sort of award for that battle, but it turned out to be just another day in the life of the 1/9th.

The men at Phan Thiet did the light work while the women worked in the fields. One day, I spotted a man working alongside the women in a rice field, so I knew that he wasn't from around there. When I circled around, he started to run, and I had Dornellis fire in front of him. After a few rounds, he just sat down, and the Blues were flown out to pick him up. Several days later, I walked past a chain gang doing heavy labor. One of the men gave me a look like he wanted to cut my throat. It took me a while to realize that he was the man from the rice field. He had been a VC recruiter from Bien Hoa.

After flying at Phan Thiet for several months, the detachment was transferred back to the main troop contingent. Charlie Troop had moved and was flying out of Two Bits North on the Bong Son Plains. We conducted operations in the An Lao Valley, the Crow's Foot, and the Tiger Mountains.

In the operations tent was a blackboard with every pilot's name listed. Beside my name was a box with a couple of cherries drawn with red chalk. They were not to be erased until the first time a pilot was shot at, which had already happened to me at Phan Thiet. However, with my youthful sense of humor, I decided to make the most of this joke.

For the rest of my tour, I never admitted that I had drawn enemy fire. I always said that it was aimed at the other helicopter. When people came and asked me about this, and I'd say it was true, they would walk away, shaking their heads in disbelief. When I was a scout team leader, they would assign me nervous people, mostly short-timers. When a short-timer found out that he was going to fly in my aircraft, he would be okay, because I never took enemy fire. The fact is that I was shot at many times, but my helicopter was never hit.

On patrol, we often received bolt-action or semiautomatic small arms fire, mostly from World War II-type weapons. The Blues captured such varied weapons as 8mm Mauser rifles, double-barreled shotguns, and Winchester 30–30s.

One day a man fired a single shot at us from the jungle. We set up a "daisy chain" pattern. The first OH-13 drew the fire and the second came in behind it and dropped a hand grenade. We received a single shot from the jungle on each pass.

When I dropped my grenade, he would shoot at my aircraft, and as the other ship dropped a grenade, he would shoot at it. Each bullet got a grenade in response. We learned to anticipate the man's direction and then lead him with the grenades. We chased him through the jungle for some time and over a considerable distance. Eventually, he either ran out of bullets or we got lucky with a grenade.

Once I spotted a bunker on the edge of a rice field. A man ran out and fired a shot at the other aircraft. Every time we opened fire, he would disappear into the bunker. When I went by, he would run out and fire at my helicopter. Again, we flew in a daisy chain, with one ship drawing his fire in front of the bunker, while the other one engaged him from behind. We were 180 degrees from each other, flying clockwise to keep our gunners in the right seats on target. The man stayed near the mouth of the bunker, and we couldn't nail him. I contacted an ARA ship (Aerial Rocket Artillery) that was flying in our area, and asked for assistance. ARA ships carried forty-eight 2.75-inch rockets in two 24-rocket pods. This one had a full load on board. I put him on a shallow, 20-mile final approach to the rice field. He was to fire all rockets in one volley.

We were still flying in a circle, and still drawing the man's fire. I looked off in the distance and saw these little black dots coming from the direction of the ARA ship, and realized that the pilot had fired his rockets. The other scout ship was just cutting across the field, so I quickly told him break left. This took the gunner off target, and the man stepped outside to squeeze off another shot.

Just as this happened, and the chopper cleared the field, all these rockets with their ten-pound TNT warheads roared by and hit the field with a big *"Ka-BOOM!"* The ground erupted in smoke, fire, dust and flying debris. When the smoke cleared, the man wasn't there anymore. I don't know to this day whether he was blown to pieces or somehow dived back into the bunker.

One day, quite near our base at Two Bits North, the gunships shot several VC. On their bodies were found maps showing the base, the names of the people living there, and the location of the tent that each of us occupied. The local villagers we had employed to build some bunkers for our helicopters had mapped the place for the VC. The perimeter around the base consisted of a few strands of barbed wire. I've always wondered why they didn't come in and kill the lot of us. Perhaps our hard-won reputation held them back.

Sometimes other events hold more importance than tales of killing the enemy. Out on the Bong Son Plains in the afternoon, I chased a young Viet Cong wearing a blue uniform. He was no more than sixteen. When I was six feet behind him, he turned his head, and from the expression on his face, I could see that he knew that in the next few seconds he was going to die. I decided that I didn't want to see his face in my dreams for the rest of my life, so I just flew away.

On another day, a scout ship picked up an old man in a paddy field. All he carried was a long hoe and a backpack. I could see that he was begging them not to arrest him. He tried to bribe the observer with the few pennies he possessed. I later flew back and picked up his backpack and hoe (which we had to tie to the skids). When I returned his stuff to him at the base camp, he just broke down and cried.

It was a dangerous life flying as a scout for the 1/9th, and not every pilot could measure up. Here's what can happen when the wrong person gets the job. A captain, an average pilot and I started flying together. Shortly thereafter, he decided that I should fly the lead ship, and he would cover me. So, I started directing the Blues, and when there was a complaint, it was the captain who went to the command tent and got chewed out by the CO. He took it.

The next day, I discovered that he was flying a thousand or several thousand feet above me, instead of two hundred feet up and five hundred feet behind. Pilots know that the higher up you are, the safer you are, so if the engine quit, you could auto-rotate from altitude. If you were two hundred feet up, you just crashed. The captain's gunner didn't like to fly that high, and made some jokes about getting a nosebleed from the altitude.

One morning, I was in a hot situation, shooting something up, and noticed that he was covering me from several thousand feet. When we returned to base, I confronted him and said, "Look, even if you auto-rotated down to save me, by the time you got to me from that high up, I'd be dead." Well, he screamed at me to stand at attention. I started to snap to, then realized just how ridiculous it was under the circumstances, so I told him that he had to be kidding. I also said that I wouldn't fly with him anymore. The CO got him to do his job by taking him aside and threatening to extend his time in the 1/9th by thirty days. A month's extension seemed like a death sentence to the captain, so he started performing until it was time to transfer to another unit.

We didn't form any lasting friendships or attachments in the 1/9th. If a pilot had any, it was a carryover from flight school. Each group of pilots in the scouts, the gunships or lift, kept pretty much to themselves. If people were wounded or killed, we couldn't even remember their faces or names after a few days. We just blotted the whole incident out of our minds and continued on with the job.

After eight months as a scout pilot, I told the CO that I wanted a transfer to the lift platoon. I wanted experience in the Huey, then known as the "Cadillac of helicopters." Few civilian pilots in 1967 were trained to fly the UH-1, so I figured that it was a good idea to build up some hours in it. Scout and lift pilots generally didn't get killed, but the slow, overloaded gunships got shot down and crashed a lot. The gunships flew into trees or fell out of the sky, because the maneuvers they were sometimes put through during combat simply caused them to fly outside of their operating envelopes.

At age nineteen, I had been a scout team leader. This was an unusual promotion for a WO-1, which had caused jealousy among the commissioned officers. The CO was not pleased that I was requesting a transfer to the lift section, where I would be starting out as a copilot.

The next morning, I flew low-level through a banana plantation. I returned to base with my scout ship liberally plastered with banana leaves. The maintenance officer sent several people to inspect the helicopter and told me that I could be court-martialed if it was damaged. I was laughing, and each man who inspected my ship returned laughing.

There was no damage of any kind. Each inspector's report said that there was nothing wrong, except that the ship was covered with all those banana leaves. The CO asked me if I had flipped my lid. I replied, "No, sir. I just want a transfer. When I got here, I was told that if I wanted a transfer after being a scout pilot for six months, I'd get one." I got my transfer.

I flew as a lift pilot for the remainder of my tour. Once we took off in a tight, four-ship diamond formation from a refueling point. As we cleared the perimeter wire on takeoff, Sam, our door gunner, saw his flight jacket blow out of the ship and fall into a pond. We broke formation and went back to get the jacket. Just as we came to a hover, our tail rotor broke off, and we went into a spin. Sam was thrown more than a hundred feet through the air before his body skipped across the water, and then sank like a stone. Warrant Officer Crawford cut the power and we splashed down into the water. We got out laughing, because we were so glad to be alive. Suddenly, Sam rose up out of the water, covered with mud and laughing, too. If we had spun out over dry land, Sam would surely have died.

Another time, we made a night landing under parachute flares, guided by hand-held strobe lights. The Blues were in heavy contact and had shot a lot of VC. It was a real tense situation, but we got them out.

My tour ended, and I returned home in early January 1968. I was home on leave when the Tet offensive erupted. I have always thought that it was better watching Tet on TV than being there. I returned to Vietnam in January 1969, and I was again assigned to the 1st Cav. I had gone to the CH-47 (Chinook) transition school, so I ended up with the 228th Assault Helicopter Battalion based at Bear Cat.

The lessons that I had learned with the 1/9th saved my life on several occasions. I was an older and wiser man of twenty-one, and I was a WO-2 (Chief Warrant Officer) with a captain as my copilot. There were times when I was in overall command of a dozen or more Chinooks. The biggest difference between the two tours was that the commissioned officers on my first tour were older. They were in their late twenties or early thirties, and were experienced combat pilots who taught me how to fly in combat and survive. During my second tour, the officers were guys my own age, and they were not up to the standards of earlier years.

The last time my path crossed that of the 1/9th was when the Cav built a firebase right in the middle of a major NVA trail network. The NVA had attacked the base the night before, and the battle was still going on in broad daylight. The base was being assaulted from all sides, which made flying in and out a precarious situation. During one of my landings at the firebase, I noticed a LOH scout hovering over the trees just outside the perimeter.

Suddenly, it was shot up, and the pilot made a forced landing in front of my Chinook. A second LOH quickly landed and picked up a wounded crewman, and then it departed in great haste—what us pilots called "hauling ass." The pilot and the other crewman from the first LOH came over and asked me to radio the 1/9th. I was to tell them that, "Toady and Irish were okay." I gave them a lift back to the main base.

During the flight, the LOH pilot pulled his fatigue shirt away from his body and showed me where a 12.7mm bullet had punched a hole through it. All he said was, "Isn't that something?"

Most people go through life wondering if they would have the "right stuff" in a life or death situation. Thanks to my tour with the 1/9th, I settled that question early in my life.

9. LZ DOG

(Gunship and Lift Pilot, Alpha Troop, 1967–68)
*Warrant Officer **Jack Fischer** was twenty-four, and older than most of his fellow pilots. When he arrived in the 9th Cav, he wrote home to his wife that he would be camping out in the bushes for a year. Little did he know the experiences that awaited him in the field.*

I joined the service in January 1966 and was sent to Fort Polk for basic training. After graduation I reported to Fort Wolters for flight training with Class 66–23. My class graduated from flight school at Fort Rucker on Valentine's Day, 1967, and two weeks later I left for Vietnam. Before the flight over, I spent some time in San Francisco with two friends from flight school, Tom Ellis and Robert Barthlemess. We bought three bottles of champagne and pledged to share them when we returned from Vietnam. I still have the three quarts of champagne. My friends and I haven't seen each other since the war, but someday I hope that will change.

My purple Braniff aircraft arrived at Tan Son Nhut on 5 March 1967. All three of us were supposed to go to the 25th Infantry Division, but the army, in its infinite wisdom, changed our orders. Bob was assigned to the 17th Aviation Group at Na Trang, and Tom and I were sent to the 1st Air Cav. In flight school, going to the 1st Cav was something you didn't talk about. Going there was supposed to be a sure sign of death.

On 15 March, I wrote home to my wife that I would be spending my time out in the bushes somewhere and camping out. I had been assigned to Alpha Troop, 1/9th Cav, and they hadn't been back at base camp since 15 September 1966. I knew that the troop was a recon unit that was supposed to fly around and find the VC. They either took care of them themselves, or called on the Air Force if the enemy units were too big to handle. The troop's missions were called search and destroy. If nothing else, this year was going to be different.

I was assigned to the lift platoon known as the "Headhunters" and began flying as a copilot on 20 March. One of my first flights was along the coast of the South China Sea. I was impressed by the beauty of the blue sea, the white sand and all the tiny sampans sailing in the ocean.

A few days later, we flew the four lift helicopters two miles south and landed in the Bong Son River. Local children washed our ships while the twelve of us (eight pilots and four crew chiefs) went for a swim. The water was as warm as what we had back home in Glenwood Springs—the world's largest naturally heated swimming pool—but not nearly as clean.

Being used to living in the cool, clean air of Colorado at 6,000 feet, the things that got to me most in Vietnam were the heat and humidity. The temperature reached over 110 degrees on many days. I seemed to be constantly drinking water, sweating and swatting at mosquitos. My watch caused a rash and I had to stop wearing it.

We spent the days flying out of LZ Dog. We would take the infantry team out into the boonies, set down at Dog, and wait to go back out and get them. Then we would either take them somewhere else or bring them home. While we waited, there might be other missions, like administrative flights to other bases, or going out and picking up VC suspects that the Blues had captured.

We would leave Dog and fly the helicopters to a different place many nights, to disperse them in case the enemy attacked or mortared Dog. Most nights I ended up sleeping in the helicopter after we had set down somewhere. It was better than sleeping on the ground. We never seemed to get enough sleep. We often started flying early and ended the day late. At night, there were alerts or additional responsibilities to keep you awake when you should have been sleeping.

On 3 April, we were scrambled for an emergency mission to rescue the Blue Platoon from a contact in the An Lao Valley. The valley begins inland from the town of Bong Son and runs about fifteen miles north, before swinging back to the southwest. It was a real spooky place to fly into. We made a one-skid landing on a mountain on the west side of the An Lao. There were several dead Blues, and fighting still going on—smoke flares, hand grenades going off, a lot of yelling, and a lot of shooting. We were sitting with our left skid touching the mountain, trying to hold the aircraft steady, as they loaded the casualties on board and climbed on themselves. That was a real experience and the first time I had seen dead Americans.

Later that day, a gunship took off and crashed only seventy-five meters from the underground bunker that I shared with two other pilots and assorted rats. Someone had forgotten to take the dust covers off the engine. The pilot later came to Blue Lift when I had four months of combat flying and was the platoon's instructor pilot. He was rather surly when I tried to explain how things were done in the Headhunters. When he told me that I could give him instructions when I had as much time in combat as him and had won a DFC, I remembered the day someone forgot to take the dust covers off his gunship.

I turned twenty-five on 6 April 1967. Three days later, the artillery observer, Lieutenant Tyree, was killed by ground fire while flying with Major Mendenhall in the An Lao Valley. The major sent three gunships to attack the VC who had done it. One ship was shot down and burned completely, but the crew escaped. Another had its hydraulics shot out, but was able to fly back to LZ English and set down safely. A lift ship was sent out to rescue the crew of the burned gunship. They needed another door gunner, so I grabbed the machine gun from my ship and jumped on board. A helicopter from the 229th got there first and rescued the crew. I was pretty peeved at them for beating us to it, but that's the way it goes.

On 12 April, I saw Tom Ellis for a few minutes, so I knew he was still around. We also built a covered patio and a grill beside my underground bunker that day. We hoped that the troop commander wouldn't make us tear it down before we could find something to cook on it.

He let us keep it. That grill was one of the few creature comforts we had, other than my fan. I later bought a three-speed, oscillating fan at the PX in An Khe, and kept it going whenever the generator was running, which wasn't often. I still have that fan today, and it works just as well now as it did back then. Three days after we built the grill, on 15 April, I received the wonderful news that I was going to be a father. It gave me something special to look forward to.

The troop commander, Major Mendenhall, was shot down in the An Lao Valley on 18 April. The aircraft was burning before it hit a steep, jungle-covered hillside. Two pilots and the two door gunners were lost. The rescue party took five hours to reach the crash site. What they found was about eight pounds of what used to be an 8,500-pound machine. There wasn't enough left of the aircraft or the crew to bring down the mountain.

On another day, I watched from Dog as a platoon from Delta Troop was inserted into some rice paddies three miles south of us. The third aircraft in was knocked out of the sky by a command-detonated mine. It pretty well destroyed the helicopter and those on board. We put our platoon on the ground to assist in the search, but they found nothing.

April 25th was the first day that my aircraft received hits. We inserted our Blues and a platoon from Delta Troop at the northern edge of the Tiger Mountains. They spent about four hours on the ground and couldn't find a thing. Later, we picked up the Delta Troop platoon and flew them to their base at LZ Two Bits. We went back for our own platoon in a staggered trail formation, and landed beside a village in a dry rice paddy that was pretty well surrounded by palm trees.

As the Blues were coming out of the village and the treeline, mortar shells started walking across the rice paddy toward us, along with antiaircraft fire from a hill to the south, and small arms fire from the palm trees and hedgerows. We sat there until the Blues scrambled on board, while two gunships and two scout ships circled overhead and tried to suppress the enemy fire. Then we lifted off in formation in the middle of shrapnel and explosions, tracers and lots of dust. The ship behind me was hit in the tail boom by an RPG as we were climbing through thirty feet. The helicopter spun around seven times and flung out four or five infantrymen before it crashed. We circled back in the other three ships and dropped off the rest of our infantry to rescue the injured people and secure the downed bird. No one had been killed, but five Blues ended up in the hospital.

Forty-five minutes after the casualties were extracted, a scout ship, part of the attempt to recover the wrecked lift ship, was shot down in flames by a .50 caliber machine gun. Both crew members were dead before they hit the ground. Later on in the afternoon, a Chinook slung out the downed Huey and our two lift ships went in to pick up the rest of the infantry. I say two lift ships, because one had been shot down and mine wasn't flyable. It had two holes in the engine compartment, and the leading edge of the rotor blade had been shot away.

Tom Ellis got shot down in the An Lao Valley on 6 May. His wingman saw the ship go down and reported that there were no survivors, but one of our gunships landed thirty minutes later to investigate. The downed ship was completely destroyed, but fortunately hadn't burned. The crew was still alive. One gunner had a broken back, and the other had two broken legs. The pilot had three broken ribs. It took twenty-five minutes to get Tom out. He was pretty banged up and he later lost his spleen. It was a miracle anyone survived that crash.

A few days before this happened, I learned that Marty Coronis, our classmate and a good friend of Tom Ellis, was flying with B Troop. He had arrived in Vietnam two months after us, because the army had forgotten to send his orders and he finally had to call them. I thought it was funny at the time, because we would be going home two months before him. Marty was killed at Duc Pho about two months later.

On 25 May, they moved some pilots out of the Headhunters, leaving only myself and one other experienced lift pilot. Captain Bill Rittenhouse took over the platoon and made me his copilot in the lead aircraft. I was going to reverse the usual trend by flying six months in lift and then six months with the gunships. Usually, pilots who first managed to survive for six months in the gunships came to the lift platoon. I wanted to do more flying, earn more medals, and most of all, shoot the miniguns and rockets.

At the time, I had one of two aircraft in Vietnam that mounted a sniffer unit. I felt very privileged to be chosen for those missions, but it also meant a lot of early flights after nights on duty for one reason or the other. We would fly over the jungle and get readings. You couldn't see anything through the canopy, but our escorting gunships would roll in with rockets and miniguns on the trees. I'll bet that surprised Charlie, if he lived through it. We found water buffalo on some sniffer missions. On another mission, we spotted a man hiding in a streambed under the trees. I tried to tell the gunship where he was, but they couldn't find him. I brought the ship back around, and we made a pass at thirty knots with our door gun. I don't know if we hit the guy, but if we didn't, we sure scared the hell out of him. I liked flying those sniffer missions.

On 25 May, another warrant officer and me were assigned to fly up the coast to Chu Lai and pick up twenty cases of soda and twenty cases of beer. We ate dinner at a navy mess hall, and it was wonderful. They had real kitchen tables with salt and pepper shakers and padded chairs. We drank glasses of ice-cold milk from a dispensing machine like they had in the States. It was real milk, too.

I met a classmate at the PX who was stationed there. He lived on a beach with lifeguards and went swimming every day. The navy had an OH-23 helicopter that flew up and down the beach all day long and watched for sharks. I lived a mile and a half from the beach at Dog and couldn't even go wading. Just before we left Chu Lai, we gave eight guys a 15-minute ride along the beach in our lift ship. They gave us six gallons of milk. We packed it on ice and beat feet for home. The milk didn't go very far at Dog, but everyone who drank some sure enjoyed it.

The next days we were back to landing our infantry in the An Lao. The gunships would kill NVA, and we would land the Blues, mostly in one-ship LZs, to search the area. After one of those patrols, some Blues brought me a nice sword and a scabbard, and a five-foot long spear with a foot-and-a-half metal point on it. They found the spear in a draw in the An Lao Valley.

Our life wasn't perfect at Dog, but in a letter home in which I complained about some hardships, I also wrote, ''I feel damned proud to be serving our country over here in the 1st Squadron, 9th Cavalry. Our little group flies more hours of combat missions, kills more VC and is more respected and talked about than any other unit over here.''

Our lives were a contrast to the living conditions of the air force boys down at Phu Cat airbase to the south. They lived better in Vietnam than they did in the States. They had streets, sidewalks, street lights, street signs, grass lawns, cement floors, air conditioning, automatic washers and dryers, hot and cold running water, flush toilets, pool tables, juke boxes, pinball machines, indoor movies, and on and on. They lounged around in Bermuda shorts and tennis shoes at night and spent a lot of time in clubs that often featured live entertainment, like strip shows.

By 10 July, we were flying even more hours than usual, starting before dawn and setting down after dark. Part of the division had been sent west to Kontum, and those of us who were left were doing a lot of flying, and shooting lots of artillery to fool Charlie into thinking that the Cav was still in the area in force. One night I flew a ''lightning bug'' mission, with a flare ship and two gunships, in the Fishhook Area northwest of the An Lao.

Every day we found new rice paddy areas that had been worked during the night. This was in a ''free fire area,'' a war zone where the civilian population had been evacuated and anyone found there could be shot on sight. We could find no one during the daytime, so the idea was to drop flares and catch them at work. We saw no people that night, but we did get shot at. We spotted about a dozen water buffalo that were being used to cultivate the fields, and killed them.

The thing about flying at night with flares was that the flares could go out and still be floating down on their parachutes. It would be easy to catch one in a tail rotor and crash. That bothered me more than the possibility of getting shot at.

By mid-August, we were loading up the Blues before dawn and flying with all the lift ships, scout ships and gunships about fifty miles northwest to the Song Re Valley. Charlie Troop had gone in there first for a few days, and had ended up with quite a few unpleasant experiences. They ran into more NVA and more .50 calibers than they had seen since the An Lao. They were withdrawn back to Bong Son, and we were sent into the Song Re. Almost every ship received fire up there and we took care of quite a few enemy soldiers. We would pack up and return to Dog each day at dusk.

I continued flying lots of sniffer missions. We had received fancy new UH-1H lift ships with the more powerful engine, and the sniffer was pulled out of the old D-Model and installed in my new H-Model. In late August, we got the additional duty of flying along the coast, counting sampans, and checking to see if they were carrying guns or ammo. After counting boats, we had to fly low level, north along the beach, and pick up suspicious looking males for questioning. The ocean and the beach were beautiful, but there was no secure area where we could swim and enjoy ourselves.

On one of those flights along the beach, we spotted a man about a mile ahead of us. He started to run into a grove of palm trees about halfway to a deserted village. When we got to him, he was trying to cover himself with palm leaves and hide from us. We circled around for a couple of minutes, then he jumped up and took off running toward the village again. I had my door gunner shoot in front of him to make him stop.

I tried to set down between him and the village. We got to about five feet off the ground, and he ran under us and kept going. I told my gunner on the left side to shoot to kill. I saw my first human being cut down and killed that day. It felt sort of odd. He was definitely a bad guy, but I was sorry for him.

By November, I had gone on R&R to see my wife who was about seven months pregnant at the time. It was a wonderful vacation. I returned to Dog and transferred to the gun platoon, the ''Red Scorpions.''

My first six months with the Headhunters had been very interesting and rewarding. I will always remember the professionalism and the camaraderie of our lift crew chiefs and pilots. The many single-ship LZs in the An Lao, and things like formation flying with overlapping rotor blades, had made me a conscious and dedicated pilot.

The sniffer missions had allowed me to fly a lot and see some remarkable scenery. On the low-level passes over the jungle, I had seen parakeets, parrots, wild boar, red deer, tiger, buffalo, river monitors, elephants and monkeys. It was like flying over a botanical garden. The clear mountain streams coming down from the mountains into the An Lao Valley were beautiful. Being from Colorado, there had been many times when I wished that we could land and go hiking through that beautiful country.

One of the things that stands out in my mind about flying with the Headhunters was the special missions. We not only did our own insertions and extractions, but flew other units as well. We often landed LRRPs or tracker dog teams, and often acted as medevac ships for infantry units in contact. In that area, at that particular time, there were many times when medevac would not land. It would be too late in the day or too dark, or there would be too much enemy fire. One excuse after another. It made us feel good to know that we were always there and would help anyone who needed us.

On Thanksgiving Day, we had a dinner with some of the children from the village. They were the ones we traded C-rations to, in exchange for washing our clothes and shining our boots. It was their first experience with a Thanksgiving meal and it was great to watch them enjoying themselves with a new type of food. One of them, a young boy, was a special friend whom I really wanted to bring home with me. At any rate, that didn't work out and we didn't know then how the war was going to end. I wish him well. My wife and I adopted a seventeen-month-old Vietnamese boy in 1975. He is now fifteen years old and doing great.

Thanksgiving day was the same as the others in some ways. I put in ten hours of flying, finished at nine P.M., and found many cards and letters from home waiting for me. That made it a special day.

On 26 November, we killed six elephants. We were going in to pick up the tusks, but changed our minds. They were in a bad location with eight-foot-high elephant grass and numerous trees. These were the first elephants seen in that area of Vietnam for eighteen months, and the sighting caused quite a commotion. General Tolson flew over the area and a Mohawk aircraft conducted an aerial photo reconnaissance. The reason the elephants had to be shot was that they were used by the NVA to haul many types of heavy equipment, including big machine guns and mortars. The meat and tusks would be used by the enemy, instead of for a better cause.

On 6 December 1967, I received a call from the Red Cross that informed me that my son had been born on 2 December. I told a friend if anything happened to me that day, to please let my wife know that I had received her letter, and how proud I was to be a father.

A short time later, our troop commander was flying up on the Bong Son Plains, about four miles north of Dog, when the door gunner spotted a radio wire, running down from a palm tree and into a well-constructed bunker. Shortly thereafter, he began to get shot at by automatic weapons.

He put in our Blue Platoon. They moved out of a rice paddy and into the treeline and were immediately pinned down by enemy fire.

A platoon from Delta Troop was put in at another location. They were quickly pinned down. Our gunships started shooting rockets and miniguns to try to cover the two platoons. This was about 4:30 in the afternoon.

By that time, we had two companies of infantry, tanks, flame-throwing armored personnel carriers, artillery and air strikes involved. Even the navy played a part with the battleship *New Jersey*. The 9th Cav infantry platoons were extracted about nine o'clock at night.

By then it was a full-fledged battle, like the kind they must have had in World War II. Seven of our aircraft had taken a total of twenty-eight hits. One of my good friends, Bart Garnsey, had been shot down in his scout ship three times that day. One crew chief was wounded. Our Blue platoon had taken one dead and four wounded, and eleven people from the Delta Troop platoon had been wounded.

I don't know how many hundreds of rockets, or how many thousands of rounds of minigun ammo my gunship expended that first day. I'll never forget the .50 caliber that fired on us after dark. I was dead tired and had been shooting so much, that I forgot the hard and fast rule to never overfly a gun position. They saw us coming and began shooting at us. I realized that the pressure was on, and about 150 yards out, began flying down the gun-target line and shooting everything we had at the machine gun position. We were flying so low and so fast that the tracers went right over us.

We continued flying long hours and attacking the surrounded NVA regiment for days. Many of the enemy dead were buried in bunkers and could only be estimated, but in the end, there were over six hundred killed.

On 17 December 1967, I was down to seventy-nine days. I had received the DFC for my part in the action on the Bong Son Plains. Now they could send me home any time they wanted. A couple of days later, my friend Captain Soltes sent me a model that was an exact copy of one of our Headhunters ships, complete with all the markings. He had gone home earlier in my tour, but he hadn't forgotten us. To this day, I am waiting to put it together and still wondering if we will ever meet again.

During this period, Alpha Troop was the only Air Cavalry troop left that far south, and we were extremely busy with action at Bong Son, in the An Lao, the Crow's Foot, and other areas. With the actions that we were having, I didn't think that I was going to make it home alive. I was ready to go anywhere on R&R, just to get away for a few days. They had one slot available for Bangkok and I asked for it. The trip to Bangkok didn't come any too soon.

I was back from R&R by 7 February. The rains were almost over, and it was getting a little warmer each day. We had been having quite a bit of bad luck on our search and destroy missions, but now I was looking forward to going home and seeing my wife and son. We moved north during Tet to Dong Ha, and I stayed with the troop until 28 February. I got checked out on Cobra gunships, but missed the old B and C models. They had their advantages. I finally came home on 6 March 1968.

I feel fortunate to have flown with the Headhunters for six months, to have been chosen to fly sniffer missions for three months, and to have flown with the Red Scorpions for six months. It was an exciting time. I look back and think of the beauty and danger of those places. I remember the naked, four-year-old girl who was standing in the middle of a river in the An Lao Valley with her arms outstretched to us, crying. We landed and brought her back to safety. I think about the recognition of sorts that I received for killing the squadron's five thousandth VC. I remember seeing what we thought were people in the trees, and firing rockets and miniguns and watching the monkeys fall through the tree limbs. Then at Tam Quan, we did find snipers tied in the tops of palm trees and took care of them.

There was the young girl and her father, both standing on the edge of a spider hole in the An Lao. I hit him with a rocket that left nothing behind but smoldering rags. We came back around and I saw her about thirty feet away with a shocked look on her face.

The door gunner had opened fire, and I ordered him to stop. It was a free fire zone and we had engaged them by instinct. We didn't pick her up and I have no idea what happened to her. I hope she made it okay.

I remember the people we shot on sight with little or no remorse. In actuality, I probably felt more remorse about shooting the elephants, even though they were a mode of transportation for the VC. The people knew where they were and we knew what they were doing there. The animals were innocent. It was just something we had to do at the time.

There were the ''lightning bug'' flights north of the An Lao, the night recon missions, the night insertions and extraction of the LRRPs, the gunship support missions and the medevacs. Those were things that I wouldn't care to do now, but I am grateful for the experiences. They gave me knowledge and a deep appreciation of life.

I am dedicating this story to the aviators who flew in Vietnam, especially those who didn't come home. A special thanks to my wife, Bonnie, for gathering my letters into a journal, and for staying by my side through all of these years.

10.   FOR GOD AND COUNTRY

(Infantryman, Bravo Troop, 1967–68)
Bob Lackey arrived in Vietnam with a conviction and an enthusiasm for the job ahead. He left a year later knowing that the war was heading downhill, and all the sacrifices he had seen were for nothing.

It was the first part of April 1967 when I stepped off the plane in Cam Ranh Bay. We had to land there because our scheduled landing site at Bien Hoa was under mortar attack. It was a great welcome to the war, but I didn't care. I was in Vietnam and ready to go out and kill VC for God and Country, and that was all I really cared about. My first thought at Cam Ranh Bay was, "Jesus Christ, it's hot!"

After a couple of days of filling sandbags and doing totally bullshit details, I was beginning to get disgusted. This wasn't what we had been trained to do. Then we got word that a battalion of the 4th Infantry had gotten the shit kicked out of it up on the Cambodian border and it was a natural conclusion that we would be sent there as replacements.

I wasn't thrilled about this at all. During my training before going to Vietnam, we were always drawn to the glory outfits like the 1st Cav or the 101st Airborne. The 4th Infantry didn't even have a good-looking shoulder patch. The next day I was assigned to the 1st Cav. They were what the war was all about, and had the greatest-looking patch—a big, impressive yellow and black patch with a horse head on it. I was about as happy as a pig in shit.

When I arrived in An Khe, I remember seeing this huge 1st Cav patch on top of this hill that dominated the division headquarters. You could probably see that thing for miles. It was like the Cav was saying to the VC and the NVA, "Hey, guys! Here we are! Come and give us your best shot."

I went through a little combat leadership school at division rear, then got orders to report to the 1/9th. That assignment gave me reason to reconsider being so anxious to get into the fighting as soon as possible. The 9th Cav was the reconnaissance element of the division and worked in very small groups. I was assigned to B Troop to become one of the Bravo Blues, and my "gung ho" spirit started to fade away. These were the guys who were considered the Cav's expendable ones, the theory being that it was better to lose an understrength platoon of Blues than a larger unit. I thought, "Oh Lord, what have I gotten myself into?"

The next day I flew up to LZ Montezuma in Quang Nai Province. The area was called Duc Pho. It was the home of the 3rd Brigade of the 25th Infantry and we were doing most of the recon work for them. B Troop had taken over from an element of the Marine Corps who hadn't managed to get out more than 600 meters from the perimeter of Montezuma. The intelligence reports on the area said that 100 percent of the villagers were either hard-core troops or sympathizers. The sympathizers planted the mines, set the booby traps and dug punji pits. So it was pretty much fair game up there. If something got in front of you in a firefight, you killed it.

On my first mission, I hadn't actually been assigned to a squad yet, so I was put under the wing of the platoon sergeant, Richard Wilkerson. I only spent one day with his headquarters squad. We spent the entire night on the side of a big hill while the VC tossed grenades down at us. It wasn't my most pleasurable evening in Vietnam. There had been a photographer out with us, and he took a picture of our landing that became very famous. It has been on a couple of army calendars, is the theme for the official Vietnam Commemorative Medal, and shows up in many books and articles on the war. That picture got a lot of publicity.

I was assigned to a regular squad as a rifleman, and soon learned how much I liked to walk point. I would walk the point and Rich Affourtit would back me up, or vice versa. It didn't take me long to learn that the point was the closest place to whatever the enemy had in his possession, as in money. We called it "gook dust."

You could always tell when Rich and I had made a strike, because the first sergeant would come running up to us, demanding, "Alright,

Goddammit! Where is it?'' By this time, we would already have converted our latest collection of gook dust to MPC (Military Payment Certificates). I would purchase money orders and mail them home. There was a limit on how much you could send home at one time, and sometimes I had to ask friends to help out. You might say I made a profit on my tour.

I learned real fast, and soon became a fire team leader, but not before we were ambushed by one of the meanest bunches of NVA in the entire country. It was 27 May and we were on our way back to Montezuma for a rest, or so we thought. We circled over this village and wondered what was going on, then we got orders that we were going in. I thought, "Oh, shit!''

I had drunk most of my water, because I thought that we would soon be refilling canteens back at the base. We were inserted at the edge of the village and started to move in. The place was deserted. We couldn't find anyone. I was thinking it was a waste of time when I came around a corner, walked into a hootch and saw a new NVA pith helmet, with a big red star, sitting in the middle of a table. From then on, I moved just a little bit slower and a lot closer to the ground.

We swept through the village and had entered a sandy hedgerow area when all hell broke loose. We got fired on by more weapons than I could even imagine, including the *''Thump-thump! Thump-thump-thump!''* of the big .50 calibers. We got pinned down so fast I was stunned. We would jump up, fire a few rounds, and get pinned down again.

This was my first meeting with the Cav's commanding general, J. J. Tolson. I had been told that B Troop was sort of his pet outfit. He always wanted to know what was happening with us. What I assumed to be a medevac ship landing behind us to pick up casualties turned out to be his command ship. Out jumped this roly-poly little two-star general with a pistol in his hand. He ran up to my position, plopped himself down and said, ''What the hell's going on, soldier?'' I didn't know if I should salute him or what. He'd get up and fire his pistol a couple of times, then plop back down. He had this shitty grin on his face like, ''Ah, this is what it's all about!''

Our casualties turned out to be surprisingly low. We had a couple of guys killed and a few wounded. The NVA suffered a somewhat different fate. This was my first real good example of the Blue Team's attitude that there really wasn't a legitimate reason to ever take a prisoner. Our job was to kill them, and that was the bottom line. It was funny the next morning when news teams arrived from UPI and the Associated Press. It was only then that we found out that this same bunch of NVA had wiped out a company of Korean Marines the month before. These reporters wanted to get the scoop on what had happened. They were asking questions, and the person who was answering them was a jackassed colonel from the 25th Infantry.

The colonel was telling all kinds of lies about how his ground troops had saved our butts, even though we had fought alone for hours while we waited for them to arrive. Every time he would say something, our platoon leader, Lt. Ted Chilcotte, would break in and say, "Well, that's not really the way it happened." He'd then give the reporters some real details.

We got further support from General Tolson who was walking around and searching out guys with the Cav patch, shaking our hands and congratulating us on a job well done. He totally ignored the guys from the 25th Infantry. Because of this, we didn't make too many points with the 25th Infantry that day, and this was further evidenced by some of the lousy missions on which we were sent.

In late September 1967, B Troop moved up to Chu Lai. A day that really stands out in my mind was 13 November 1967. Our CO, Maj. George Burrow, got shot down in a huge rice paddy between two large village areas. Two squads went in to secure him. We got on the ground and got to him and his crew, then all shit broke loose. We seemed to be getting shot at from eighty-five different directions. Our headquarters squad tried to come in and get on the ground with us, and hundreds of rounds of ammunition were being shot at this single ship. Amazingly enough, only one man was hit. My friend, Jimmy Chryster, was shot through the neck and killed.

This was not a good place for us to be. George Burrow loved being on the ground, but I think he would have preferred being there in some other way than being shot down. A call went out for assistance. One of the nice things about being in the 9th Cav and the 1st Cav in general was that we were never inserted without a few gunships for cover. Unfortunately, this wasn't the place for gunships. We were in the middle of an NVA regimental concentration that was supported by an antiaircraft element. They had AA guns everywhere.

By the next morning, we had lost over twenty helicopters from B Troop and the Aerial Rocket Artillery, one of the heaviest losses in a single battle of the entire war. It took our gunships and ARA birds quite a while to figure out how to hit these guys. One ship would fly without any running lights, while another one would make a pass and draw fire, then the blacked-out ship would make a rocket run and knock out the gun. It was a risky maneuver and we lost a lot of ships and crews. They took a tremendous beating.

That was one of the scariest nights of my life. There was nowhere to crawl off to sleep. I spent the night standing almost neck-deep in rice paddy water and trying to sleep. It was a wonder I didn't fall over from exhaustion and drown. Eventually, a large force of ground troops humped in to our location. The next morning, a helicopter flew over at about 900 feet, which was absurd. We heard the *"Whop-whop-whop"* of chopper blades and looked up until we saw it. We had lost all these helicopters the previous day and night, and here was a 4th Infantry Division colonel flying over to take a look. Across the rice paddy was a huge grey rock, and behind it, two barrels reached up and went *"Boom-boom-boom!"* The AA gunner was an absolute pro, because all three rounds broke around the colonel's helicopter.

One knocked off the tail rotor. The pilot did a very good job of trying to auto-rotate, but he was too high up and it was too much of a strain on the transmission. He got down to about 300 or 400 feet when his transmission locked and the main rotor stopped turning. The chopper started a real violent whipping around. At about 250 feet off the ground, the crew chief was thrown out of the ship and we watched the guy screaming and falling to his death. Then the main rotor blade snapped off. The ship nosed over, headed straight down to the ground, crashed and blew up on impact. That is the sequence of events as I remember them.

The helicopter lost both rotor blades, then crashed and exploded. It hit about ninety yards from where we were standing. We could see the crews, their faces, the flailing of arms. It was one of my most horrible experiences. We didn't feel good about what happened. We had gotten our butts kicked and had lost one of our nicest men, Jimmy Chryster. Jimmy always had a knack for knowing what was coming up. He could describe the types of battles we were going to be in, and had even predicted his own death.

We got our own back about three weeks later. Gunships were just blasting the hell out of the place. The next thing we know, we were being inserted on top of the largest hill in the valley. We weren't too happy about it after seeing the gunships working out, but we were always kind of bloodthirsty.

We were under fire as soon as we touched down. A few of us crawled up to the top of our hill with M-60s, opened up on this force on top of the next hill, and neutralized it enough to run across to it. All the bodies over there seemed to have pistols on them. Pistols denoted officers, not enlisted men. Guys were grabbing pistols and stuffing them in their shirts. They were the best war trophies you could get. Naturally, I discovered a paymaster and took the pack off his back and put it on mine.

As we were checking out the bodies, I saw a guy who didn't seem to have any bullet holes in him. I leaned down with my Car-15, put the muzzle to his forehead and pulled the trigger, just to be sure. This sucker came flying up off the ground and scared the living shit out of me. I must have done a 48-inch vertical jump. It must have been reflexes or something, because my finger never left the trigger. He was already dead. There was another guy underneath him who was killed in the barrage of bullets. I was standing there with brains all over my face and sunglasses, which got a few laughs, but not from me. The man under this guy I had shot was the 3rd NVA Regimental commander, the commander of the force that had hit us on 13 November. We had just killed off his entire staff.

We were thrilled, because we all had great war trophies. I had a lot more money. They put us on the hill a few days later, because it took that long for intelligence to go through the documents and figure out what we had. We should have reported all the souvenirs, but being the greedy fuckers that we were, what the hell did we know? The survivors had dragged the bodies off or buried them. We got some medals out of it, so we were happy. Anytime you got a medal it was a big deal and meant a little article in the hometown paper. We had gotten back better at them than they had at us. All we really wanted was someone to kill and we got more than our fair share that day.

One of the biggest finds was the outfit's entire battle plan for the Que Son Valley Offensive. We recaptured one of our maps from 13 November, and they had taken plastic overlays and marked all the locations of their forces for the entire valley. There were hospitals, camps and weapons caches. We didn't know if it was legit, so one day Major Burrow picked a troop location at random and went out to see what he could find.

I think they got over a hundred kills. The hill overlooked the entire valley and they had a pretty good idea where we were, so we took the battle plans to heart. Where the plans showed a human wave, the Americans set up claymores, foogas (napalm) and everything else you could imagine. Places where diversionary attacks were planned were alerted and pretty well ignored. The NVA just got the shit kicked out of them.

By March 1968 we were north of Hue, and Bravo Blues were not seeing the type of action that we were used to. The regular strength NVA units seemed to have disappeared into the air. Of course, the massive numbers killed by arc lights (B-52 strikes) around Khe Sanh had reduced an estimated 40,000 NVA regulars by about 75 percent. It seemed that the war was finally starting to wind down. Our bombing above the DMZ and along the Ho Chi Minh Trail was so effective that the troops, supplies, and just about everything else from the North were not getting through. We were starting to encounter NVA regulars who seemed to be too young and too small to be packing AK-47s.

It was the end of March and we were sitting around the troop area, hoping that something would happen, when 2nd Squad was told to saddle up for a hawk flight. Our gunships had killed three NVA on a trail a short distance northwest of Camp Evans. Our job would be to pick up the weapons and military gear and get out. It was no problem—real simple and quick. When we landed near the bodies, things turned out to be a little different than we had planned.

After we policed up the weapons and gear, Vic Carter and I started to move down a trail, quickly followed by the rest of the squad. As we walked down the trail, it turned into what would later be thought of by me as a scene from a Sam Peckinpah movie where everything happens in slow motion. All along both sides of this trail were the AK-47 rifles and khaki uniforms of NVA soldiers. Holy shit! I'd shoot one. Carter would shoot another one. The guys behind us were shooting still more of them, but they were not returning our fire. Some of them ran, or at least tried to run. I fired at one NVA soldier who was fleeing through the brush, not knowing whether I had hit him. A scout gunner later told me that the burst from my Car-15 had literally cut him in half.

Anyway, the squad finally reached a place where a small stream cut across the trail before it continued into a cane field. We could hear a lot of voices as we stood there. As they started to move toward us and around us, it became clear that it was time to get the hell out of there. Carter radioed for a slick to pick us up. We each threw a frag into the cane field across the stream, turned around and hauled ass. After we were extracted, artillery and ARA was called in to blast the area. The ground unit that went in later learned that we were smack in the middle of a battalion of NVA teenagers. They were children. One of those captured was the battalion commander, and he was said to be twelve years old.

Our bombing was working so well that we were probably weeks away from winning the war. Then it happened. A certain president decided to limit the bombing of the North. He also decided not to run for re-election, or accept his party's nomination for president. Within a few weeks after that, we were seeing fresh NVA troops, tanks and the other stuff that had not been around for a long time. I guess we all know how things went from then on.

We got our Silver Stars for gallantry in action. The U.S. was getting a new president, and our effort in Vietnam was about to begin an irreversible slide. Oh, well.

11.   DAI DONG

(Infantryman, Alpha Troop, 1967–68)
*Joe Kelbus tells the story of the beginning of the long battle of Dai
Dong, also known as Tam Quan. These real events are the kind that
usually aren't found in the standard after action reports.*

On 6 December, 1967, Alpha Troop scout helicopters spotted radio
antennas protruding above village huts, and Six (the troop commander)
sent the Blues to investigate. At that time I was the radio operator for
Blue, the platoon leader. It was mid-afternoon when we got the report
of signs of enemy activity near the village of Dai Dong, about 5,000
meters northeast of our small base camp at LZ Dog.

My platoon of twenty-four men were the first Americans inserted
into the area. It wasn't a hot LZ and no rounds were fired, so it was
just a very ordinary, routine patrol to recon potential enemy activity.
While we were walking through the rice paddy water toward the palm
and coconut trees, we started getting reports over the radio that our
scout ships had spotted people running on the ground near the village.
We were ordered to move quickly into the treeline. Apparently, the
scouts thought that they had caught a few VC by surprise. Next, the
scouts and gunships started to receive heavy automatic weapons fire.
Our new orders were for us to be a blocking force against enemy evacuation
from the area.

We formed a perimeter and waited, listening to weapons firing from
the ground and the gunships shooting back. It was heavy, loud, and
furious action. As the platoon radio operator, I could hear all the messages
during the entire battle. I knew from the number and content of those

messages that this was very serious fighting. It wasn't going to be any ordinary patrol like I had at first thought. Even though we were hearing all this weapons fire, we were still not part of the action, but the gunships and scout ships were, and they were flying all around us.

We heard that a Delta Troop platoon was being inserted into the rice paddies near us, about 500 meters away, to help block Charlie. Then came the bad news. As they landed, they were pinned down by heavy automatic weapons fire from a treeline. Their platoon leader and radioman were killed, the platoon sergeant was wounded, and a squad leader took charge. They told us that a mechanized unit of APCs was on the way, but they never made it. The APCs got stuck in rice paddy muck. So much for the rescue attempt.

A much larger unit from the 1/8th Cav was inserted nearby to help us block. Then began a tragic mistake. In the confusion of the battle, Charlie fired on the 1/8th Cav and us at the same time, and both units began firing back. Charlie crawled back into his tunnels, and we ended up shooting at each other. The brush was thick and it was getting too dark to see anyone. There wasn't much that we could do at first. All of us hit the ground, stayed in our defensive perimeter and continued to return what we thought was enemy fire. As the firefight continued, Blue and I moved from place to place to give situation reports to the troop commander.

I had a new friend, PFC Norm Williams. Two days earlier, I had given Norm a fruitcake that I had received from home. I hate fruit-cakes, but he ate it and enjoyed it. I liked him. At one point during the firefight, the lieutenant and I picked up and exchanged positions with Norm. He was shot through the eye as soon as he took my position. He didn't look like he was going to live, and later that night he died.

That bullet could have been for me. I went to the wall in Washington twice and saw "NORM WILLIAMS" engraved on the black granite. I wonder why he died and not me. I don't know if it was a matter of a minute, or luck, or God's wishes. To this day I don't know. There are no answers. Only God knows.

We laid low until we made contact with the 1/8th Cav and realized that we were shooting at each other. It was already too late. Williams was dying and four more Blues had been wounded by friendly fire. I don't know what injuries the 1/8th Cav had. It was dark by then. We could still hear the gunships blasting away, but we were told to hold our fire and pull out so the artillery could fire on our position.

Six told us to carry our wounded back to a rice paddy dike about one hundred meters away. He said that the slicks were ready and waiting for a night helicopter extraction, without landing lights or any other illumination. We were to call them in as soon as we were in position. I helped carry Norm Williams to the dike. Bullets were splashing in the rice paddy water all around us, and again, I don't know why I wasn't wounded or killed. One hundred meters is a long, long way to walk in mud and water when someone is shooting at you.

Once we reached the dike, we formed a line of four squads and spaced ourselves for the helicopters that were coming in to pick us up. Blue was positioning the squads in pitch-black darkness, and the slicks were coming in blind—no lights from the choppers and none from us. As the platoon radioman, I was given the job of guiding the helicopters by sound alone. Boy, was I scared. I remember screaming into the radio handset, "I can hear you! Keep coming! You are to my right! You are getting louder! You are two hundred meters to my left! Move to my right! You are getting closer! I can see you (silhouettes against starlight)! You are getting real close! Slow down! You are on top of us! Land Now!"

All four choppers landed in a row, right on the button. In spite of the pitch darkness, I was able to help my platoon out of that horrible mess. I felt so good and so very proud. I have never been so relieved as when I set foot on solid ground that night at LZ Dog.

Days later it was discovered that Alpha Troop had tripped into the entire 22nd NVA Regiment. They had come down from the mountains near the An Lao Valley, and occupied the village of Dai Dong between the South China Sea and Highway One. A very large base camp, LZ English, seemed to be the regiment's target. English was the supply camp for weapons and fuel, and it also had a field hospital. The NVA never got that far, and their dead at Dai Dong eventually totaled 650. Alpha Troop Blues returned two days later for another recon. This time it was extremely quiet and desolate. There was no contact. We found the dead Delta Troop platoon leader in a rice paddy and carried him home aboard one of our slicks. End of mission.

I received a Bronze Star for my actions on 6 December 1967.

12. FLYING WITH MAJOR BEASLEY

(Gunship Door Gunner, Bravo Troop, 1967–68)

*Sergeant **Ron Chapman** was on his second tour in Vietnam when the B Troop commander chose him as his personal crew chief. This story shows why so many of the squadron's aviation crews were called "crazy." Ron is working on a book about his adventures in Vietnam.*

Maj. Lewis Beasley was a West Point graduate, and you could tell. He had close-cropped hair, spit-shined boots, and fatigues so perfectly starched and pressed that you would think he had arrived from the Point a few minutes before. If he removed his helmet (no cavalry hat for him), he would carry it like a cadet—between left arm and body, as though he was at a fancy dress ball with his lady. He stood out from the rest of us like a rose in a field of weeds. He was tough, too. Not just because he did the "Daily Dozen" exercise drill every morning, but mentally tough as well. If you ever heard him say, "THIS IS SIX!" you damn well knew who was in command. That's how he talked, all capital letters, not yelling and screaming like a rabid drill sergeant, just forceful.

We were a scruffy lot with our shaggy heads of hair, wrinkled and tattered fatigues and rundown boots. Camouflaged boonie hats with wide brims were favored day-to-day wear, and many of us pinned up one side, just like the Aussies and New Zealanders. Cavalry hats were for off-duty time, because no one wanted to get his prized possession screwed up. Almost everyone tried to grow a mustache with varying degrees of success. We were baby-faced killers with peach fuzz on our upper lips. You would think that we would have been spit-shined, too, but the major ignored the way we looked. Your performance was another story.

I was Major Beasley's crew chief. It was my second tour in Vietnam, and I had gotten damned good at maintaining the aircraft and handling an M-60 machine gun. I was a free-gunner. That's to say that I "John Wayned" the gun—no mount, no bungee cord, just hang onto about thirty pounds of weapon and ammunition (in a can bolted to the weapon's left side) and have at it. My freedom of movement was limited only by the length of a "monkey belt" harness that could be adjusted to suit me. I could climb almost completely out of the gunship, except for one foot hooked around a pole inside, and have a field of fire in a 240-degree arc horizontally, as well as directly under the ship. This was a big advantage in covering your tail, literally. The major liked that.

Major Beasley loved white phosphorous, and at least half of our rockets were always "Willy Petes." He also wanted lots of Willy Pete grenades on board for setting hootches and things on fire. At first, I couldn't throw grenades accurately, for love or money. I couldn't hit the side of a barn from the inside with a grenade, much less from a helicopter doing 100 miles per hour and dodging bullets at fifteen or twenty feet off the ground. When the major discovered this, he sent a couple of pilots over to take me out for grenade practice. We spent several hours flying around a free fire zone with me hanging out the back door, pitching grenades at whatever struck our fancy—hootches, spider holes, pigs, anything. It's sort of like throwing empty beer bottles at road signs from a speeding car, but you've got to consider the vertical, as well as the horizontal, speed. I finally got proficient enough at grenade throwing to satisfy him.

As much as the major liked white phosphorous, he also wanted some CS grenades aboard. These were a form of tear gas. While I was game for almost anything, I didn't believe in using gas, even if it was non-lethal. It's strange how you can kill people and don't think that it's wrong, but are not willing to do something that will not hurt them in the long run. I "forgot" to put CS grenades on board, and we flew a couple of weeks before a situation came up and he wanted me to heave one. Of course, I didn't have any of them. The ensuing silence on the intercom was so thick you could have cut it with a knife. Worse yet, he didn't say anything else about it during the entire flight.

When we got back to base and the major was out of the ship, he said, "Next time, there'd better be CS on board!" Fortunately, he didn't call for tear gas often, and only once did I have a visible target. That turned out to be a stubborn old man who wouldn't come out of his hole until after the third grenade. The major let him go. "Ah, he's just an old man. Let him be."

"Six" was always the radio call sign for a commanding officer. "Saber Six" was the Bravo Troop commander, "Apache Six" was the Alpha Troop commander, "Long Knife Six" was the squadron commander, and so forth. Major Beasley had a large number "6" painted inside the yellow squares on the pilots' doors of his gunship. The squares identified those helicopters belonging to Bravo Troop, and he wanted the whole world to know which one of them was his ship. When we referred to him, it was usually as "Six" or "the Major." I never heard him called the "Old Man."

It wasn't just the people that he outranked who had to mind their manners around him. We were supporting an infantry battalion one day when he got into it with the colonel commanding the group. The area was one of those typical rice paddy, treeline, mangrove swamp combinations that were so common in the lowlands near the South China Sea. The rice paddies were like an ocean with islands in it. The islands were hamlets of eight or ten Vietnamese homes with thatched roofs and walls constructed of bamboo, straw or clay. The islands were connected with low paddy dikes, running this way and that, and canals cut across the entire tableau. In this case, the area was almost fifty-fifty—half rice paddies and half islands.

We were scouting ahead of the grunts and searching for the enemy, flying along treelines, looking for bunkers, spider holes or anything else that looked suspicious. On this particular day, we found what we were after: quite a lot of enemy activity. It was obvious that the area belonged to Charles, but the infantry was headed the wrong way. We were there to find the enemy and direct the division's troops, so Major Beasley passed the word to the colonel and suggested a change of direction. The colonel refused, expressing concern over some light sniper fire that his troops had received from the area.

Six advised the colonel that we had neither received fire, nor had we seen any signs of a major enemy presence that would warrant this cautious attitude. He again suggested that the colonel change his plans and head for our area of interest. Again, the colonel refused. Major Beasley was more forceful now. He ordered the colonel to change direction. I know that colonels don't particularly like taking orders from majors, and this one was no exception. Once more he said, "No."

With a voice that cut like an Arctic wind, the major now informed the colonel, "This is Saber Six, and we are here to find the enemy. If you do not move your troops into the area where the enemy is, I will take my helicopters and my troops and return to base camp, right now!" The colonel changed direction. I never saw anything like it. Our commander had actually faced down a superior officer and gotten away with it.

Six loved to get in close and duke it out. He seemed to have absolutely no fear. Commanders are never supposed to show fear, but he displayed eagerness and affinity for closing with the enemy. We would be right on top of them before he would open fire, sometimes with unpleasant results. I had to repair or replace the Plexiglas chin bubbles on the "Laggin' Dragon" several times, because he had flown too close to a tree, or through one of the rocket explosions. One day he flew through a tree and caught a big branch, bending it back as it slid alongside the fuselage. It reached my open door, whipped inside and struck me square in the chest, slamming me against the aft cabin bulkhead. It would have broken some ribs if I hadn't been wearing my "chicken plate" breast armor.

Then there were the rockets. The 2.75-inch rocket has to travel a couple of hundred feet before arming, then it explodes on contact. It was not unusual for us to watch a rocket bore into the target without exploding, because we were too close to whatever Six was shooting at. Other times rockets went just far enough to arm, so whatever had been hit was still in the air when we flew through the debris. The crew chief and door gunner rode halfway out of the ship, and we would get pelted with pieces of flying mud, wood, people or what have you. Once I was hit by a chunk of mud that was large enough and hard enough to make me think that I had been shot. On another occasion, I was hit in the helmet visor so hard that it shattered and put a piece of Plexiglas in my right eye. I became more afraid of being hit by a piece of flying junk than by enemy bullets. It didn't seem to bother the major, even if the result was one of the most beat-up ships in the troop. He was happy as long as I kept the bird flying.

As hard-nosed as he was, the major was extremely concerned about the welfare of his men. Once we were inserting the Blues into an area held by the enemy, and an ARA (Aerial Rocket Artillery—48-rocket Huey gunships) bird lost its tail rotor during a turn and spun into the jungle. Within seconds, we were circling over the trees around the crash site. There was no room to land and assist the crew, but we could see them struggling to get out of the wreckage. They were obviously seriously injured. The pilots couldn't get their doors open and the crew chief appeared to have broken his legs or back, maybe both. He was trying to pull himself out of the rear compartment using his arms, but was making little progress. He would struggle, then stop, then struggle again. Even if he got free, there was no way he would be able to help the trapped pilots.

Six ordered a ship with a squad of Blues over to help. The slick found a small break in the canopy about one hundred meters from the downed bird, hovered down as far as possible, and the Blues jumped the rest of the way. The Blues could see our gunship over the wreckage and quickly thrashed through the undergrowth. As they arrived and were rushing to help the injured crew, we spotted the fire. The fire itself was small, just under the left side of the wrecked gunship, but also beneath the fuel cell and the rocket pods on that side. Six yelled into the microphone for the Blues to clear the area, but it was too late. The ARA chopper blew up while our troops were reaching for the crewmen.

Men disappeared from sight. One pilot was blown, seat and all, over two hundred feet through the dense forest. Other bodies could be seen lying around the blasted area, not moving. They weren't all killed instantly. One man stood up, staggered a few feet from the burning ship and looked up at us. We could see him, naked, black and horribly burned, and he could still see us. He raised his arms vertically over his head, at once the signal to land there and a gesture of supplication. Blue, the platoon leader, was on the radio, calling for us to help them. He died in mid-sentence, still trying to call us in. The standing trooper was moving from body to body, trying to help his fallen comrades. Now and then he would return to the center of the clearing and raise up his arms to us. Eventually, the condition of his body overcame his will to live and he collapsed.

Six was on the radio, calling for more Blues, trying in vain to reach Blue Mike, and fending off the ARA platoon leader. The platoon leader was naturally concerned about his own men and had begun jamming the frequency with his own inquiries. Six shut him off quickly and bluntly. "I have my own people down there, too!" Then more gently, "Go back to base. We'll get your people out as quick as we can."

In spite of the explosion, there were still a lot of tree stumps and brush that would wreck any ship that tried to land. The tree trunks were too thick for machetes, so a new squad of Blues called for chainsaws.

The saws arrived from the base camp about twenty minutes later, and an opening was finally cut that would just clear the spinning tail rotor of a Huey. There were still stumps and debris everywhere, so the rescue ship had to hover down inside the tiny clearing. You can't imagine how hard it is to hold a chopper perfectly still in good conditions, much less while people are getting aboard and constantly changing the center of gravity. I hope the pilot got a medal.

I have never forgotten the sight of that ship blowing up, the vision of human beings burned beyond recognition, but still alive and appealing for help, and the sound of Blue dying in mid-sentence. They have died in my dreams over and over again for more than twenty years now, seared onto the wall of my mind.

I'm positive that Major Beasley was affected, too. There was little said on the way out of there, as if a pall hung over the gunship. I couldn't see his face while we were flying, but you could read his frame of mind by the way he talked and the way he sat in his seat. You could just tell. When we arrived back at base camp, and I opened his door, he got out with a look of great sadness, visibly affected by the tragedy. For all his hard exterior, he had compassion. He didn't seem to show it, but if you were around him long enough, and paid attention, you could see it.

He didn't want anyone to see anything that could be mistaken for a sign of weakness, but he cared and he knew how to speak gently. Once we were low-level with a new copilot, circling around a tree and checking out a dink hiding underneath it. The new pilot was watching us instead of tending to business, and let the airspeed and rotor RPM get too slow. As we began to mush downward, Six took the controls and softly said, "Keep the RPM up, son, or you'll kill us all." His tone of voice was soft and almost sad, and no more was said. Once things were under control again, he gave the controls back to the copilot and we went on about our business as though nothing had happened.

That incident was a typical situation. Six loved getting into the thick of things, and often pulled back a White Bird (scout ship) so he could go in and take a look himself at whatever had been spotted. This is a good way to draw fire or get ambushed, and you never knew which it would be. One time, I spotted a VC with a rifle in a tree. He was hiding there, probably waiting for some unsuspecting grunt. We came upon him too quickly for him to react. I called the sighting over the intercom, the major brought us around to circle the tree, and I blew the guy away with a few rounds from my M-60. No big deal.

Another time I saw a VC in a tree. I called the sighting as usual, and we came around. Only this time it was a dummy or a scarecrow, tied to the branches of the tree. Our rotor wash made the branches move, and the dummy appeared to be alive. They were waiting for us. Three machine guns opened up, and it sounded like a popcorn popper going full blast. We had no choice but to get the hell out of there. Six gathered the two fire teams that were with us and set up a daisy chain that hit the ambushers again and again with rockets and machine-gun attacks. The Air Force took over after we had finished. Soon there were only tree stumps and churned up dirt where, a few minutes before, there had been lush growth.

Often after a shootout, Six wanted a closer look at what had been killed. Sometimes we would land. This always scared the bejesus out of me, because you never knew what sort of shit you were stepping into. It went like this. We've just shot the crap out of a bunch of VC and there are bodies all over the place. Six wants a closer look, so we hover down over the largest group of bodies and my gunner and I jump out to search them and check out the area. Six keeps the ship running to be ready to get the hell out if things get unpleasant. There are no "friendlies" there, otherwise we wouldn't be doing this crazy stunt, just dead VC (I hope), the four of us and the gunship.

I always searched the body with my left hand and kept a .38 Smith & Wesson ready in my right hand, just in case. Once a man wasn't dead. When he moved, it scared me so much that I jumped back and emptied my pistol into him. He didn't move after that. It put the fear of God in me. I grabbed what equipment I could see and hustled back to the gunship.

Major Beasley watched the entire incident with an apparent lack of concern, and after I had scrambled back aboard and hooked my flight helmet into the intercom, he casually asked what had happened. "The SOB was still alive, sir." I was shaking so bad that I could hardly talk. He just nodded his head, almost imperceptibly, and went off in search of more people to shoot.

I never envied the grunts, knowing that they had to face that sort of thing regularly. Eyeball to eyeball killing is tough to do, and I wouldn't have wanted their job. On the other hand, I had grunts tell me that they wouldn't have my job. Hanging out the door of a helicopter with no cover was sort of like being a target in a shooting gallery. I suppose it was a matter of perspective.

One day in late September 1967, shortly after we arrived at Chu

Lai, the major got a captain from the 101st Airborne Brigade to fly out with us and show us the AO (Area of Operations). As we flew low-level down a road, the captain told Six not to go beyond the village that we were approaching. "Why not?" inquired the major.

"Because everything on the other side belongs to Charlie."

"Not anymore, it doesn't!"

The gunner and I looked at each other across the cabin as we zipped past the village and kept on going. A single ship, heading into the enemy's turf. "Oh, shit," our expressions said, "now we're in for it." There wasn't much we could do except check our weapons and be double sharp on the lookout. The captain got real quiet. We hadn't gone more than a couple of klicks past the village when some dude took a shot at us. Six was furious. As we came around, he was yelling over the intercom, "Do you have him? Where is he? Who does he think he is, anyway, shooting at us? Can't he see the '6' on the door?" The major wasn't frightened. He was just mad as hell that some SOB had the unmitigated gall to pop a round at him.

It looked like an easy kill. The offender was standing in the middle of a rice paddy with what appeared to be an elephant gun, bigger than he was. To add insult to injury, the fool didn't have the sense, or the courtesy, to run or hide. This incensed the major even more. "Kill him! Show them what happens when they shoot at us! Shoot him now!"

So I shot him—a lot. As we hovered around and I pumped more bullets into the body, his buddies in the treeline got pissed off at us and opened up with automatic weapons. Now Six reached a level of indignant rage that would put fear in the soul of the bravest warrior. He broke off circling and began a sort of bobbing, weaving hover around the rice paddies, shooting rockets like Zeus hurling thunderbolts, while we fired our M-60s in all directions. Our guide, the captain, had only a sidearm and was yelling for a weapon. I pointed to my M-16, which was hooked over the back of the major's seat. He grabbed it and began firing.

We silenced one of the guns almost immediately but were still taking heavy fire from all sides. It was not a good situation, and Six quickly realized it. We were a lone ship, we were in heavy contact with at least three automatic weapons, and no one knew where we were. If we were shot down and survived, it'd be five of us (maybe), outnumbered and surrounded, with no way out. We were in deep shit. So he broke contact and left with the vow that we would be back. We returned with all of Bravo Troop.

In the next month, the troop killed 350 North Vietnamese and Viet Cong at Chu Lai. We went out in the morning with blood in our eyes and returned in the evening with blood on our hands. It was a particularly good time to be a gunship gunner or crew chief, because most of the confirmed kills were made by scout gunners or gunship door gunners. We would all mount up at first light and head out to a place called LZ Porazzo which was not much more than a big mound of dirt in the middle of a bunch of rice paddies. An armored unit was stationed there. After we finished with the day's work, we all flew back to Chu Lai in the evening. Our helicopters were too tempting a target for the NVA to leave them on an exposed LZ overnight.

The area west of Chu Lai proved to be a fertile hunting ground for us. We had pretty much eliminated the competition in Bong Son, and there had been days when it was tough to find something worth shooting at, but there were lots of NVA in the Que Son Valley. We caught groups of them in the open, day after day. They were used to the more conventional tactics of our Marine predecessors, and we were happy to "educate" them about ours. They were slow learners, but we taught them not to mess with us. The whole area was hot. I spent two weeks not only getting shot at every day, but having my helicopter hit every day. Each hit was a maintenance discrepancy that had to be logged at the end of the day, so I began to date the holes with a grease pencil to remember which ones were old and which ones were new.

One day we didn't get shot at, and it was the scariest day of my life. They say that you never hear the round that gets you, and I believed it. I had gotten up with a bad feeling that morning, like this would be the day I would get it. Everything was just like it usually was—up early, launch, out to LZ Porazzo, launch again, look for the enemy. No one was there—no one in the rice paddies, no one in the treelines, no one in the villages. It really spooked me. We got back to Chu Lai that evening and I found myself still in one piece. I secured my bird, went to the NCO club and commenced to tie on a drunk that left me hung over for two days afterwards. The next day, things were back to normal.

Sometimes the killing could be damned near funny in a morbid sort of way. Death was our constant companion, and guys would say things like, "Can I have your camera if you get killed today?" Once Major Beasley wanted to get a close-up look at this little farm village on what must have been market day. People were all over the place, going about their business and ignoring the mechanical grim reaper above them.

This was the thing to do if you didn't want to get shot. Go about your business, don't run, don't hide, don't wear a uniform, and above all, don't shoot at us.

Everything would have been fine, except that in the middle of this idyllic rural scene walked some fool in a North Vietnamese Army uniform. He must have been on pass and on his way to visit his girlfriend, intending to impress her or something. We were so surprised that we were past him before we could get a shot off. He began running as we came back around, running right down the middle of the main street with us in hot pursuit.

Villagers scattered like a flock of chickens as I began to walk machine-gun rounds toward him. My gun jammed, and we were past him again before I could clear it. The NVA was running for all he was worth, trying to get to a hut at the end of the street, and he made it, too. The major had held off firing his rockets to avoid hitting any civilians, but he couldn't resist this shot. One of our rockets went right through the door at the same time as the NVA. It blew up the hut with a satisfying *"Boom!"*

It was funny when it happened. I visualized the people in that hut and their initial reaction to the sudden arrival of this guy. Did they know him? And as he dashes in the front door of their house, they look up and see a rocket right behind him. Imagine their surprise and consternation. Perhaps it's not funny from where we sit today, but it sure tells a lot about our attitude back then.

I rode with Major Beasley until he left from Chu Lai to go home. He was replaced by Major Ryan, and not long after that, I was asked to become the technical inspector for the troop. Crewing for Six was a trip, but technical inspector meant getting promoted to E-6 and more money. The present inspector was soon going home, and there was no replacement en route, so I didn't have much choice. Besides, Major Beasley was gone and I was getting short. A couple of weeks after I got off the gunship, Major Ryan was killed.

Being a tech inspector was good duty. My days were spent inspecting helicopters and doing paperwork, and it was slowly driving me crazy. I had been used to going out and getting in the shit, and now I watched the troop go out in the morning and return in the evening. I wanted to be with them again, but couldn't get out of the job. I knew more about ships and gun systems than any of the others, and the CO wouldn't let me go back on the line. He said that I was needed where I was.

Then we got a new maintenance officer. His name was Mark Watkins and he was fresh out of pilot training. He was young and eager to get into it with the enemy, and being with the maintenance platoon rankled him. It didn't take long for the two of us to figure out a way to get out and try to find some action. We were in Quang Tri Province by then, an area that was mostly free fire zones. Finding the enemy was no problem because it was all enemy territory. Since helicopters needed to be test-flown after repairs or inspections, we had ready access to what was needed to get out and around. Our excuse was that the armament systems should be thoroughly tested as well, whenever we test-flew the aircraft.

Getting ammunition and rockets was no problem. All we had to do was hover over to the rearming point and load up. No one ever questioned anyone who pulled up with a helicopter. You wouldn't believe what we could get, just by walking in and taking it with no questions asked. We would arm a ship and go on a test flight. After the regular checks and tests were complete, we would continue along, "testing" the armament systems. This probably wouldn't have mattered to anyone, except that we were a lone ship and no one knew where we were. That was definitely against the rules.

Scout birds were our favorites, mainly because I was able to ride up front and check the instruments and things like I was supposed to do, yet still man a door gun. You got the most kills with the door gun. Riding up front in the pilot's seat of a gunship meant no door gunning, only the rockets for Watkins and the miniguns for me. A slick had no armament at all.

We had great fun for several weeks, shooting up whatever we found. It wasn't much, to tell the truth—old bunkers, hootches, pigs, water buffaloes. We didn't know where the enemy actually was, and couldn't go into the really hot areas alone. We spent a lot of time together off duty, and one of us always seemed to be in trouble, like the time I accidentally burned down my tent, or the night I drove a mule into a ditch.

Word about us got around among the troops. What we were doing was sort of a secret, but not too secret, if you know what I mean. People knew, but they didn't tell. The other guys in maintenance and other noncombat positions always wanted to come with us on test flights, because they knew we were looking for something to shoot and wanted in on the action. Eventually, they started calling us "Dennis the Menace and Joey."

One day we hit paydirt. We left Camp Evans in a scout bird and were several miles east of the camp when I spotted two dinks in a rice paddy. They saw us coming and beat feet for a hootch that was out in the middle of several rice paddies. Watkins headed the ship for them, but they were too far away to hit and made it to the hootch. We circled a couple of times, then backed off and fired all of our rockets at the hootch. I had an M-79 grenade launcher, and we fired all forty of our grenades, then hosed the place down with my M-60 machine gun. The hut was rubble by now, so we circled around, looking for bodies or signs of life. Seeing neither, we decided to move on and look for something else to shoot at.

We were flying along, excited as a couple of young studs after their first visit to a whorehouse, when I spotted a whole squad in uniform in a roofless hootch. I yelled "Come right!" in the intercom and had a clear view of ten NVA, who had also seen us and were scattering for cover. I got two of them before they could get out of the hootch, but the others were running in all directions like a flock of scared hens. Another was out the door and about twenty feet away when he went down with a half dozen or so rounds in him. Then I dropped another one. He was down a path and turned to fire at us, but not for long. He got off a burst that missed, and I put him down.

We were out of rockets, so all we could do was manuever around at treetop level, trying to keep them all within range. The problem was that they were going every which way and, being alone, we couldn't stay over all of them. The others made it into the brush and began firing back. We managed to silence two more in a clump of bushes with fragmentation grenades, then another NVA broke cover and ran. That was a big mistake. I shot him and reached for another box of machine-gun ammo—my last box.

We were down to 200 rounds of machine-gun ammo and our sidearms, and in the middle of a fight. I told Watkins that we were low on ammo and better get out while we could. He agreed and we broke it off. Five sure kills and two probables in a couple of minutes wasn't bad work at all, plus the two probables from the hootch. Not bad for a "test flight." We headed home the same way we had come, and that was dumb.

We flew right over the hootch that had been shot up earlier, and the two guys' buddies were waiting for us with a machine gun. We could hear the rounds zinging past and through the ship, and I felt my leg fly back and up. I was hit. Holy shit! That wasn't the time or the place to belly-ache about it, so I returned fire at the treeline to our right. The enemy machine gun was someplace in there. I couldn't tell exactly where, and hoped to keep their heads down until we could escape.

Watkins began coming around to go back after them. We were alone and out of almost everything and he wanted to go back after them. I motioned for him to get us out of there, and he resumed our westward heading. But since they were still firing at us, I fired back at them. He started to come around again. I had been afraid to look at my leg, but knew I was hit. Usually, I was respectful to officers, but there wasn't time. I stopped firing and yelled, "You get this machine the fuck out of here! Now! I'm hit!"

Watkins' eyes got as big as saucers and he didn't say a word, he just nosed over and hauled ass. I never knew one of those little helicopters could fly so fast. As soon as we were out of range and clear, he went to 1,000 feet and called operations. He told them what we had found and asked for infantry, artillery, air strikes and nuclear weapons. He actually asked for a nuke. Then the operations officer began asking some embarrassing questions, like who we were, where we were, what we were doing there, etc. Then the XO broke in on the frequency, ordering us back to camp.

As we headed back, I looked at my leg, my ankle, actually. To my relief, it was not as bad as I had feared. There was a small hole in the side of my boot and some blood was soaking through the fabric. My foot was still there, so I figured that it would be all right. It turned out to be just a piece of shrapnel.

The CO and the maintenance officer were waiting for us back at camp. The CO took Watkins inside and the maintenance officer took me to the dispensary. I was stitched up and taken back to the maintenance office. I imagine my ass-chewing was mild compared to what Watkins got. We had really pissed them off, especially when they saw the helicopter. The chopper had been repaired and had been scheduled to go back on the line. Now it was so shot up that we had to put it back into maintenance for battle damage.

Sneaking out to go flying became a lot tougher after that, especially since we crashed a helicopter in a cemetery the next time we did it. But, that's another story for another time.

13. SOME FOOL MADE A PILOT OF ME

(Infantryman, Bravo Troop, 1967)
Terry Young was first assigned to operate a radio in B Troop headquarters, then he was sent to the Blues to carry one on his back. This is a serious/humorous story about some of his experiences with the troop.

The first time I almost got killed was over a Montagnard village. I had been in the B Troop Blues for a little over a week and had just received an "Instamatic" camera in the mail from my folks. I was behaving like a tourist and trying to take pictures of anything that was interesting, and just about everything was. Our flight of slicks approached the village on the way to an insertion, and I got my camera ready for a couple of shots. The thing about the Montagnard village was its extraordinary geometric neatness. Unlike the usual random clusterings of Vietnamese hootches, the village was comprised of long, rectangular dwellings raised on stilts above the ground and arranged in meticulous rows. I wanted to capture that marvelous precision on film. As we flew directly over the village, I leaned as far out of the cabin as I could to take a straight-down shot. Closer, closer, a little more, almost there. . . .

The male fascination with the female body is a curious thing sometimes, and that curiosity was about to strike terror into the deepest part of my heart. Just as I undid my seat belt to lean out a little bit farther, the pilots noticed a bevy of unclad Montagnard maidens bathing in the river ahead to their "two o'clock." The Huey veered, and so did I. For a split second I was suspended in mid-air with heart constricted and bowels loosened. I would have screamed, but my stomach was in my mouth. I grabbed for straps, tubing, bodies, anything at all, with an enormous degree of panic. My buddies helped me back aboard and then laughed hysterically. Never again did I try that trick.

When I first joined the troop in the field in early June 1967, I was assigned to the troop operations section as a radio operator. I figured that some of my luck had already been used up just in being assigned to the 1st Air Cav. Ever since I was a kid, a lot of my adventure fantasies had centered around the cavalry. When I first arrived at the troop area at LZ Two Bits in Bong Son and saw the cavalry Stetsons worn by some of the pilots, I knew I was where I had always wanted to be. From Two Bits, we journeyed north to LZ Montezuma, a Marine camp at Duc Pho, to take part in Task Force Oregon.

The first casualty after my arrival at Duc Pho was a Blue; a young, diminutive kid who was suffering from an ego problem and had joined the Army to acquire the heroic stature of its uniform. He was so excited about killing his first gook that he jumped for joy, jumped up in the middle of a firefight. I guess he thought that he was now a hero, but the timing was awful. It was the last thing he ever did.

On one memorable day in June, a tunnel complex was sealed and CS gas pumped into it. Suddenly, from a hidden entrance, dozens of enemy soldiers emerged and started to flee. I listened on the radio as Major Beasley, the troop commander, swept in on a strafing run with miniguns and door gunners blazing away with deadly effect. Major Beasley was later credited with thirty-three enemy killed, while the executive officer, Major Burrow, killed eleven more. This was the power of the Air Cav.

My own excitement was limited to the action I heard on the radio, and to the evening card games with the warrant officer pilots, especially Flannigan and Bressem.

There were two troop mascots. One was a black dog kept by the Blues. The other dog, Irving, named after the operation that was taking place when he adopted the troop as his new home, was the favorite of the pilots. Thanks to the generosity of the pilots, Irving got drunk every night during our card games. Then he spent most of the following day sleeping it off in my tent.

Bravo Troop was back at LZ Two Bits in July, and I was now part of the Blues. Their 3rd Squad was so grateful for my communication skills that they made me the RTO, which meant that I got to lug around the heavy PRC-25 squad radio. Some welcoming gift!

Smoke grenades were part of my radio attachments. They were used as markers for extractions. Then I started carrying a couple of white phosphorous grenades and at least one incendiary grenade. I thought that I was ready for anything until I heard about the officer with a gun belt loaded with grenades who was hit during a night attack. All they found of him was a hole in the ground. I stopped wearing all those grenades.

Soon the Binh Dinh rice paddies became as familiar to me as the Kim Son and An Lao Valley jungles. Everybody hated the An Lao, mostly as a result of the heavy fighting there in the early days. Charlie was still there, but he was more difficult to find now. Once after an insertion, I was following another Blue across the top of a dike when a line of bullets holed the ground right between us. It had been an errant burst from our gunship overhead. "That's really great," I thought. "My own people nearly wasted me." Again, the aura of luck had held.

Every now and then we would have a stand-down. There would be a lull in the action or maybe some birds down for maintenance. The Blues would not have to hump the boonies that day, but it meant we would have to find productive work elsewhere. Namely, putting up more barbed wire around our perimeter. There were countless rolls around it already, but since the stuff did not reproduce itself, we were obligated to help continue its steady growth. One day we were laying wire when three or four VC fired a dozen shots at us from about fifty meters away. Everybody scrambled for cover, but no one was injured. I was lucky again.

Then there was the trapping mission. We were situated around the treeline segment of jungle while another unit was supposed to be herding some Charlies toward us. As I waited anxiously, I attempted to flip the safety on my M-16. Nothing. I pushed harder—still nothing. I pulled and twisted, but the safety wouldn't budge. Sweat—the nervous kind— began trickling down my face. My fingers hurt from trying to move the switch, but the rifle was essentially useless. Quite possibly, the enemy would soon emerge from that jungle. "Bushey!" I whispered to another Blue. "I can't get my safety off!"

Bushey considered this for a moment, then answered. "How are you at prayer?"

Not too bad, I reckoned, but I started to improve in a real hurry, said all the ones that I knew and made up quite a few. I never did get the safety off that day, but the enemy vanished before they got to us. I made sure that the problem, caused by dirt, never happened again.

Another time, the B Troop Blues were brought back to An Khe after it had been hit by a mortar attack the night before. We were being sent after the attackers because of our swift mobility. We followed their trail and discovered the mortar tubes hidden in a grove, but the enemy eluded us. We spent that night in the troop rear area in An Khe and had a great time drinking at the squadron bar. I didn't have any money with me and allowed Kenny to buy me five beers. The next day would be his last in the field. After that, it was five days and a wake-up.

The original mission was over, but Major Beasley decided to try another area the next day before we returned to Bong Son. In our rotation scheme, it was 3rd Squad's (my squad) turn for point, so we were the first to be inserted—no opposition, no problem.

As my squad was going in, the ARA bird that was providing us some prepping cover crashed 300 meters behind us. We were already on the ground, so the command squad was dropped near the wreckage. The Doc was with them and they would undoubtedly be needing him. After a few minutes, the command squad reached the crash site and began to extricate the crew of the downed bird. *"Ka-rooomph!"* The ground shivered as a white cloud appeared above the wreckage. "Oh God, no! Please, no!"

The ARA ship had blown up. Our stomachs churned when we realized what had happened and what it meant. First and 2d Squads were dropped into the area. As my squad waited to be lifted there as well, I heard Blue, the platoon leader, pleading for help on the radio. His voice was agonizing, barely more than a moan, and I knew that he was in a bad way.

By the time we got over there, several members of the other squads were virtually in shock at what they'd seen. Blue was dead, and so was his RTO. Warrant Officer Bressem, the Doc, and three other Blues had already been extracted by medevac. All were messed up. Bressem was a pilot, but he had chosen that day to persuade Six (the troop commander) to let him spend some time with the Blues to see what it was like. That timing had cost him dearly.

There was someone else on the ground, someone dead, without a face. They were still debating his identity, but I knew who it was immediately. It had been Kenny's last damn day—no more missions, no more patrols, no more hawk flights, no more danger. I was not going to get the chance to repay him for those five beers. I took what was left of one ARA crew member back to Graves Registration in An Khe in my handkerchief.

Six tried some consolation, even lamented that their deaths were not caused by enemy action. Hell, it didn't matter to them how they died. They were dead. I got totally smashed that night—we all did. The troop had to cut back on operations for a while until some volunteers from other 9th Cavalry units replenished our numbers. There was even a cook among them who no longer wanted to stay in a mess tent. Then the patrols continued. A sniper was spotted in a tree ahead of us and Red, the weapons section commander, rolled in hot, with everything blazing. The tree and the sniper were destroyed.

We were returning from another day of humping the boonies—hour after hour of pulling our straining bodies up craggy hills, struggling through mazes of wait-a-minute vines, slopping through rice paddies, stalking along dense jungle trails. This day we had found nothing but fatigue, and in the evening glow of dusk, the lift birds were taking us back to "the barn." Iridescent beams of light shot through the ranges of mountainlike clouds and accented the exquisitely beautiful landscape of hills and valleys below. The cool breezes flowing through the Huey cabin heightened the visual effect.

Suddenly, I felt a sense of elation, an exhilaration that is beyond description. It seemed at that moment that I could reach out and touch the face of God, just like the poem I'd learned in high school. Some might call it a divine revelation. So sublime was this feeling that I was sure that I was about to die and meet my Maker. The moment passed and I was still alive. Before Vietnam, and despite my religious upbringing, I questioned the existence of God with arguments of reason. Never again would I do that.

Our never-ending searches continued. Blue was what we always called the platoon leader, and we went through a couple more of them after the ARA crash tragedy. Both were pilots who had originally been infantry officers, and Six thought the experience would be good for them. Both were wounded by booby traps. That made three pilots so far.

The colonel got miffed at this expenditure of trained flight personnel, so B Troop finally got another regular infantry lieutenant, the notorious "Baby Blue." He was doomed by the most angelic, adorable countenance a mother could wish for a child. He was just out of OCS and he was a jerk.

He was broken in by Lt. Lou Porazzo, a popular guy who was to be the last of the pilots to serve as Blue. We were going to miss Porazzo, because we had no confidence in his replacement. A few days later, one of our teams spotted a suspect and went after him. There were ravines, undergrowth and some thick canopy. There was a burst of gunfire, and Lou Porazzo fell dead. He had been so close to being back where he belonged, back to being a pilot. We didn't forget him, ever.

Shortly after that, I returned to operations as radio operator. Ahead were more adventures—some time at LZ Baldy; the move to Chu Lai; the Tet Offensive; and being part of the advance party of Operation Pegasus (the relief of Khe Sanh)—but nothing compared to my tour with the Blues. Well, almost nothing. There were still some challenges to my protective shield of luck, or whatever you call it—a near mid-air collision, rocket attacks and so forth.

One day in the Que Son Valley, while we were flying to LZ Porazzo, we happened into a huge swarm of ducks. Apparently spooked by our approach, thousands of them lifted into the air right in front of us. There was no way to avoid them. *"Whump! Whump! Whump!"* Ducks splattered against the Huey in bloody, messy smears. By some miracle, none of them fouled vital equipment that might have caused a crash. But this was beyond belief. It wasn't enough that the VC and NVA were trying to kill me, that random events could drastically alter my expectations of a long life, now it was ducks.

"Tell me, Mrs. Young, just how did your son die in Vietnam?"

"Well, he was ducked."

Right! That night we had a lot of fun with the incident. Jokes like, what a fowl way to die, and at least he wasn't chicken. Somehow, it set the tone, especially after a few beers, for us to loudly sing the theme song that had been recently composed by one of our bards. The song belonged to all of us—pilots, Blues, everybody:

I remember when I was a barefooted boy,
Climbing in a Sycamore tree;
But now I'm a young man—
Got a cyclic in my right hand—
Some fool made a pilot of me!

CHORUS:
Some fool made a pilot of me, ah-ha!
And I fly in the First Cavalry;
Got an old worn-out Huey
That I fly in the Army;
Some fool made a pilot of me!

I told her we'd marry and build us a home
And raise us a big family;
Now she's giving her charms
To a blue uniform—
Some fool made a pilot of me!

I told General Tolson that I want to go home—
Just to see my sweet Sandra Lee;
He said have no fear—
Sin City is near—
Some fool made a pilot of me!

I went to Sin City, nice as could be
Just to see what I could see;
But when I returned, 'twas then that I learned—
This fool had caught the V.D.!

This fool had caught the V.D., ah-ha!
I'd seen what I went to see;
She said she was a virgin—
Now I'm at the Flight Surgeon—
Some fool made a pilot of me!

14. SUPER SCOUT

(Scout Pilot, Bravo Troop, 1967–68; Echo Troop, 1970–71)
*Warrant Officer **Larry Brown** earned the title "Super Scout" during the days of Task Force Oregon at Chu Lai. He returned to Echo Troop as a lieutenant and scout platoon leader in 1970. A handful of men survived one tour of scout flying, but Brown lived through two.*

I was a scout pilot with Bravo Troop in early November 1967. We had been working the sand spit area on the coast north of Chu Lai, jumping on things out there and finding lots of enemy activity. On this particular day, the troop commander was over an infantry contact with two gunships. A kid on the ground was calling for help. He'd give his call sign but wouldn't respond when we tried to get him on the radio. I was on the way out, and finally got close enough to contact him myself. We figured if everyone took turns on the radio, he might answer somebody. He responded to me, probably because I always made an effort to give my whole call sign and talk slowly and calmly to people on the ground, especially those who were in heavy contact. It was like saying, "This is Saber White One-Four, and we're all here to help you."

The kid was calling, "White One-Four! White One-Four!" I asked him what was going on. "They're all dead! My platoon leader, everybody's dead!"

An infantry company had been sweeping the area. The bad guys were dug into dispersed spider holes and little bunkers all over the place, and they had let the infantry walk right through them. Everyone in the lead platoon was basically cut off and surrounded. The entire company was in the same situation and could not help them. The NVA were in the middle of them and around them in every direction. A guy would shoot, roll to cover and get shot from a new direction. I told the kid on the radio to hold still and do nothing.

The problem for the dinks was their overhead cover. They couldn't shoot up at us very easily. We were able to hover over their positions and engage them with machine guns and hand grenades, without taking a lot of fire back up. It took two or three hours to kill off enough dinks to allow the infantry survivors to consolidate and get some protection for themselves. I never did find out what happened to the kid on the radio. I don't know how many bad guys we took out that day. I got to 170 or 180 kills on my first tour and stopped counting. Numbers didn't matter much after that.

On another day at Chu Lai, we jumped a company of NVA engineers north of Baldy. We got a call that "Snoopy Scouts" (the 3rd Brigade Scouts) had found an enemy unit and shot them up, and they wanted some help. One of the Snoopy Scouts showed me where he had seven guys lined up, supposedly dead. I made a pass over them and realized that those sons of bitches weren't dead. They were just lying there. We kicked back around, came back over and shot them. A guy with an AK jumped up and fired before we could take him out. We were coming head-on into him, and I kicked the bird around to get out of the way. We took one hit. It went right through the wiring bundle on the side of the aircraft. We lost all instruments and radios, and finally had to return to Baldy. In the meantime, Maj. George Burrow, the troop commander, got up there and started mixing it up. Most of the time, the engineers just jumped up and ran down the road in an attempt to get away. The major got about seventy KIA in that turkey shoot. My bird didn't get back up there until it was damned near over. We only got two or three more bad guys. I got my first AK-47 from that fight, and always carried one in my aircraft after that.

I will never forget the day my observer, Buchanan (we called him "Blade"), got hit in the sand spit area. We had shot up some dinks there earlier in the day. The first flight had been with a Marine Corps liaison officer, who was not an experienced observer. We had basically ended up having to point everything out to him. He would get distracted by things, like watching a pig run, instead of shooting the bad guys.

Blade flew with me on the next mission. An infantry company was sweeping north along the coast, and wanted a hunter-killer team to scout an area before they entered it. We took off to the northeast with Bobby

Zahn flying gun cover for me in a Huey "Hog" with 48 rockets. Zahn was a real rocket shooter. He didn't miss very often. As we headed out to the possible contact site, the operations officer called Zahn and told us to be careful. Bobby relayed the message and I popped off that I was too short not to be careful. I wasn't all that short, but I was trying to say something smart.

We came ripping up on this infantry company from behind. Their battalion commander was overhead in a C&C (Command and Control) chopper, telling them to get their asses moving. The company commander wanted an aerial recon. He wasn't sure what was in front of them, but said that it didn't look good to him. We went right on by them and over the front, then swung back around toward them. There were little clumps of brush dispersed all across the open sand spit area. The brush wasn't the kind of foliage that was supposed to be there. Blade opened up on a couple of bushes and took out two guys. The Vietnamese had little brush patches on their backs. They had dug fighting positions about two feet deep and bent over in them, and they looked like bushes growing on the sand.

I slid back over to the infantry and told them that the whole area on the other side of the berm where they were lying was full of people. The Charlie-Charlie (C&C) was pretty well pissed off, and still wanted them to move out. The infantry started getting ready, but I told them to wait. I called the infantry battalion commander and told him that there were people right in front of his men. We wanted to mark the area with smoke before they moved out. The ground commander offered to give us cover fire. I told him, "No." We needed to know when we were being shot at, but he should be prepared to get us out of there if something went wrong.

We headed back north, and were fifty meters in front of them before we started encountering the first bushes. We turned sideways, so that Blade could toss smoke. A bad guy jumped up to pop some caps at us. It started with a few isolated *"Pops!"* then rapid fire all around us. I was shouting at Blade to shoot, and hollering to Bobby Zahn that we were taking hits. I looked over at Blade, and he was slumped over in his seat. One of the first rounds had gone through Blade's visor and hit him just to the right of the nose, over his eye. The whole inside of the aircraft went blood-red. It took seconds, but seemed to last an eternity. Zahn later said that the whole ground appeared to light up under us. He rolled in and pumped all 48 rockets around us in one pass.

I wasn't flying my own aircraft that day, so there was no skid gun. I was watching Blade and holding down the trigger, and nothing was happening. I felt something slam into the side of my leg. A bullet had gone through the ammo can between the pilot and observer, continued on through the two AK-47 magazines I carried in my leg pocket, and lodged against the skin. I looked down at that instant and watched a bullet enter my pant leg just above the boot, then exit at my knee. It never touched me. Another bullet hit the same leg and left a nasty, bleeding cut. The whole cockpit was getting hot from the heat of the rounds passing through it. We were getting the hell kicked out of us. Then the whole instrument panel exploded. My face felt like someone had hauled off and slapped me with a wet towel. I started having trouble seeing.

We tried to get back to LZ Baldy, but were flying the wrong way. I could just make out a few things outside the aircraft, so we weren't flying totally blind. Bobby Zahn started talking us back as he flew wing beside me. My eyes were really burning, and everything outside was hazy. The shield below the saddle fuel tank was supposed to drain gas away from the engine, but it was full of holes, and fuel was spilling everywhere. The gunship crew saw this and they knew that we were in bad shape.

About that time, Blade tried to sit up in his seat. He kept putting his foot down on his foot mike to talk, but I couldn't hear him. He could hear me. I told him to hold his head back and stop moving around. We would get him to safety. They finally talked us back to Baldy. I set the bird down at Baldy by compensating for lost tail rotor control. The two gunship door gunners got out and started towards us. I reached up to shut down the engine and it quit. We were out of fuel.

Then someone was tugging at my harness to help me out of the aircraft. I thought that it was the gunners, but it was Blade. He had gotten out and come around to my side to help me. Then the door gunners arrived. They loaded us on an ambulance for the ride to the aid station.

I was covered in blood, but most of it was from Blade. The people at the aid station took care of him first, then worked on me. I had the cuts on my leg and pieces of metal around the eyes, but was in pretty good shape. The doctor kept saying, "I think I know you." He had recognized my yellow scarf. I had been hit earlier in October and had gone AWOL from the hospital to get back to the troop. He wasn't too happy to see me again. I spent the night in the "Dust Off" bunker with a couple of classmates who flew medevac.

A new doctor changed my dressing the next morning. Mr. Flannigan flew in to pick me up, and took me over to inspect my OH-13. There were three hits in the erector set tail structure, and more than twenty hits in the main rotor blade. The tail rotor cable had been shot in two, and Blade's harness lock had been cut. Crosby and I had installed extra pieces of armor behind the seat backs. Blade's plate had nine hits. Mine had seven. The engine, the radios, and the instrument panel had been hit. An antenna had been shot off, and the fuel tanks had five or six holes in them. The mechanics said the aircraft shouldn't have been flying after that kind of damage. It should have crashed on the spot.

One day at Chu Lai, a new M-60 came into the troop. My main observer, SFC Don Crosby, had a machine gun that had been around for a long time, but it was a real worker. He went over to the scout gunner that had been issued the new weapon and pulled rank. He felt that he was the senior scout observer, and we were the senior scout crew, and he should have that gun. I was kind of happy with the old gun. I told him that he had better be able to get back the old one if this one didn't work.

The next morning, we were on first light, running up the sand spit in front of a mechanized infantry outfit. I spotted four guys in a ditch. I came around slowly and crossed over them again as if continuing the same search pattern, with Crosby's gun out the door away from them. This allowed Crosby to glance over and confirm the sighting without spooking them. I would go in at an angle on the trench and rake them good, then turn around and let Crosby take them out. The skid gun stitched a trail that went right across all four of them, stopped at the other side, then walked back over them.

I kicked it into a hard right turn. Crosby got off about six rounds and the new machine gun jammed. He cleared it, fired about five rounds and it jammed again. Every time he cleared the gun, it would fire a few rounds and then jam. We had already wounded these guys, and now couldn't finish them off. We were trying to take them out with Crosby's M-16, by standing the bird up on its nose and firing the skid gun straight down, and by dropping grenades. He wanted to throw the machine gun at them at one point. I told him that what would probably happen is that they would get the son of a bitch to work. We finally got three guys with weapons and a radio, and the fourth one managed to hobble off somewhere into the bushes. When we got back to LZ Porazzo, Crosby went hunting for his old gun. It was back in the rear at Chu Lai for some reason, and they had to fly it out to us. I told Don to make sure a gun worked before he made any more swaps.

In the last part of November, my Pink Team was sent on a mission to a valley about eight to ten kilometers south of LZ Ross. Don Crosby was my observer again that day. John Fegg was flying gunship cover over us. Communications intercept had triangulated transmissions coming from a ville in a valley. This was in a three-kilometer radius of the place where we had stepped into a big mess and had 27 helicopters shot down about a week before, on 13 November.

We flew over the ville and couldn't find a thing. It wasn't unusual to fly over a place and not find people, but usually there were animals. You might see a chicken take off or some livestock moving around. What made this eerie was that nothing was moving. The hair was standing up on the backs of our necks as we kept looking around. I told John Fegg that it just didn't look right. Then we spotted a little stream, about four feet wide, running through the ville.

After a couple of passes over the stream, Crosby told me to come back around. He thought he had something in the stream. Some leaves in the middle of the stream were hanging up on commo wire stretched just below the surface of the water. If it hadn't been for the leaves, we never would have spotted the wire. We found where it ran out and discovered a lot of empty spider holes along the banks, but still no sign of anybody. Something was out of place, but we just couldn't put our fingers on it.

Then Crosby spotted something in a trench and told me to come back around. I told the gunship that we were going to do some shooting. I went to a slow hover while Crosby fired his M-60 machine gun into a pile of leaves at the end of the trench, and *"Bang!"* Something went off. I jerked the aircraft away from the trench, then headed back for a look. Our bullets had hit the end of a mortar round and ignited the primer. It had fired down the length of the trench without exploding the warhead, but it scared the hell out of us. The detonation had exposed more mortar rounds. Then it hit us. There were piles of banana leaves scattered around the place, and the ville didn't have any banana trees.

We uncovered something every time we threw a frag at a pile of leaves. We found a 60mm mortar, recoilless rifles, a .30 cal machine gun and a .50 cal; just all kinds of stuff. They had been put in position on their carrying poles and covered with the wrong camouflage. Those banana leaves were the only reason we found them. We hovered across a big area, about fifty or sixty feet across, that was covered with leaves. Crosby tossed in a frag. It was full of NVA rucksacks. The gunship was reporting all this stuff back to brigade, and they were skeptical. They didn't know how we operated, hovering around on the deck. They were saying things like, "How can you spot commo wire from the air?" We were low on fuel by then and had to leave station. The team that replaced us had a new scout pilot on board and a new observer. We told them what to look for.

We hadn't been on the ground for fifteen minutes at our base at LZ Porazzo when the major came over to Crosby and asked him what a recoilless rifle or a mortar looked like. The major said that he wasn't too sure. Crosby told him, then came over to me and asked what the hell was going on. What we didn't know was that while we were refueling and rearming, the other scout had gotten on station and couldn't find anything. That had reinforced brigade's idea that we were making all this stuff up.

Major Burrow came over and asked me to show him what we had found. Crosby and I were irked, and a little upset, as we headed back out to the ville. We told the major about the banana leaves, "Now, here's what you're looking for." Pretty soon, he found a foot-deep ditch with some leaves in it. Crosby tossed a frag, and we came back around. The grenade had laid down right next to this recoilless rifle, put a ding in the barrel and kicked it up out of the ditch. I was being a little facetious in the next transmission. "Six, I don't know for sure, but the last time I was told, this was called a fifty-seven reckless rifle."

We kept uncovering stuff while Six flew north to talk to brigade and try to insert some infantry there. The brigade was so overcommitted farther to the west that there was nothing to spare. We couldn't land the Blues, because we didn't know how big the enemy unit was. There was an armored unit about five klicks away, but they were afraid to send it without infantry support. Meantime, we had found some tunnel entrances that were about five feet across. They went straight down for twelve to fourteen feet and had big tunnels running off of them at the bottom. By that time, we could have reported sighting thirteen pink elephants and they would have believed us.

All brigade could give us was a TOT (artillery Time on Target concentration) and air strikes. By the time we broke station to get out of the way of the TOT, we had found thirteen crew-served weapons. We had jumped on a unit of the 3rd NVA Division and their heavy weapons support as they were deploying into the ville. They had made the mistake of using banana leaves from the mountains around the valley. The Air Force fighters put in delayed fuse 500-pound bombs. The ground would fall away in places, just cave in. There was one tunnel that was about forty feet wide and a hundred feet long that collapsed. The whole village was networked.

We only found one dude. He crawled up out of a spider hole by a hedgerow, and Crosby took him out. It was basically a case of being in the wrong place at the wrong time. After that day's action, the major dubbed me "Super Scout." We went back in at first light and, of course, nothing was left behind by then. We found the leaves scattered everywhere. On the northwest corner of the village was a beaten-down, four-foot-wide trail, heading across the rice paddies toward Dragon Valley west of LZ Ross. A lot of people had escaped.

Like I said before, that had been the same bunch we had engaged on 13 November. I was supposed to have the 13th off, but they were short a lift pilot and I had volunteered to fly a slick with Mike Covey. We were the only lift bird that didn't get shot down, or shot up so badly that it had to set down and shut down. We used the bird to lead in lifts of infantry reinforcements for our surrounded Blue platoon. The next morning, I flew our last surviving scout bird back to the contact site to shoot up a ridge and a ville, while the Blues and the major's crew were flown out, one load at a time, on the last lift bird.

December 5th was a day where we basically sat around. We hadn't been finding much in the AO. We had a new Red (gunship platoon leader) and Major Burrow thought it would be a good time to take him out and show him around. We started working around the area, and Six suggested that we go back and look for the commo wire I had discovered a few days before. We were flying with my scout ship low and Six and the new Red flying gunships over us.

Pretty soon, we all started taking fire along the ridgeline. Six and Red took some hits, and we started shooting up a knoll. There were people everywhere. It was toward last light, but Six wanted to put the Blues on the ground. They had to get in and out quickly. The Blues landed and were pulling off souvenirs like a son of a gun. They found nine pistols, 27 pounds of documents, one of our captured maps from 13 November, and many other items.

The documents gave the plans for the upcoming Que Son Valley operation, and prelims for the Tet offensive. We had killed the 3rd

NVA regimental commander and his staff, and two 2nd NVA Division staff officers, including the division's commissar, a full colonel. General Westmoreland and his staff were up there the next day to review all the documents. It was a hell of a find.

In the same time frame, we were working west of Ross in a nasty place called Dragon Valley (Antenna Valley). We had been making contact and taking out some bad guys. There was an infantry company in the area, and the Pink Team on station told them to be careful. The team was about ready to break station and couldn't give them support.

We didn't know how many people were in there, and the team leader cautioned the company commander not to send too small an element to check out our contact. He sent about five men. They got part-way across some rice paddies before the gooks opened up from spider holes and bunkers in a treeline. One kid was lying in the rice paddy, just short of the berm. Another one was lying on top of the berm. Two guys were pinned down in a bomb crater. The infantry started screaming for cover, so they could break contact and get their people back.

Two Pink Teams set up a daisy chain over the top of the boys who were pinned down. When the first team had to break station to refuel and rearm, we stayed to provide cover. A couple of guys tried to crawl out to help and got shot. Finally, I told my observer that the only way to save those guys was to get between them and the bad guys.

After a few more passes and hand signals from me to tell the guys when to make their break, we hovered slowly down the paddy between the treeline and the grunts and opened fire. One of the infantrymen in the bomb crater jumped out and ran back, using the aircraft as a shield. On the next pass, we got another one out. Finally, we got three of them back, but had to leave the boy on the berm. It's hard to leave somebody behind like that.

A few months later at Evans, an infantry kid came up and introduced himself. He asked if I was White One-Four, and when I told him I was, he said that he remembered me from the buckskin gloves and yellow scarf I always wore. He was one of the guys we saved that day. He told me, "I'm here to tell ya, I'm the only one of those guys going home. All the rest have been killed since, or died from their wounds. I want you to know I'm going home because you were there, because of what you did that day."

With all the medals and other bullshit I got out of this, those few minutes with that young man were more of a reward than everything that I have ever received. The only thing I feel bad about is that I don't remember his name. I'd like to say hello to him again some time.

We were at Camp Evans, northwest of Hue, during Tet of 1968. One day, we were working with Swift boats off the coast and flying near a village that had been hot all morning. A VC flag was flying in the middle of it. I had been on a couple of missions around the village. The guns had worked it over, and the Swift boats were shooting it up, but we were having trouble getting into the village itself, because of the heavy NVA fire.

Toward the end of the day, a last light team arrived to replace us and I knew we weren't going to be coming back. I made a run on the center of the ville from the ocean side and drew a lot of fire on the way in. Right when I got where I was going, I did a "Whoa boy!" on the OH-13 and came to a hover over the flagpole. The observer leaned out and cut the lanyard on the flag and we took off—trailing rope. All hell broke loose behind us. The last light team came in later. "You son of a gun. It was bad enough in that ville, but when you cut that flag down, they really got mad!" I still have the flag.

One of our tricks at Camp Evans was playing games with .50 cals. Once we spotted one of them, the gunship would climb up to altitude and stand off out of range and lob rockets at it. The scout bird would come on the deck, 180 degrees out from the direction the rockets were coming, and make a run on the position, just going like hell. The gunship would tell you when the last pair was on the way. As soon as that last pair hit the ground, you'd pop up from behind and spin right over the top of them as the gunner took out the crew. They couldn't elevate the barrels on those things straight up.

That was a fun trick to do once in a while, until the day I was moving out to get in position for the low-level run and something told me to break. A .30 cal opened up on us. We were flying right down the barrel, but this guy had waited too long to shoot. I think if he had a bayonet on the end of that gun, he could have got us. He just couldn't traverse fast enough. After that, I just didn't want to play "chase the .50" anymore.

We had a guy by the name of Lieutenant Ricktaun. We called him the "Red Baron" because he spoke with a German accent. He took over the scout platoon after we moved up to Camp Evans, and decided that he was going to become the all-time Super Scout and take over the title from me. He didn't like the fact that Major Burrow called me that. He told me one day after a briefing that he was going to be the number one scout and take over the lead in kills. He said, "The way we'll decide this is to have a challenge. The one with the most kills by the end of the day tomorrow will be the winner." He was flying an OH-6 (LOH) and I was flying an OH-13. We still had both types of aircraft at the time.

He got one or two people on the first light mission the next morning. We got one down towards Hue later on. By later on in the day, he had seven kills and I had four. They gave me the last light, because he had flown first light. They sent me to a bad place called the Ba Long Valley, one ridgeline over from Evans. I hated flying there. It was one of those real spooky places. The Red Baron called and said that we wouldn't find anything there. He had just been through it and hadn't found a thing. He had been razzing Crosby and me like that for most of the day. We dropped down and were scooting along the valley floor over a trail network we could see through breaks in the treetops. All of a sudden, Crosby yelled, "Come around!"

We started hovering along the trail as Crosby engaged with his M-60. He got four or five through holes in the trees, then shouted, "Look up front!" I thought he meant we were going to hit a tree. Ahead of us was a big bomb-blast clearing with forty or fifty people running across it. I had jerked the aircraft around, so my skid guns weren't lined up, but I turned it so Crosby could engage. He spotted one big guy with an army flight jacket and dropped him. He looked Chinese. I saw a guy with a white pith helmet and then lost track of him. We were finding a lot of other people, but didn't see him again. Crosby was razzing me that I hadn't really seen a guy in a white hat. I kept easing back over the creekbed where I'd seen this guy, then working down it, and pretty soon we picked him up again. The guy had a motor for a 122mm rocket strapped to his back. Besides hitting him, the tracers ignited the solid fuel motor. Fire shot out of the bullet holes in the sides of the motor, and this guy started doing flip-flops down the creekbed. It was a little hard to keep from laughing at that one, because it really looked funny.

We got back in to Evans and reported our situation, and Division's G-2 decided we should go back out there. They wanted us to pick up the big guy in the flight jacket who looked Chinese. It was getting pretty dark by then. Mr. Flannigan flew in one slick with a squad of Blues. We told him that it was a tight spot and we couldn't cover him very well. I thought we had gotten everybody, but it was hard to tell. We hovered around and couldn't see anyone alive down there. Mr. Flannigan landed the slick, and told us that he was keeping the chopper on the ground in case he had to get the Blues out in a hurry.

The Blues started out of the bombed-out area and began following the trail back to where we had initially found those folks. I couldn't cover them very well under the canopy. They reported four KIAs, then, *"Bang!"* A wounded dink had tossed a grenade into the helicopter in the clearing. It had bounced across the floor plates, went clear through the bay, and exploded on the other side. I couldn't shoot, because the guy was under the rotor blades of the slick. Someone at the site gunned this dude.

The Blues came back up the trail, crossed the bombed-out area and headed uphill on a trail where these guys had bugged out to the west. They were finding more bodies. I told them to forget it and get back to the slick. They got back to the clearing, toting a .30 caliber machine gun. Mr. Flannigan exclaimed over the radio, "They've got the biggest damned Army gun I ever did see!" The Blues policed up the big guy in the flight jacket.

The G-2 was waiting for us when we got back to Evans. There were no markings on the flight jacket to tell us where it had come from, and the G-2 said he was just a big North Vietnamese. I knew better than that. We took him out to the "Street Without Joy" and dumped him. We got twelve in that contact and that made us the day's winners. The Red Baron told me that evening that the matter was settled. I could keep my title. It was Crosby's eagle eyes that made the difference. He had been gunning for ten months when I got there, stayed for my tour and six months beyond, and then came back in 1970 for another tour as a scout gunner.

Five pilots had arrived at Bravo Troop on the same day in March 1967. Two of us, John Flannigan and me, completed our tours. One of the others was dead. The other two were severely wounded and medevaced. John and I looked out for each other. One of us had to make it home. The excitement of scout flying, the adrenaline rush of contact, kept me going. Some of the things that I said and did in those days followed me home.

Every now and again, we would have a beer challenge where the troop commander would buy a case of beer for the ship with the most kills. I won it more often than not, and one day he asked me over the radio how I always came up with the numbers to win. I responded in typical scout fashion that I knew how to hunt. "Oh yeah?" he said, "How is that?" I said, "The villages around here have all these little buildings with funny colored flags outside. When you find one of those things, you throw a Willy Pete in the front door and shoot the guys when they run out the back."

Of course, it was a joke and I didn't go around shooting up Buddhist temples, but some of the guys overheard it. I was sent to see the chaplain. I told the chaplain that it was scout humor, and he let it go. Then they sent me for an interview with a shrink. His report stated that I liked what I did and could joke about it. I probably was crazy, but you couldn't get sane people to do that job. The truth was, we found those dudes so far out that we were often afraid of running out of gas on the way back to base.

Then there was the famous hover-down. The story went that Crosby and I hovered down into the jungle and engaged NVA on all sides of us with machine guns, skid guns and hand grenades while I spun the scout bird around. We did go down into a bomb crater to better engage bunkers on two sides of the blast area, and there were trees all around us. But I could attack them with the skid guns, and Crosby could use his machine gun, if I swung back and forth in a 60-to-90-degree arc. We got four confirmed KIAs and maybe some more in the bunkers, but the exploit grew each time it was retold. We got away with doing crazy things like that because we knew that everyone else in the troop would be there to help if we got into trouble. I still sometimes hear about temple hunting and the hover-down.

I was back with Charlie 3/17th (Charlie Horse) in 1970. I had come back as a Flying Crane instructor pilot and ended up back with a scout platoon, flying OH-58s. The troop had a policy that new scout pilots fly fifty hours in the left seat before taking off on their own. No one asked me what I had done on my first tour, and they put me out flying with guys who had two or three hundred hours of scout flying. I had over a thousand hours of scout flying from my first tour, but nobody seemed interested. By the time of the Cambodian incursion, I had enough time in and had my own bird. The crews would pick who they would fly with, and I was the new guy.

One day at Tay Ninh, a couple of the more experienced kids decided that they were going to fly with me to try me out. We were sent to an area where there wasn't supposed to be much activity. It was one of those deals where somebody had just come out and hadn't found anything. I was hovering around in ten-foot-tall brush over a trail network and spotted a piece of blue poncho material. The kids didn't see it at first, so I pointed it out to them. Then we started finding people. We got five KIA on that mission. The other crews came over and asked my observers how I had done, and if they had to show me everything. "Hell no, he showed it to us."

These two observers started flying with me every day. At first, the platoon sergeant thought that I was ordering his two best observers to fly with me. I set him straight on that. I was pointing stuff out to them that they had never seen before.

A few days later, we found a trail that was heavily traveled. The footprints were just too fresh for us not to find something. I was so sure that we were on to something, that I called on the radio to verify that there were no friendlies in the area. A few minutes later, we started jumping on people. The observers couldn't believe it—"Here's more! Here's more!"

After we had shot up all the folks on the ground, I called the gunship and asked how many we had. He didn't know. I told him, "That's why we tell you how many we get each time, so you can write it on the windshield or something, and get that front seat to keep track of it." We had to go back over and try to count them, and came up with twenty-one bodies. The kid in the back seat, my observer, wondered if we should report more kills, but my philosophy was that you report what you see and not add anything. If somebody came out and discovered that we had reported too many kills, they'd never trust us again. Sure enough, an infantry company swept through the area and found twenty-two bodies and more blood trails.

Guys from the other troops started asking who was this Charlie Horse One-Nine (my call sign). The platoon leader came to me that evening and asked for the first time what I had flown on my first tour, and what unit I was with. I had sat through my fifty hours with guys who weren't finding anything, while they told me all about flying scouts. They quit laughing at my first tour flight helmet, my buckskin gloves and my yellow scarf. They stopped pestering me and calling me "new guy." All that shit stopped.

After Cambodia, we were based out of Di An, between Saigon and Long Binh, and were flying teams out of Zuan Loc in support of the 199th Light Infantry Brigade and the 11th Armored Cav Regiment. I was going with Carol at the time. She was a nurse with the 24th Evac Hospital. Carol complained that she never got to see anything in the hospital, so we took her out to Zuan Loc to see how boring it really was. I put her in the front seat of a Mr. Gibson's snake (Cobra). We called him "Teddy Bear." His front seat (copilot) flew out with somebody else. In the stair-step rubber, about five klicks out from Zuan Loc, a couple of ARVN companies were in heavy contact. Teddy Bear and "Hump" cranked up their Cobras and we took off. We were laughing and joking. It was going to be a great day, and everybody was going to get a chance at a medal. Ha! Ha! As long as it wasn't a VC sharpshooter badge (Purple Heart).

We made contact with the ARVN's American advisors, and they told us they had been taking heavy automatic weapons fire and some mortars. We went to check it out. We crossed over a jungle area beside a plantation and immediately began taking fire. Teddy Bear wanted to know if he should shoot it up. I said, "No." I had a good idea where the fire was coming from and wanted to take another look and mark it with smoke. Just as I got back over the same area, they opened up on us with an M-60. We started taking hits. Hot transmission fluid ran down my back, and the kid next to me hollered that he was hit.

We lost power and hit the 200-foot tall canopy, then slid nose-down into some tall bamboo. The kid in the back seat was hit in both legs, and the observer beside me was hit in the back and in both legs as well. We got out on the ground and I tried to establish a perimeter. We were down on one side of a ravine, and the bad guys were trying to work up on us on the other side. I got the wounded observer out. The crew chief from the back seat took both M-60s and started putting out fire across the ravine. Everyone at Zuan Loc could see the two Cobras start to work out over our crash site.

Carol was sitting on the ramp at Zuan Loc when everybody scrambled. The RTO beside her told her, "Don't worry, ma'am. We got a bird shot down, but the guns are okay. It's one of the scouts." He had seen her in the Cobra earlier and thought that she was dating a Cobra pilot. She sat there for a while and listened as they reported a scout down. They had no visual on us and no radio contact. Then we made radio contact and the Cobras reported casualties. Carol was getting more nervous and concerned as she listened to all this. The RTO asked her, "You are going with a Cobra pilot, aren't you?" No, she replied, she was with the scout that had just gotten shot down.

Where we had hit the trees and made the first hole, we slid along under the canopy instead of going straight down, and the Cobras lost sight of us. They had seen us roll over and hit the trees upside down, and they thought we were dead. The Cobras were making passes, but still couldn't see us. I got on the survival radio when one passed overhead and told them that "The Rebel," one of the Cobras, had just passed over us. The XO flew out to us in his ladder bird.

About twenty minutes later, the CO came by and picked up Carol in his aircraft. The XO's bird had a .50 cal on the side of this thing, so he could give us some covering fire. The ladder was just long enough for us to reach it, if we climbed up on top of the downed aircraft. I had gotten both wounded boys on top of the aircraft and was getting ready to get the M-60s when 60mm mortar shells started impacting in the treetops near the ladder bird. The bad guys were trying to knock it down with a tree burst. The shells started coming down around us, too. The two wounded boys were already sitting on the ladder, so I waved him on.

I had the two machine guns and needed to get the hell out of there. A cover bird told me that there was a clearing about 500 or 600 meters away, so I took off running with both M-60s and my own weapons, the AK and my .357 magnum, "Old Thunder." I was still wearing a chicken plate and helmet. It was one of those days when nothing stopped me. I had a place to go and a reason to be there. No one followed me and I couldn't figure out why. I got to the clearing with my tongue hanging out, really exhausted from carrying all that shit, and like a fool, moved out into the middle and slumped down.

Teddy Bear flew over and saw me laid out below him. He thought I'd been shot. He called back for a Blue insertion. The Blues were called Arps in the 17th Cav. Meanwhile, the ladder ship hovered over me, and a door gunner climbed down to help. He was a big, husky guy. I was hanging the machine guns on the ladder by their carrying handles when someone thought I had a grip. The bird took off. The kid had one hand and one foot on the ladder and they started to lift him up, so he reached down and grabbed me by the harness and cloth around my neck. Then an M-60 opened up. I thought that it was a door gun from the lift ships that were bringing in the Arps, but we later found out that it was fire from the guys who had been following me. They had set up to ambush anybody landing to help me. We had surprised them with the ladder rescue.

By the time I had the M-60s hung on the rungs of the ladder and was able to get my foot on one of the rungs, we were fifty to a hundred feet in the air. They sat us down in a safe place, and we climbed on board. My two wounded kids were still there, even though they had been rescued at least a half hour earlier. There was a medic to take care of them, but I was pissed that my boys hadn't been evacuated yet.

Carol had gotten the word that I was missing, then that I was rescued. The CO flew her to the wrong hospital first, then to the hospital where my two boys were being treated. I was already back at Di An, getting another OH-58, and preparing to head back out with two Cobra pilots who had volunteered to act as observers. The CO landed at Di An with Carol. She saw me and asked how I was doing and where I was going. "Back out to fly again." She told me that she couldn't take that kind of stress. "Fine, I'm going back out."

We broke up for about a week, but eventually worked it out. Later on, we were married at the 24th Evac. The wedding party was composed of second and third-tour 9th Cav veterans. After the wedding, we flew Carol up to a reception at Quang Tri where Charlie Horse was now operating.

One morning at Quang Tri, we were working out by Khe Sanh along the Laotian border. I smelled the cooking fires and saw the signs and requested an air strike. In the meantime, I was replaced on station by a second-tour veteran who had been with the Special Forces ground troops his first time around. When we got back out there, he told me that I had found a phony base camp, one of the decoys that had been mentioned about in recent reports. He had found the real camp and diverted my air strike there.

I told him that the NVA in that area had no reason to build phony camps, and that he had just bombed an abandoned camp. He wouldn't believe me, so I told him I'd prove it to him. I landed in a clearing beside a trail and walked fifty to a hundred yards to some old bunkers that hadn't been used for months. It was one of those foolish things a guy does once in a while, like the kind of thing we used to do on the first tour with Bravo Troop—land, get out and walk and look for something.

We put in another air strike on the right area. The first pilot missed and blamed it on an electrical problem. The second pilot missed and blamed it on the smoke dissipating too much. We marked again and both jets missed a second time. I hovered over the top of the complex and called the FAC (Forward Air Controller). "My observers miss. I miss. Do the jets ever miss, or is it always just electrical problems or smoke dissipating? Do they ever miss just because they miss?"

I told the FAC to keep me in sight and let me know when they got lined up on final. He told me they had us in sight and were heading in. The observer held the smoke until we were streaming it, then let it drop on target. I told him we could stay there as long as they needed us to mark the target. This time they hit the complex. We enjoyed razzing the FACs. I never heard a jet pilot say he had missed a target. It was always bad ordnance or an electrical problem or something.

The weather was too bad one day to get into Khe Sanh, so we decided to just work in our backyard, between the coast and the foothills of the Ba Long Valley. We found a mech unit and wanted to beg some C-rations. I landed next to the tracks and asked the crews if they had any rations to spare. They had Cs, but this was the third night that they were staying in the same stop, and they were a little worried about it.

They asked us if we would do them a favor and recon an area of rolling hills above them where they couldn't take their tracks. We eased up over a little ridge and found an old bunker complex. Something about it just didn't look right. Finally I realized that none of the spider holes or bunker entrances had any spider webs across them, as was common in the area. Just inside each of these entrances were signs that somebody had been sleeping there.

We soon found footprints along a little stream. They were still filling up with water. We hovered along a trail over eight-foot-tall scrub brush that was pretty thick, and all of a sudden, there they were. They were right under us. The rear seat hollered, and I kicked it around so he could fire and put a smoke out for the gun. The Cobra made one pass as I got lined up, then we got back in the middle and killed six of them.

They had a radio and a mortar, and one of the guys had a pistol. We had wiped out a mortar squad that was moving into position to hit the tracks after dark. I briefed General Hill, the 1/5th Mech commander, about the mission that night. He asked me why my report estimated six to eight people, when I had reported six killed. How did I know how many there were in all? He invited me to dinner and asked the question again.

"Sir, you take a six-foot piece of ground, count the footprints and divide by two. Everybody's going to step in it about twice. Or, you can just count the right footprints.'' He probably still doesn't believe me, but you can't give all your secrets away.

I returned to Echo 1/9th from November 1970 through March 1971. I was the Scout Platoon leader with the call sign, ''El Lobo White.'' We had Crosby and Leathers back as observers. They had flown with me at Chu Lai. Some of the young observers were skeptical of us, but we showed them what we could do and find when others couldn't. Squadron put out an order not to let the three of us fly together in one scout ship.

Red, the Gunship Platoon leader, came back from one mission with a bullet hole through his Cav hat. When I got back, I went into the officer's club to get a drink. I was wearing my Cav hat. ''White, you don't have a bullet hole in your hat.''

''That's right, Red.''

He pulled out his .38 revolver and shot the hat off my head, putting a bullet hole dead center between the captain's bars (''Railroad Tracks''). The place went dead silent. I looked at him and said, ''Red, if it had been anyone but you, you'd be dead right now.'' Needless to say, there were a whole bunch of guys who didn't want to mess with Red and White, if that was the kind of games we were playing with each other. Red had been with the squadron about twenty months and was kind of crazy himself.

I flew scouts about 1,000 hours on my first tour, and about 800 or 900 hours on the second. It's hard to express the excitement and emotions of those days. Some times things went a hundred miles an hour. Other times, everything moved in slow motion. In the H-13s, it was easy to get that, ''I'm all alone and the bad guys could be anywhere'' feeling. You were looking out one door and the observer was looking out the other door.

On the OH-58s or OH-6s, that wasn't so much of a problem, because you could see the gunner in the back seat on the same side as you. The observer in the left seat probably felt all alone as we made right-hand turns, and the gunner and I looked down at the ground. Sometimes we talked a lot. Other times, we didn't say anything at all, unless we spotted something. At the end of a day, you often had that euphoric, good feeling from the adrenaline.

I was lucky. I was shot down nine times and went down once from engine failure. But I never had anyone killed in my aircraft. Blade and

Leathers were hit on the first tour and a couple of my guys got hit on the second tour. I had one Cobra shot down over me by .50 cal fire. That crew was lost. Most of the observers who flew with me made it. I came out of it with three Silver Stars, four DFCs, four Purple Hearts, and a lot of other decorations. The story would have been different if it wasn't for guys like Crosby and Leathers, who covered us on those missions and kept us alive. They had very different styles, but their skills and eagle eyes were life savers.

When I first started flying scouts, Sergeant First Class Crosby taught me many things and demonstrated how to perform some important maneuvers. He had been flying scouts long enough to be able to do everything well, except hovering over one spot. He liked to lean forward and be aggressive on missions. The first time I found PAVN, early in the first tour, Crosby and I were working low in the scout bird. We spotted some guys in clean blue uniforms running away from a position.

I had never seen the PAVN light blue uniform, but Crosby immediately knew those were bad dudes. I made a pass, but wasn't sure who they were, or what to do. Meantime, the gunship on the deck with us went after them. I was a foolish young scout pilot and tried to read a map and fly at the same time. Then someone opened up on us with an automatic weapon. It took me a while to realize that we were being shot at. Just one mistake after the other. I ended up being hit, and Crosby flew the aircraft back to base. I told him later that I had made a mistake out there and had learned from it. It wouldn't happen again. We were tighter after that.

Staff Sergeant Leathers was so laid back and relaxed that you would have thought he didn't know where he was. Then he would quietly say, "Come around. I think I've got something." He'd lean forward long enough to engage a target, or take out some bad guys, then relax again and drape his arm over his machine gun. The day he was wounded west of LZ Ross, he just said very calmly, "We'd better leave now." People like that made all the difference.

I served with Bravo Troop from March 1967 to March 1968, with Charlie Horse (C/3/17) from March 1970 to November 1970, and with Echo Troop from November 1970 to March 1971. There was a saying I used to let people know that we could have cared less about our image, just about being the best at what we did. "We may not be well liked, but we are sure as fuck well known."

15. QUICK STRIKE AT QUE SON

(Forward Observer, Bravo Troop, 1967)
*This is **Matt Brennan**'s personal account of the Que Son Valley operation in which B Troop played a significant part. The cavalry raid described here might well have been the most successful one of its type during the entire war.*

Our first low-level recon flights over the "liberated zones" were turkey shoots as the scouts and gunships caught squads and platoons of North Vietnamese Army troops in the open, day after day. The NVA would stand frozen in their columns, gaping at the low-flying choppers until the gunners killed them. No NVA unit in the Cav area farther to the south would have dared to cross open areas in broad daylight.

Bravo Troop was usually assigned to conduct screening and reconnaissance for the 3rd Brigade of the 1st Cav. The scouts and gunships flew in teams, with an H-13 on the deck and a gunship covering it from a slightly higher altitude. These were the "Pink Teams." Battles started by the Pink Teams were exploited by a landing of the Blues. While a more pure form of scouting (fixing locations and guiding larger units to the contact area) may have been the troop's mission when it arrived in Vietnam in 1965, by 1967 we were more concerned with killing enemy soldiers ourselves. Other units were involved only after it became clear that a fight was just too big for us to handle without some help.

The troop moved north from operations in the An Lao Valley in early October 1967. We were to scout for an Army task force called "Oregon" that was replacing the Marine infantry in the Hiep Duc-Que Son valleys northwest of the Chu Lai airbase. We screened at various times for elements of the 4th Infantry Division, 1st Brigade of the 101st Airborne Division, 3rd Brigade of the 1st Air Cav, and the 196th Light Infantry Brigade. As had happened during a similar arrangement in the spring of that year at Duc Pho, those other units took credit for some of the troop's kills and most of the captured weapons.

The Que Son Valley was roughly divided into three zones when we arrived. There was a secure zone along part of the coast, centered around the Chu Lai airbase. This was bordered by a contested zone that began just west of Tam Ky and contained a string of fire support bases. Further to the west were "liberated zones" which showed almost no evidence of the war up to that point. While the contested zone held half-destroyed villages and populated areas, the "liberated zones" consisted of green rice fields that were ready for harvest, and neat, populated villages that often supported NVA garrison companies.

The "liberated zones" appeared to be the most prosperous part of the valleys for three reasons. First, they had the most fertile soil. Second, the farmers must have still been under the illusion that the communists would allow them to keep their rice fields as family holdings. Communization would proceed only after the war was won, and the farmers were still unaware of this little detail. The third factor concerned Marine operations in the region. The Marines had been occupied farther north, along the DMZ and west of Da Nang. In much of the Que Son Valley, Marine operations consisted of raids, with little capability for prolonged operations near the western mountains. There were more pressing problems further north, and the "liberated zones" appeared to have been left pretty much alone.

In the last week of November, a Cav line company captured a directive instructing the NVA not to shoot at choppers with the crossed sabers on their noses (Bravo Troop's choppers). It was raining more each day, and either the weather or the directive was causing poor hunting in the Que Son Valley. The troop had killed about seven hundred NVA in less than two months, and the rest of the task force was taking a heavy toll as well. Targets were just not as easy to find as before.

Our best day was 5 December 1967. The Blues had not even left the armored base where we had waited for a mission since dawn, and all the troop's recon flights had only killed eight NVA. The Pink Teams were on "last light" missions around the Que Son Valley. When they returned, the troop would fly in formation back to Chu Lai.

Light was just beginning to fade when the platoon sergeant dropped the handset he was monitoring and shouted, "Let's go, Blue! On the double!"

The platoon rolled away from underneath the bellies and tails of the slicks, saddled up and climbed on board. We were airborne within a minute. The door gunner on each slick always briefed his squad on the mission. Ours said, "Somebody shot at the major's gunship in the Que Son Valley. Broke the gunner's arm. Major's mad as hell and wants the gook that did it." He didn't tell us that the major's gunners had already killed four NVA. I assumed that we were after one man. Blues on the other slicks were getting their briefings and may have known more than we did, depending on what their slick gunners had learned.

Our slicks dropped toward the ridges that separated the An Hoa Basin from the Que Son Valley. Gunships were rocketing a grassy knoll while Larry Brown's lone scout ship hovered over a twin knoll about forty meters to the south, pumping tracers into a jumble of huge grey boulders. We jumped onto the grassy knoll as the last gunship climbed out of its rocket run, and quickly took cover in a ring of old spider holes. Red smoke, marking an enemy location, was floating over the short trees and boulders on the other knoll.

One squad ran into a saddle between the knolls while a machine gunner fired over their heads at two boulders on the military crest directly above them. When they reached the boulders, the machine gun stopped and platoon headquarters and the other two squads ran to join them. The first squad had already swept past the boulders by the time we arrived. To the left of the boulders were four bodies in American camouflage jungle fatigues, and I thought that we were attacking an ARVN recon unit and would land in some deep shit because of it. Then two men in green NVA uniforms were spotted in a trench in front of the two boulders.

The opening was very narrow and almost invisible unless you were standing on the edge of it. Two Blues were standing there, and they nailed two NVA from a distance of about one foot. Bob Lackey, one of the Blues, got his helmet and face sprayed with blood and pink brains in the process. He wiped the brains off his face and cursed. The other NVA was a middle-aged man who was wearing bifocals—the first enemy soldier I had ever seen with glasses of any type. I tried on the bifocals, then slipped them into an eyeglass case he carried in his breast pocket and left them on the ground beside him.

My main contribution to the battle was almost getting shot. I walked around the right side of the boulders and saw a narrow trench with a man in khakis lying face down in it. When I looked again, he was pointing an SKS rifle at my stomach. Two Blues, a machine gunner named Jim Borsos and a rifleman named Gary DeFries, were walking on either side of the trench. They both shot the man and didn't even bother to look back to see who he had been aiming at.

Gary DeFries still wears the NVA's leather belt with the star on its buckle. When the two Blues shot the one in the trench, a bush moved just enough to get a spraying. Result—one more NVA killed. He hadn't been camouflaged like a bush, but was wearing black pajamas and had wrapped himself so closely around the base of the shrub and under its branches, and lain so still, that he was almost invisible. They were very good at that trick.

The lone scout helicopter was back with us. It hovered slowly along over the first line of Blues, the machine gunner firing like crazy, as we moved toward the top of the knoll. Hot brass cartridge cases rained down on us, but we didn't mind them that day. Seven more bodies were strewn on both sides of a path that began beside the trench and extended about thirty meters to the top of the knoll. The scouts had been busy.

Each body received another burst, just to be sure. I was always a souvenir collector and this was a bonanza. The path or trail was littered with leather map cases, binoculars, compasses and other equipment. I was interested in the rings the NVA were wearing. They were golden with Vietnamese inscriptions. I assumed they were wedding rings, although I had never seen the enemy wearing them. They were probably command rings of some sort. I didn't take any of them.

We reached the top of the knoll and moved down the other side in a line, firing rifles, machine guns and grenade launchers into the jungle that began at the base of another saddle, again about forty meters away. Two NVA in khakis ran out of the jungle and charged us, running forward in a crouch and firing AKs from waist level, until they were shot down. More AKs flashed from the jungle below us to the left, and in front of us where the two NVA had appeared. We could catch glimpses of thatched roofs in both directions, probably temporary shelter for the conventional security around the knoll. A good idea, but worthless against vertical assaults. Gunships rocketed the jungle below us to the left, then another one hovered over us and blew apart the hootches to our front with rockets and 40mm grenades. One roof was blown straight up into the air about ten feet above the trees, then burst into flames before falling back. All enemy fire abruptly ceased.

We were ordered to withdraw and walked backward toward the top of the hill, firing to the left and front and grabbing everything we could carry. Some of the Blues had slung their rifles and were carrying armfuls of weapons, pistol belts and documents. We found an M-79 grenade launcher and a map taken from our choppers in the battle on 13 November. The map still had the 9th Cav crossed sabers under the lamination and had been marked with the locations of units on both sides. I noticed that the main NVA units were located in the mountains on the very edge of the Hiep Duc–Que Son valleys.

Documents and the other evidence confirmed that we had killed nine officers and eight enlisted men. The officers included a full colonel (2nd NVA Division commissar), four majors and four senior captains. Our major told us that the highest confirmed dead NVA officer in the war up to that point was senior captain. Among the NVA officers was the regimental commander of the 3rd Regiment, 2nd NVA Division, the 2nd Division's intelligence and operations officers, and members of the 3rd NVA's regimental staff.

The major didn't tell us that a battle plan had been captured for a coordinated attack on fire bases throughout the valleys on the morning of 4 January 1968. The only other high-level kill and intelligence coup of this magnitude took place at Khe Sanh on 2 January 1968. There an alert Marine outpost killed six NVA officers, including another regimental commander and his operations and communications officers. Again, high-ranking officers were personally inspecting a future battle site.

We landed again on the grassy knoll about four days later in a steady drizzle, and found a miserable place. The bunker beneath the boulders and the narrow trench had been used as graves. The back of one of the bodies in the trench was partially exposed and swarming with large, black beetles. One bloated, purple corpse had been left in the middle of the trail leading to the top of the knoll. He was lying on his back with wide open eyes staring up at the sky. As I looked down at him, one of the black beetles crawled out of a bullet hole in his forehead.

After a year with the 9th Cav, such things no longer left much of an impression. It was just business as usual. We argued on the spot over whether this was a prisoner who had been executed or the man who had taken the first shot at our commander's gunship. The only thing good about that day was that they didn't make us dig up the bodies.

The gunships completed the destruction of the 3rd NVA Regiment's command post on 11 December 1967. This time it was the common soldiers—the privates and the sergeants—who died. They were found wandering through the rice paddies north of the armored base toward Ross. A company of the 4th Infantry swept through the area as our choppers hunted down each cluster of enemy soldiers. Many of them were carrying two or three rifles from men who had been hit in other battles. Most of them hardly bothered to resist. When the fight was over, ninety-nine more NVA were dead. It would be hard to find a parallel in all of the Vietnam War for a single unit being so thoroughly destroyed by another unit, almost as if by vendetta.

The two victories made us media stars for a few weeks. Almost every recon flight or Blue landing was accompanied by newsmen. There were magazine writers, newspaper correspondents, still photographers and network camera teams. Our greatest honor was when Cathy LeRoy, the brave French photographer (she took the pictures of the Marines at Hill 881 and the NVA inside Hue) stepped off a chopper one day. She had come to the Cav to find some action, and division had sent her to us. She stayed for two weeks and later published pictures of the troop in *Look* magazine. We learned to know and respect her.

Cathy had dropped out of college in France, sold her possessions and purchased an expensive camera and a ticket to Vietnam. She told us that she never again wanted to lead a quiet, boring life. She wore fatigues, had her hair in pigtails and carried a canteen of brandy on her hip. She served me a cup of spiked coffee each morning at the armored base as we waited for the first mission of the day. I wonder if she remembers me—the young staff sergeant with the rifle called "Grim Reaper." She said she knew my kind in the Army and the Marines. I would go home, but I was too hooked on the action to stay away very long. I told her she was wrong about that. She was right.

Cathy was able to fly a lot of gunship missions and make some relatively quiet landings with the Blues. I remember one mission to the one-man bunkers. A Chinook with a full load of bodies had been shot down and we had to load them, plus the bodies of the Chinook crew, onto a shuttle of Hueys. Cathy helped with some of the work with one of the saddest expressions I have ever seen. She later said that the Marines were brave like the French Foreign Legion, but the 1st Cav was her favorite unit. They could do anything. I like to think that she was talking about Bravo Troop.

The NVA attack came off as scheduled on 4 January 1968 and was stopped cold. Long Range Patrol teams were inserted into the Que Son Valley and had watched the enemy units assembling per the original battle plan we had captured. The bases were already on full alert. We were taken to Ross to stand by as our scouts and gunships hunted down stragglers escaping toward the western mountains. As the slicks circled over the knoll where it had all begun, then dropped toward Ross, we passed over a staggered line of teenage bodies in green uniforms, faces up, feet pointing toward the perimeter wire about eighty miles away. They all had fresh NVA haircuts. Heavy machine guns had killed them while they were lining up for the assault. A two-wheeled farm cart, pulled by a water buffalo and filled with more bodies, was traveling down the single dirt road toward Ross. The farmer was taking them there for burial.

The attack had been conducted by the 2nd NVA Division and units from the 3rd NVA Division, our old friends from the An Lao Valley and the Bong Son Plains. They had marched 100 miles north to participate. It had proceeded on schedule, even though they should have known that we had captured their battle plans. So much for arguments about communist flexibility in that war. The attack concentrated on three American firebases and had managed to penetrate the wire of only one, Leslie, on a ridge on the far western edge of the Que Son Valley. Fire from quad .50 machine guns saved the day at Leslie. Most of the attack was the usual one-sided slaughter. Things would have been different if a man hadn't gotten nervous on 5 December and fired at the major's gunship.

Bravo Troop left the twin valleys with a Presidential Unit Citation and 915 enemy dead to its credit. We had captured 305 more, mostly in the early days there. Many of the captives had been young NVA soldiers who were helping the local farmers harvest rice as part of their political education. They were picked up by "hawk flights" (one infantry squad on a single slick) in areas that the NVA considered safe. Many of them were working in their green uniforms, and the best hunting was on rainy days when they didn't expect to encounter helicopters. The captives were typically unarmed—at least the hardware was hidden by the time a slick roared in at rice paddy level to snatch them. Farther to the south, in Binh Dinh Province, we had taken the time to form a line to walk across paddies in search of military equipment. We couldn't afford that luxury at Chu Lai. The nearby villages were often garrisoned by NVA companies.

If you don't consider the battle damage to so many helicopters, our losses were slight—almost ludicrous, except that no friend's death is ludicrous. One Blue radioman and two scout crewmen were killed. I don't know how many were wounded, but there were probably many among the air crews. The important thing was that we were not an elite formation, except through experience and on-the-job training. The unit was composed of volunteers and draftees, paratroopers and legs.

The air crews had a particular shortage of pilots on their second and third tours in Vietnam. Veteran pilots knew what flying in the 1/9th was about and didn't ask to be sent there. Most of us were in our late teens or early twenties and didn't think that what we were doing was anything special. We really had nothing with which to compare ourselves. The only difference was the mission, our superb and plentiful equipment, and the strong bond of comradeship that held us together.

Chu Lai was Bravo Troop's finest hour.

Note: A longer version of this story was first published in *Soldier of Fortune* magazine, 1989.

16. BREAKING THE TRUCE

(Troop Commander, Bravo Troop, 1967–68)

*Maj. **George Burrow** is as close to a legend as a 9th Cav troop commander ever got. In the slightly over three months that he commanded B Troop, it killed over 1,000 enemy soldiers, captured more than 300 and won a Presidential Unit Citation. Here is a small part of his story.*

Bravo Troop had been ordered further north to join the division and its squadron headquarters at Camp Evans, just south of the DMZ and north of the old imperial capital of Hue. It was unknown at the troop level why the deployment was ordered, but it appeared to be unrelated to Tet, 1968. The troop had moved progressively north from Bong Son to Duc Pho, from Duc Pho to Chu Lai, and now from Chu Lai to Camp Evans. Instructions were issued at the squadron operations and intelligence briefing that the Tet truce would not be violated unless we were provoked, or if American or ARVN soldiers and facilities were endangered. I made careful written entries to this effect in my small notebook and returned to Bravo Troop to conduct a troop briefing. As soon as the briefing was over, I conducted a recon of the area of operation with my gunship and a chase scout helicopter.

Our team lifted off from Camp Evans and proceeded in a lazy zig-zag flight across the landscape while looking for anything out of the ordinary. It was a beautiful, sunny day and there were no frantic calls for support from friendly forces engaged with VC or NVA forces. The country seemed to be at peace in every respect. This was the first day in over ten months that I had not been fired upon, or had initiated fire upon hostile forces. The truce was holding.

After about a half hour of this, we spotted a lone VC soldier who was riding a bicycle down a dirt road towards a small village. He had his AK-47 rifle slung over his shoulder and several grenades tied to his black pajama uniform. We hovered around him and closed to within ten to twenty meters, but he just grinned and continued on his way. The village itself was bedecked in bright flags, and there was some sort of celebration going on. The women were all dressed in colorful, flowing silk dresses.

We followed the VC until he was in the village square. He dismounted from his bicycle as we hovered in a slow circle just above him. He looked up at us again, grinned and gave the crew chief the "bird" (the finger). In my opinion, that was sufficient provocation. I ordered the young eighteen-year-old door gunner to "zap him!" The gunner responded with a short burst from his M-60, and the VC fell dead. His blood-soaked body lay motionless, still surrounded by the gala-dressed inhabitants of the village. It seemed like we received hostile gunfire from everywhere as immediately we left the area. It was so intense that it sounded like we were flying inside a popcorn machine. We flew back to Camp Evans thinking that we had broken the truce. What we didn't know was that the VC and NVA had no intention of honoring it anyway.

We received orders the next morning to conduct a reconnaissance mission over the city of Hue and the surrounding area. Communications between U.S. forces and ARVN forces inside the city had been cut. My gunship and an accompanying scout helicopter lifted off in very low overcast conditions and proceeded at low-level, nap-of-earth altitude toward the city.

Almost immediately we encountered large formations of NVA and VC troops. They were marching in battalion-sized columns toward Hue. We were so low that you could see the enemy soldiers' gold teeth as they gaped in amazement at our choppers. In some cases, we were probably the first gunship or scout helicopter that they had ever seen. Needless to say, we were equally taken by surprise. It wasn't long before all hell broke loose and the ground lit up with gunfire of all calibers, from all quadrants. We shot back while attempting to fly to a safe area.

We made it to the walled city section of Hue by flying down the Perfume River. A large VC flag was flying over the Citadel in the center of the city, and fire from the ground and rooftops was so intense that both choppers were taking multiple hits. Our console was lit up like a Christmas tree with warning lights for transmission and engine problems, so I decided to fly to the nearby Air Force base at Phu Bai. We made it. My crew and I immediately transferred to a second gunship that had arrived safely in response to my request for assistance. The ship we left behind had been hit over one hundred times. The maintenance crew chief quit counting at that number.

We headed back to the AO to attempt to determine the situation, and the location and strength of the NVA/VC forces that were occupying Hue and the surrounding villages. Again, we flew over marching columns of enemy. Again, we received continuous hostile fire from all quadrants. Air support was virtually impossible because of the low cloud ceiling, but where there were holes in the overcast, air strikes were in progress.

The big VC flag was still flying over the Citadel, and this was much more provocative than that lone soldier who gave us the finger the day before. The flag was symbolic of the NVA and VC thumbing their noses at the United States. My comments were similar to the slogan painted on the underside of my chopper—"F—k Communism." That slogan was also painted on a red, white and blue sign in Bravo Troop's operations bunker. It read, "F—k Communism . . . Sponsored by the Daughters of the American Revolution."

As we proceeded west of Hue at nap of earth, we approached a small village. On the south side of the village was a stone wall surrounding a cemetery. As my gunship approached the cemetery, the ground erupted in more gunfire of all calibers, and this time it included RPGs (rocket-propelled grenades). The gunship shuddered, the engine quit, and the chopper rolled violently to the left and crashed into a rice paddy about fifty meters from the cemetery wall. My crew survived with minor injuries and we began moving away from the village. We left so fast that I didn't have time to grab the AK-47 and shotgun that hung on either side of my armored seat. At least forty or fifty NVA soldiers crossed the wall and advanced toward the downed chopper. The scout chopper attacked the advancing NVA with machine-gun fire and killed about thirty of them.

I tried to engage some of them at close range with my .38 service revolver, but it failed to fire. Then I attempted to wrench an M-16 from one of the injured door gunners, but he refused to give up his weapon. Meanwhile, the scout chopper was placing accurate fire on the NVA. The survivors eventually took cover or retreated to the safety of the cemetery wall. Almost as if it had all been planned and coordinated, a Marine Corps CH-46 landed and picked us up. The Marine crew was not aware of the serious situation and the extreme danger they were putting themselves in by landing. I quickly briefed the pilot and directed him to return to the Phu Bai airbase. As the CH-46 lifted off, the Marine crew applied suppressive fire into the village and cemetery. They returned us safely back to Phu Bai.

There I was informed that another Bravo Troop gunship had been downed and the crew captured. A heroic action by the crew of a troop lift ship had rescued two crewmen, but could only recover the bodies of the other two. They had been executed by the NVA as the lift ship came in for the rescue. I had to identify the two dead crew members at the Air Force morgue, then proceeded back to Camp Evans to plan the evening reconnaissance effort and prepare those difficult letters to next of kin.

The only choppers flyable that evening were the small OH-13 scout ships. They were ordered into the area of operations to conduct a "last light" reconnaissance around Camp Evans. The scouts encountered more NVA and VC formations and killed about eighty enemy soldiers. They described them as bumblebees or wasps swarming in attack of a predator.

That night, word came down from squadron headquarters that I would relinquish command of the troop to Maj. Jimmy D. Weeks, a fellow Texan. I was to become the Squadron Adjutant (S1). I had been shot down thirteen times and the division commander was concerned about me. They felt that thirteen was a charm and number fourteen might not be. I was medevaced to Japan for eye surgery the next day. About three months before, the windscreen on my chopper had been blown away by hostile fire, with Plexiglas fragments penetrating my eye. My left eye had been virtually closed for three months now, and it was time to repair it. It was one of those "million-dollar wounds."

While I was in the hospital in Japan, I received the notebook I had lost when shot down near the cemetery. It was found on the body of an NVA officer who had been killed in the recapture of Hue. It still contained the instructions from squadron headquarters, detailing the conditions of the Tet truce. "Attack only when provoked, or U.S. and ARVN soldiers and facilities are endangered." Now the truce was broken forever.

Being in harm's way each day was routine, rather than the exception, for all Cav troopers in Bravo Troop. They were all heroes in their own way. Nobody wanted to be a hero, but it was thrust upon them by the circumstances associated with being in the 1/9th Cavalry.

Col. George Burrow retired recently after thirty-nine years of service, twenty-two of which came after the extraordinary events described above. What follows is a letter from Wayne D. Phipps, the young gunner who shot the VC on that first day of Tet, 1968.

I came into the Army in the mid-60s, during the height of the Vietnam conflict, and was immediately assigned to Vietnam as a door gunner crew chief on a UH-1C helicopter gunship. My first assignment was to the 1st Air Cavalry Division, B Troop, 1/9 Cav. I was a kid at the time, just eighteen and scared.

I was fortunate to have drawn that assignment. My future was about to be shaped and a pattern for my entire life would shortly be laid before me. The commander of the unit was a young infantry major by the name of George Burrow. Never before or since have I met such a man. He was the kind of commander we all wished for, a good friend, compassionate, understanding, and a good commander; but above all, he was a soldier.

My first personal experience with Major Burrow came in the A Shau Valley. On this particular day, we'd taken heavy enemy fire, which had caused severe damage to my aircraft, and I had lost a couple of good friends. At eighteen, this was traumatic (it was my first mission, the first time I'd drawn enemy fire and the first time I'd returned fire and killed someone). There was a sixth sense about George Burrow. He knew about his troops without asking. Later that night, after he'd finished his duties as commander, George Burrow, the friend, appeared at my tent. He brought a couple of beers and we sat and talked a long time. I got hold of a bottle of wine to cap it off. The next morning, I was back in the air behind my guns again. I was hung over, but morally, I felt a hell of a lot better.

To watch this man develop his soldiers into the professionals he made of them was like watching a maestro conduct an orchestra. All parts of the unit began to come together in harmony, and the final result was an amazing 200 to 1 kill ratio, the best in all of Vietnam.

George accomplished this record by leading by example and showing an honest concern for his soldiers. When I say leading by example, I mean he was where you were and was doing what you were doing— and more. His fame was such that Hanoi Hannah mentioned him by name on the radio, and there was a bounty placed on his head. Several newspapers and magazines wanted to write about him. I still have one of those articles in which we were dubbed "Burrow's Bastards."

I watched George over the next few months. He seemed invincible. When he got shot down, he didn't show fear. He showed dedication to the cause and was back in the air in minutes after the same target. It wasn't unusual for him to bring back an aircraft with twenty or more bullet holes in it. If anything upset or scared him, he didn't show it.

I can't ever recall him saying to anyone that he was the commander, or having to use his rank. Respect came naturally for him. His soldiers followed him willingly into the heaviest of battles, because they were proud to be with the best, and they would fight to their last breath without regret.

There are so many specific missions and instances I could relate. However, this isn't intended to tell war stories, only to paint for you a picture of a soldier of days gone by. George was truly a soldier, because when the action was heaviest, he was at his best.

When George left the troop in 1968, he left behind a legacy. Although his legacy is not tangible, it produced tangible results. I don't remember anyone mentioning his name when we flew or when the action got heavy, but what he had instilled into his soldiers was a desire to succeed that produced those results.

I stayed with the troop until 1970. When they phased out the old gunships and replaced them with Cobras, I was phased out too. On the day I departed, I remember looking down the flight line at the old gunship. She was never to fly again. She had taken us out and brought us home for nearly 2,000 hours of flying. She shook laterally and vertically and had high-frequency vibrations. Each new mission meant more rivets lost somewhere over Vietnam. There's no telling how many bullet holes the ship had in it over the years, probably hundreds. Some were patched with beer cans, and those in non-critical areas were often taped and then spray-painted. Some of the crew members she had taken out didn't come back alive. Still, I felt I was leaving a good friend behind.

I didn't realize it at the time, but I had brought to close an era. I was the last of Burrow's Bastards. Some were dead, some were missing, some had been medically evacuated from the country, and some went home normally, but they were all gone.

I lost track of George over the years. One fellow Cav trooper told me he had died. In 1987, I found that George was alive and well and still in the Army. He'll be retiring this spring. I'll be retiring this fall. As I look back over these past twenty-two years, one man shaped my future more than all the others combined. He taught me to care for my soldiers and my equipment, to lead by example and to understand my troops.

I only hope that when this country goes to war again, there are more Georges around to take care of this Army and our soldiers. May God help us if there aren't—goodbye, George!

Note: This letter was presented at Colonel Burrow's retirement ceremonies. My thanks to Wayne Phipps and George Burrow for permission to reprint it.

17. SHOOT-DOWN

(Gunship Pilot, Bravo Troop, 1967–68)
*Warrant Officer **William Neuman** arrived at B Troop during one of its most intense periods of action. This is the story of his first shoot-down during Tet, as he flew copilot to the troop commander. This re-tells part of the previous story from a different perspective. Major Burrow acknowledges the air strike, but attributes the downed crew's survival to the scout ship's attacks. Undoubtedly, both elements played their parts.*

On the morning of 2 February 1968, I was flying 6X (copilot) for the CO of Bravo Troop, 1/9th Cav, out of Camp Evans. Our aircraft was a UH-1B (Huey) gunship with a crew of four. Our mission, with the assistance of WO Charles P. Inman and his observer in an OH-13, was to accomplish a visual recon of a possible LZ northwest of the Imperial city of Hue. The marines and ARVN were struggling with the 7,000-plus NVA troops inside the city. We were supposed to find a suitable LZ for the insertion of the Cav's 3rd Brigade to block NVA supply routes into Hue. This was happening only two days after the beginning of the Tet Offensive, and things weren't really going well. We all felt that we didn't have the degree of control in the AO (Area of Operations) that we wanted.

We were reconning the trees surrounding the large rice paddy that had been selected as a possible LZ. When I say reconning, I mean flying low and slow, twenty feet up and at seventy knots, down in the zap zone. It seemed that the only place the major knew where to fly (against my recommendations) was in the zap zone. At the north end of the LZ was a fairly large cemetery, containing the familiar circular graves. As we flew west past the graves, we started receiving intense automatic weapons fire. All the while, Charlie Inman was orbiting over-head in his OH-13. This was not the usual practice for recon team operations. The gunship usually orbited over the scout ship, but the major wanted to "snoop and poop" from the Huey.

We advised Inman that we were receiving fire. He immediately in-formed us that he could see seventy-five to one hundred NVA troops dug into the graves of the cemetery. Just as he completed his transmission, we received numerous hits in the cockpit area and felt a tremendous shudder and yaw in the aircraft. Sergeant Laudner, who was manning the M-60 on the starboard side, yelled over the intercom that we had been hit by a recoilless rifle shell or an RPG. By now we knew that Flashing Saber Six was going down. We had no fore and aft cyclic control. The CO and I were both pulling back as hard as we could on the cyclic, trying to keep the ship from nosing over.

The grinding noise was deafening as we crashed into a rice paddy and slid to a stop. We could see the NVA coming after us from off to our right. We heard their yelling above the noise from their weapons. Bullets were splattering mud all over the wrecked Huey and piercing the already crumpled skin. A small fire appeared under the engine, just forward of the tail pipe.

Specialist 4 Hooker was the first man out of the ship, followed by me, then the CO. We were about ten meters away when we realized that Sergeant Laudner wasn't with us. Pistols in hand, we suddenly realized that we had no firepower against the AKs and whatever else the NVA had. Hooker ran back to the wreckage to check on Laudner and to retrieve my M-16, which was hanging on the back of my seat. By now, Inman in his OH-13 had rolled in on the NVA with his skidgun and the M-16 fired by the observer. As Inman attacked, the NVA quit firing at us and trained all their fire on him. This allowed us to crawl a few more precious feet in the putrid rice paddy. The OH-13 accomplished this maneuver several more times, allowing us to get approximately fifty meters away from the crash site.

Believe me, there isn't much consolation in firing a .45 automatic pistol at one hundred NVA troops. The sound of the .45s was almost comical against the roar of all those AKs. Then Hooker began running toward us, M-16 at port arms and a smile on his face. Our firepower was almost here. A long burst of AK fire hit all around, splattering mud and dung all over us. When I looked back up, Hooker was falling face first, and rifle muzzle first, into the mud. He had taken an AK round through the left thigh, and his smile was suddenly replaced by an anguished, mud-covered frown. The M-16, full of mud from the muzzle to the breach, had been rendered useless. Hooker grimaced as he told us that Laudner was alive in the wreckage and would take his chances by playing dead.

As we lay there, huddled in the stench, my thoughts wandered. I wondered if we would be rescued or captured. Should I save one round for myself? Had Inman called for an air strike? I said the Lord's Prayer over and over to myself. Charlie Inman continued to make passes on the NVA, even though he was out of ammunition and surely low on fuel. Only fifteen or twenty minutes had passed since the crash, but it seemed like hours. Just after Inman made his last pass, the NVA headed for the crumpled Huey, shooting and yelling. Our concern for Laudner, who was still lying in the wreckage, was at a peak. We were sure he didn't have a chance.

Then we heard the sound of jets coming in low from behind us. This was the most welcome sound I have ever heard. I don't think the NVA felt quite that way. They turned around and ran back toward the treeline and the safety of the graves. I looked back and saw two A-4 Skyhawks coming in fast from the south. The Skyhawks streaked over us at approximately one hundred feet and dropped two napalm cannisters on the NVA. The heat was intense, even across the seventy-five meters that separated us from them. I remember thinking what an awesome weapon napalm was. It seemed to vaporize everything in its path.

After the initial fireball, the silence was unbelievable. No more NVA, no more jets, no helicopters, only the sounds of our hearts pounding. We had truly been "delivered from evil." We laid there in silence for a few more minutes, contemplating what had happened to us and trying to comfort Sergeant Hooker. The experience was one I hoped that I would never repeat again. Fighting on the ground was for the infantry, not for helicopter crews. Unfortunately, I was destined to repeat the experience two more times before completing my tour.

The beautiful sound of a helicopter broke the silence. A Marine CH-46 had been dispatched to pick us up and take us to the hospital at Phu Bai. Saber Six and I were debriefed and sent back to Camp Evans. Hooker and Laudner remained in the hospital and, I suspect, were evacuated to Japan or the States. I wrote Charlie Inman and his observer up for Silver Stars, but was medevaced myself two months later. I assume that they received the Stars, but I don't know for sure. Maybe I'll run into them some day at a 1st Cav reunion.

18. DOC

(Infantry Medic, Alpha Troop, 1968–69)
*Spec-5 **Lloyd Brockney** cared more about the men in his trust than he did about himself. This kind of courage often made medics the most respected members of Vietnam combat outfits.*

I remember seeing all those young guys coming into the Nam, fresh out of AIT. I wondered what was going on in their minds. Not only was the army new to them, but they were being sent directly into combat at eighteen or nineteen years old. I had already been in the army for three years, and being a Spec-5, at least had a comfortable knowledge of how the army worked and how to get things done. I felt like an old man at twenty-two, especially standing next to those green recruits.

After basic training at Fort Dix, I attended Medical AIT (Advanced Individual Training) at Fort Sam Houston, Texas. I had originally wanted to be in armor, as a turret gunner, but the army sent me to medical training because of my flat feet. I went to Germany after the medical training. That cost an extra year of enlistment. Germany was a good place for a medic to train. You had to learn to speak some foreign words and get used to communicating without using much language. That helped me later in Vietnam. I really got into in-depth training for a while—doing hard duty in the O.R. (Operating Room). I found that you don't have to be in combat to die of wounds. Each of us had to do a case study—from O.R. to outcome. The man I had chosen died of shrapnel wounds to the brain from a grenade explosion during a training exercise.

After that temporary duty, I returned to my outfit (546th Medical Company) and learned that they were looking for volunteers for dust-off duty. I took a flight physical, but as sometimes happens in the army, they screwed it up. My unit rotated back Stateside before I could complete another physical. We spent several months on "The Hill" at Fort Benning, where I met a returned Vietnam medic from the Big Red One. I never asked any questions and he didn't volunteer any information, but you could see the look of combat in his eyes. Then I got my orders for Vietnam. I got used to seeing that look a lot over there.

A couple of other medics had gotten orders and gone over, so I figured it was my turn. While I was home on leave, a man told me that I could probably get out of my tour, because I was an only child and my father had died when I was nine years old, but I didn't like the idea of men my age skipping off to Canada or finding some excuse not to go. My philosophy was that everybody should do his own dying, if it comes to that, and not send someone else to do it for him. I don't see how anyone can live with himself if he knows someone may have died in his place.

I arrived at Tan Son Nhut on a Caribbean airliner in December 1968. I'll never forget how sad the stewardess looked when she said goodbye and watched us deplane. The first thing I heard somebody say was, "Just pray your orders aren't for the 1st Air Cav. They have a lot of casualties." Naturally, my orders were for the Cav. That was okay with me. I was already hoping to be assigned to the 1st Cav or the Big Red One.

I had an uneasy feeling being in a combat zone at An Khe and training. I had the same feeling every time I got into a situation where I was powerless to do anything. We had all our gear those first days, but no ammo. I always felt better with plenty of full clips and a couple of frags. We rappelled off a tower, then had a practical exercise where you climb up a ladder to a hovering chopper and climb down the swinging ladder on the other side, all the while trying to keep someone else's boots from stepping on your hands. We learned to field-strip an M-16 and reassemble it without looking at the parts. I didn't like pink grapefruit, but in An Khe I had the most wonderful piece of it. Some trooper asked why we were having such a nice breakfast that particular morning, and we were reminded that it was Christmas Day. We had forgotten about that. It seemed like we had dropped out of "The World" onto a different planet. People in America watched the same sun set and the same moon shine, but led normal lives, without others trying to kill them, and without having to kill other people just to survive.

I was assigned to A Troop at Tay Ninh. The short-timer, Doc Ketzner, showed me around the troop area and familiarized me with the duties of a Blue Platoon medic. We went on a couple of missions together and he was gone. The troop had Light Observation Helicopters, Huey lift ships and Cobra gunships, so I had the pilots' health and flight status to attend to as much as the infantry boys and the support troops. The health of my people was "number one" as far as I was concerned, and I made up my mind that this was going to be the best cared-for unit in Vietnam. That included the daily routine of sick call, shot records, malaria pills, to whatever it took to keep people alive in the jungle.

I was always ready to burn a clip of ammo if somebody asked for recon by fire, or to lay down some cover fire on a treeline when we took fire in the air. Some of the guys wondered why a medic was so willing to pull the trigger on the enemy. I know that some medics were conscientious objectors and didn't carry weapons, and that was fine with me, but I felt that any enemy soldier that I could dispatch before he wasted an American was an opportunity to keep the Blues healthy and my medical work at a minimum. They tried to give me a .45 pistol and that was okay until I found out it meant giving up my M-16. I stuck with the rifle.

A war zone is a strange place. Sometimes time flew by. Other times, it crawled by when we were waiting in base camp for a mission. We spent a great deal of time on regular duties like sick call, filling sandbags, and other work details, all performed in either sweltering heat or sloppy mud. I worked out of a conex metal shipping container with a makeshift screen door. It would be 110 degrees outside and 130 degrees inside the conex medical station.

Ice, cold soda or cold beer were luxuries. When cold beer was available, I never dared drink more than one or two. I didn't want to be less than sober in case we had to "saddle up" and fly out to the bush. I carried my morphine styrettes with me even to the shower. I was always afraid someone would steal them and I would be caught short when we needed them in the field. On a regular schedule, a Vietnamese would spray our tent area for bugs. He almost choked us to death each time, and we were sure that he was a VC.

Our troop area was right on the perimeter of Tay Ninh. You could look out and see nothing but flat land, except for Nui Ba Dinh, the Black Virgin Mountain, which towered over the region. It was a strange sight out on the plain. The mountain was supposedly sacred to the Cao Dai, a religious sect that had a temple in Tay Ninh. The pilots used the temple as a landmark for their flight path to Phouc Vinh. Nui Ba Dinh had a U.S. commo station on top, and rumor had it, a VC hospital somewhere inside it. Our LOHs used to catch VC coming in who were sick or injured, and swoop down and grab them as prisoners for interrogation.

Headquarters had found a recording of the old cavalry bugle call, "Boots and Saddles." Whenever we heard that call over the loudspeaker, we had to run for the ready racks where we kept all of our combat gear, then out to the flight line. It never seemed to fail that we were called out every time we went over to the engineer compound to take in a movie. The projectionist would break into a movie and call for all 1st Cavalry to report to their area immediately. The movies were usually old ones and not that great anyway. Missions could come at any time, and although it was hot as hell on the ground, it was much cooler in the air.

My first mission was at night. Our choppers stayed at high altitude, because the enemy had a quad .50 working out on the ground. You could watch the tracer ammo streaming into the sky after us. We had come to extract a LRRP team. That was done without the need for a Blue insertion. Our missions were usually of two kinds. Either the LOHs would see something suspicious and we would be sent to check it out, or one of the birds would get shot down and we would go out to secure it and bring in the crew. Sometimes we came under sniper fire while doing this. The chopper itself would be slung out under the belly of our maintenance bird.

One thing about 1st Cav pilots is that they never refused to come when we called for them. They would fly into LZs and PZs so tight that they would chop salad out of the surrounding trees with the main rotor. They didn't hang around long when it was hot, but they always came when you needed them. In one LZ, the pilot wanted to get up and out fast, so he didn't touch down. The men were exiting from both doorways, and I was sitting in the middle of the aircraft, waiting to see which doorway would empty first. There was a new guy in the door and our Vietnamese interpreter was behind him. The new guy stopped while I hollered, "Jump! Jump!" Then the Huey was too high and it was too late to jump. I went up one side of those guys and down the other. I'm sure I made a lasting impression. The CO put me on the radio answering calls on top of a hill while we waited to extract the Blues. I think he wanted to give me something to do and keep me separated from the other two soldiers.

The platoon found a tunnel complex and threw in some concussion grenades. They came up with an old man that they wanted to take back for questioning. I cooled down and climbed on an empty ship to pick up the prisoner. There was no place to land out there, so the pilot dropped down until he was chopping green. The Blues tied a rappelling rope to the prisoner, I secured it to a seat strut, and off we went with the old man twisting at the end of a rope. I had first tried to haul him aboard, but he was just too heavy. We sailed over the countryside with the VC dangling below us until we could find a safe place to land, then the door gunner and I carried him to the ship. A concussion grenade doesn't leave much to look at as far as external damage, but this man's internal injuries were another matter. I could tell his eardrums were ruptured and he was in shock. He was still alive when we got him back to base, but I wasn't too sure about his chances of survival, either before or after interrogation.

The Blues returned home with a couple of kills and flew over the flight line, popping and trailing smoke grenades, shouting and rebel-yelling in a low-pass fly-by. They deserved that moment of glory. They had met the enemy and every man was still in one piece. Most of us were close to each other. A few kept to themselves, not wanting to get too attached or familiar with people who could be dead the next day, perhaps from fear of the sadness and anger that goes with it. But the majority of us took life as it came and made friends more or less easily. Some of those people I knew better in one month than others I had known for years at home. I trusted them with my life, as I hope they trusted me to try and help them.

On 15 February 1969 we got a distress call. One of our ships was down. The platoon scrambled to the ready racks and the flight line to the sound of "Boots and Saddles," the whine of lift ship turbines and the smells of hot, oily dirt and aircraft interiors. There was never a great amount of chatter as everyone scrambled and anticipated the coming insertion. I would mentally and physically go over my gear, making sure everything was in place before the birds were ready for lift-off. Then it was skids up, a slide to the left out of the revetments, forward and a turn to the right onto the take-off strip, and a tilt forward as the aircraft churned up speed and altitude for the jump over the perimeter fence. The lift ships climbed into the cooler, more pleasant, high-altitude air of Vietnam as the infantry stared down from open cargo bays onto a blur of passing greens and browns, pockmarked with hundreds of water-filled craters from the B-52 bombing raids.

The lift ship dropped into an LZ just long enough for us to jump out and form a perimeter. Everything went fine at first. The maintenance Huey flew in and slung the downed chopper under its belly to take it back for repairs. The Blues set up for extraction after first reconning the area by fire. There was no return fire, so the lift birds were called back to the clearing. The pilots must have been nervous. The PZ was very tight and the birds bunched closely. We jumped back on board and began to lift away.

I was in the first chopper in line, sitting on the floor in back of the pilots' seats. In the doorway to my right was Jim Fields, the RTO who bunked with me in back of the briefing shack at Tay Ninh. Jim was planning to get married after his tour. In the opposite doorway was Frank Kulbatski, a machine gunner. "Ski" was a new guy who had been with the unit only a few weeks. We had talked often. He had just written a song and had it published and was really flying high about that. The seat on the back bulkhead, directly across from me, was filled with other GIs.

We were only a couple of hundred feet in the air when there was a slight jolt. We were in major trouble. An RPG round had slammed into the second bird in our tight formation, sending it out of control. Its main rotor cut off our tail rotor and sent us into a spin. I looked out the left door and saw green flashing past. I looked right and the doorway was empty. Fields and his radio were gone. I looked back left and now Ski and his machine gun were gone, too. Everything went into slow motion. It seemed like half an hour had passed since the jolt, but it must have been only seconds.

I had my M-16 standing upright between my legs. I put it on the deck plate between the pilots' seats so it wouldn't fly around and spear somebody. Then I hooked the chin strap on my helmet, slid back against the seats, grabbed a strut and braced for the inevitable crash. The last thing I remember was looking into the eyes of the trooper across from me. Everybody was sitting tight, waiting. I thought, "Is this it? This is the way it ends? This is all there is? Are we all dead men?" Everything went black.

Even before I could open my eyes I could smell the JP-4 aviation fuel. That brought me back to the present. All I thought was, "This is going to blow." I knew that I had to get out, but couldn't move and didn't know why. The chopper was on top of me. My head and shoulders were the farthest under. I fought in desperation to get out of my helmet. I got the strap off and my head out. The helmet was caught tightly under the metal belly of the fuselage. If I had lost it or not strapped it on, I would already have been dead. I tried to move again and could not. It was dark and I could still smell fuel. I was in shock by then and didn't know it.

"What am I going to do?" I thought. "I'm not the kind of person who does this" I thought as I became embarrassed at the idea of yelling for help. But I did it anyway. I yelled more than once, three or four times I think, as I was extracting myself from my backpack full of medical supplies. That was also holding the ship off me. I slipped out of the straps and crawled toward the light, and realized for the first time that I was under the chopper.

Two people in flight suits and helmets ran toward me through the field. I tried to get up, but couldn't understand why I felt so weak. I tried to get my left leg up and did, but couldn't feel my right leg. I panicked when I couldn't see it. I felt the ground where the leg should be and found nothing. I started down from my belt with my hand, got about a foot down and still found nothing. "God! My leg is gone!" I felt wildly around and found the boot and leg. They were buckled under my back, still attached, but pointing toward my head. The crew members got to me by then, but I had seen someone lying out in the field in front of the chopper. I pointed and said "Help him!" I was trying to get my leg straightened out and didn't see much blood, so I was semi-relieved as well as semi-coherent.

"Hurry up!" somebody said. "She's going to blow!" I knew that. I had a mental picture of JP-4 dripping onto a hot engine and knew what would happen. The other man must have been knocked out before, because now he was up and moving. The crewmen came back for me. Our hands kept slipping as they attempted to carry me away, so I showed them how to drag me—fast—by linking our hands like a locomotive coupling and making a fist.

I looked back and saw Sgt. Harold Tyson with his lower body pinned half under the chopper door on the copilot's side. He wasn't moving. I had never felt so helpless. I was a medic and should be there to help him get out, not being rescued myself. I felt guilty for being dragged away and leaving this man who had a wife and daughter waiting for him. He had often talked about longing to get back home and trying to save his hardscrabble Georgia farm. It was too much for his family to manage alone, and he just wanted to hurry back to them. Now we were leaving him behind.

We were in high grass and the ship hadn't been long out of my sight when there was a loud explosion and ammunition began cooking off like popcorn. The blast set the field on fire. I asked the crew to stop and gave them my two grenades and a claymore bag full of ammo. "Here, you might need these." Then we went on. I heard Lieutenant Buholtz holler, "Where's the medic?" and answered "Here, sir!" I hoped to be put to work and finally be able to do something to help, but the lieutenant never said another word. I felt useless again.

I was left in a small crater with my head pointed almost out of the other side. I lay there for a while as they evacuated the wounded. There were five dead and five wounded. The gunships began working over the treeline with everything they had, and I hoped they got whoever had done this to us. I felt better about that, but I was beginning to feel pain in my right leg and was choking on the acrid smoke from the fire. As flames appeared over the rim of the crater, I began crawling away by thrusting myself forward with my left leg. I didn't want to be cut off from the platoon again. I hadn't gone far before the crewmen were back and we were off again to the PZ. One of the LOHs came in and I was dragged over to it. As I lay on the ground, ashes were stirred up by the rotor blades, and I used a handkerchief over my nose and mouth to breathe. I was hoisted onto the LOH and we were airborne. A crew member was watching over me, so I lay back.

I'm not sure if I was conscious on the flight back to the Tay Ninh hospital. I was off-loaded from the LOH and taken inside. They put me on the table, and a Vietnamese girl took off my uniform and cleaned me up. I was given a shot and the pain went away. Then I was taken to the cast room and put in a cast from my armpits to my toes on the right side, to the knee on my left. I remember looking up and seeing a familiar face. A corpsman, whom I had gone through basic and medical training with, was putting on the cast. I called him by name, but don't know if he recognized me. I was put back in bed with an IV, and later got some new blood. I realized that my morphine styrettes were still with me and turned them in.

The troop commander came around and thanked us for what we had done. I didn't think I had done much and told him that I wished it could have been more. I had the "million-dollar" wound and wouldn't be back in Vietnam, but I didn't want to leave. I knew a fellow Alpha trooper who was on his second tour, had been wounded, had been in one chopper crash, and now had been in two of them. When the time was right, I had wanted to ask him why he put in for a second tour. I never did ask him, but now I believe I know why. Not many people actually wanted to be there, fighting in the mud and the dust for their lives. However, no one wanted to leave as long as any of their buddies had to stay behind. Most of us would have stayed and fought until the war was finished, if we thought that we could save lives and all of us could come home together. If that could only have been possible.

The bonds that form between members of a combat unit are hard to explain. I probably can't do them justice, and maybe they can't be fully explained. They are the kind of "you had to be there" feeling that is shared only by participants in a place where life and death are a fifty-fifty proposition, where life is fast and hard, and where death is the same, and sometimes asked for.

I spent eleven months in different hospitals in traction, surgery and more casts. I was in wards where men screamed at night and cried for some kind of relief from their pain. I will never forget that experience, or the war that put us in that situation.

As I was writing this, four Hueys flew in formation over my home. That's all it takes, even twenty years later, to bring Vietnam flooding back. The men I knew there, both dead and alive, will be with me and other combat veterans always. They will stay with us until the day we make that final mission and meet again in "Cav Country."

19. FLYING TIGERS

(Scout and Cobra Pilot, Bravo Troop, 1968–69)
*Warrant Officer **Rick Chesson** left for his second tour in Vietnam and told his wife not to worry. At least he wouldn't be flying scouts in the 1st Cav. Things didn't work out quite the way he had planned.*

John Wayne was one of my heroes. I dropped out of college and volunteered for the Army, because I wanted to be part of the Vietnam War before it was over. I have never regretted that decision, but the way we left the country after the sacrifices and loss of life by so many brave Vietnamese and Americans still doesn't set well with me.

In October 1966, I graduated as a helicopter crew chief and went to Vietnam. The cultural shock of being out of the country for the first time when you are eighteen years old is hard enough to handle, even without being assigned to a war zone. I flew as a crew chief with the 336th Assault Helicopter Company out of Soc Trang. We supported Vietnamese Army units all over the Mekong Delta. We had our battles and our losses, but they were nothing compared to what came later. I left Vietnam in 1967 and was brought back to the United States to attend flight school. Flying was something that I had wanted to do since I was a small child, and the Army gave me that opportunity. I graduated from Fort Rucker in March 1968, along with my good friend and stick buddy, John Burt. He had already spent a tour in Vietnam as a forward observer with the 4th Infantry Division.

John and I were assigned to Fort Knox, to a unit that was supposed to be building up to go over to Vietnam. There we were both checked out on the OH-6 Light Observation Helicopter (LOH), or Loach as it was called by the troops. Many of the things we learned about flying the Loach would later save our lives in Vietnam. In September, we were sent to Cobra School in Savannah, Georgia, enroute to Vietnam for our second tours. We lived fairly close to each other in the San Francisco area and saw each other on our short leave home.

John's leave ended before mine and he left for his second tour, hoping to return to the 4th Infantry Division. I hoped to return to the 13th Aviation Battalion in the Delta. I didn't have much apprehension about going back to Vietnam because of my experiences on the first tour. The 13th Aviation Battalion was a good unit. I had a new wife who was concerned about me, but I told her not to worry. I was going back to my old unit in an area where I had flown in before. She should be grateful that I wasn't going to be a scout pilot or assigned to a unit like the 1st Air Cavalry Division.

I flew to Vietnam this time on a commercial airliner which was quite a contrast to my first trip over on a military C-141 cargo plane. Sitting in the cold, dark, crowded cargo hole of the C-141, while staring at a pallet of duffle bags covered with cargo nets for twenty-five hours, is quite different from traveling on a commercial airliner. We landed at Cam Ranh Bay, a thriving version of a Stateside military base. The same hot, muggy air hit us and clung to us. The same smell was there— the alien smells of tropical flowers, local cooking fires, and even rotting garbage. Things were much more efficient and controlled this time around. In 1966, I had been assigned to a unit and had made my way south to the Delta by hitching rides on helicopters from various units. This time we were transported on buses, briefed and efficiently processed. The next day, I truly expected to grab my duffle bag and hitch south to Soc Trang. Much to my surprise, we were ushered into a large, tin-roofed building. A larger-than-life major with a big Cav patch stood in front of my group of about 200 replacements. He advised us that we had just been assigned to the 1st Air Cav.

I was sure that he had made a mistake, and what he was saying applied to everyone else in the room, except me. I told him that I was on my second tour and by regulation could choose my unit of assignment. He quickly told me that the needs of the Army came first, and I was now in the 1st Cav, like it or not. I was loaded on a CH-47 and flown from Cam Ranh Bay to An Khe. There they divided us up and sent most of the replacements to the 1st Cav "Charm School" (jungle school). Pilots were sent directly to their units. My dreams of the good life in

Soc Trang went down the drain. I arrived at Camp Evans on 1 November 1968.

Instead of buying stereo equipment and living in a comfortable hootch in the Delta, the people here were living in underground bunkers. My nightmare continued. I was assigned to the 1/9th Cav. The stories of their exploits had filtered throughout the Army by then. Their casualty rate was very high, and the worst assignment was to the scouts. I tried to remove all evidence from my flight records that showed that I was an OH-6 pilot. Besides, I had always wanted to fly Cobras, to be a fighter pilot like my hero, John Wayne in "The Flying Tigers," bringing death and destruction on the enemy in my Cobra gunship. I was assigned to B Troop and found that most of the unit had already departed for a new area of operations 350 miles to the south.

I helped pack up the rest of the equipment, then climbed aboard a UH-1H (Huey) with Major Colley, the incoming troop commander. I would serve under five troop commanders in one tour. This constant rotation of commanders was one of the problems with the way the Army ran the war. By the time a man learned his job, he was replaced. Hard lessons had to be learned all over again, and each period of training cost more casualties. It took us about seven and a half hours to fly south to Quan Loi. During those periods when I was not flying, I looked out in amazement at the beauty of the country—the blue waters, white beaches, emerald green jungles, and shimmering rice paddies. It was easy to see that Vietnam had been a colonial paradise. The substantial buildings were built of white stucco and brown brick with red tile roofs. These contrasted with the simple, thatched huts of the villagers.

As we flew into Quan Loi, I found myself in a beautiful rubber plantation region of a type that I had never seen before. There were miles of rubber trees planted in perfectly straight rows. The east-west airstrip at Quan Loi was established on a ridge in the middle of the Terre Rouge rubber plantation. On the east end of the airfield were the large white homes of the plantation manager, his wife, and his two beautiful teen-age daughters. On the north end of the airstrip was a large colonial building with an Olympic-sized swimming pool. Our base camp was like a scar on this beautiful plantation.

Compared to Camp Evans, Quan Loi was like moving uptown. We slept in GP (general purpose) medium tents with wire-screen sides and wood floors. There were walkways made of ammo crates, and the flavor of the place was like a mining camp in the California Gold Rush days.

Our flight line was on the edge of the perimeter in the southeast portion of the base. Behind our living quarters was the 3rd Brigade Tactical Operations Center (TOC) bunker. Because of the operations bunker's proximity and Bravo Troop's activities, we became the favorite targets for North Vietnamese and Viet Cong gunners.

I was assigned to the gun platoon. As I was checking in, I ran into my good friend, John Burt. He had been hijacked to the 1st Air Cav the same as me. As I listened to pilots relate their exploits during Tet, the relief of Khe Sanh and the A Shau Valley campaign, I realized that this was a tight unit that took care of its own. Stories that sounded boastful were later found to be understated fact.

I was briefed over the next couple of days about our mission and the new area of operations. We operated over free fire areas, just as the British had done in Malaysia. The local people knew about the policy and where they could go. The free fire areas had been in existence for a long time by then, and anyone in them was fair game. The friendly population had been relocated to government-controlled strong points. Within the protected areas, we could not return fire without the authority of the local government, even if we pinpointed the precise location of the fire. Outside those protected areas, in the war zones, people were immediately taken under fire and killed. It didn't take long after we arrived for the enemy to retreat to the fringes of the Cav area or across the border into Cambodia.

Cambodia was a sore point with us, because we could not engage enemy units that sought sanctuary there. We were responsible for patrolling a couple of hundred miles of border. In typical Cav style, we crossed the border many times. On our flights along the border, we watched U.S. military helicopters flying Special Forces teams on deep interdiction missions into Cambodia. Those helicopters used our refueling and rearming points. They had American crews who wore the same uniforms as us, but officially, they did not exist. On our cross-border missions, we would engage a target ourselves, or mark a target with smoke and try to convince the forward air controllers or artillery batteries that the location was really inside Vietnam. They usually looked the other way and helped us.

Being a former crew chief myself, I helped the Bravo Troop crew chiefs work on their aircraft. This earned their respect, gave them a hand with a hard job, gave me more knowledge of my own aircraft, and brought us all closer together. One of my first tasks was to teach the crew chiefs how to boresight the gun systems on all the Cobras, so that they would basically all shoot in the same direction and pilots could exchange aircraft and know what to expect from the weapons systems. I also taught them how to keep the guns and ammo feed system operating with a few tricks I had learned as a crew chief. Later, when we could not obtain a gun system for our old Charlie-Model Huey gunship, I rigged a couple of Cobra 40mm grenade launchers to the gun mounts. They could really smoke Charlie with those 40s.

Besides working long hours in the dust and dirt, the crew chiefs were exposed to frequent mortar and rocket attacks. All you could do on the flight line during a rocket or mortar attack was lay flat between the aircraft and the low, L-shaped revetment. During one of those attacks, we actually watched the rockets coming in. They looked like white, flying fence posts. One landed behind us and destroyed the maintenance tent.

The Cobra was a mean machine. It carried seventy-six rockets and a minigun in a turret that could cover 120 degrees to each side of the aircraft. Later, a 40mm grenade launcher was also installed in the turret. The pilot in the back seat fired the rockets and the copilot in the front seat fired the minigun. The miniguns had an electrical shut-off, so their bullets would not set off the rockets when they were fired, but this often resulted in jams. The only way to clear those jams was to land in a safe area and manually rotate the minigun barrels. A good pilot would alert the copilot when he was going to fire rockets, and the copilot would stop firing the minigun.

The 2.75-inch HE rockets had the explosive power of a 105mm artillery round. Another weapon was the flechette rocket. It had 1,500 inch-and-a-half nails with stamped fins. The rockets would travel approximately 1,500 feet before arming, then an explosive charge would propel the nails at near supersonic speed. Two flechette rockets would cover the area of a football field with nails spaced about 18 inches apart. They traveled through tree limbs, bunkers and people with great ease. Returning fire with flechettes generally meant you didn't have to worry about people ever shooting back. The limitation on flechettes was that they couldn't be fired as close to troops on the ground as the HE rockets, miniguns or 40mm grenade launchers.

Most of my first missions were routine recons. This changed on 14 November, when a large NVA force attacked LZ Dot in the early morning hours. The LZ was situated south and west of Quan Loi, astride one of the main infiltration routes from Cambodia. Our bases along the border were frequently moved. They consisted of an artillery element and hasty field fortifications such as earth berms, sandbag bunkers, rows of concertina wire, claymore mines and other devices. They were spaced with overlapping fields of fire for the artillery so that they would be mutually supporting. Our mission after a base was attacked was to break up any new concentrations of troops and track down survivors as they retreated toward Cambodia. The problem was that they usually broke up into small groups of ten or fewer people. They only assembled in larger formations in safe areas or to launch an assault on a fire base.

My Pink Team arrived at Dot just as the sun came up. The devastation was just unbelievable. The NVA had concentrated their attack on one side of the camp and the artillery had lowered their tubes and fired canister rounds. There were hundreds of bodies around the perimeter of the camp. I am sure there were another hundred and fifty or two hundred people killed or wounded. There were large stacks of human bodies as the soldiers collected equipment and piled the NVA dead for burial.

Bulldozers were busy digging open trenches for mass graves. There would be fifty to one hundred corpses in each grave. We found no large concentrations of troops, but there seemed to be hundreds of blood trails leading back toward the border. We did occasionally find groups of four or five NVA soldiers and take them under fire.

In late afternoon on the same day, we were shaken by our own losses. A klaxon went off in the troop area and everyone scrambled the one hundred yards to the flight line. A scout helicopter had been shot down near Song Be. I was copilot to Major Colley that day. Capt. Frank Miller was already on site, organizing our gaggle of aircraft into a fighting force. The Loach had gone down in a large clearing, by a treeline near the fork of two rivers. The NVA had rushed out of the treeline and had been held off by the Pink Team's Cobra. Each time the Cobra made a run, it was fired on by 12.7mm machine guns and AKs. The downed crew headed for the closest river, but the pilot, Dave Morris, was cut down by the NVA. The other crew members, Sergeant Tranham and Specialist Lofton, made it to the river bank and slid into the water. They were spotted by a Loach almost by accident as they frantically waved for help. It was only after repeated air strikes and artillery fire that the Blues were able to land and recover Dave Morris's body. It was only after I got back to the troop area that the realization of what had happened hit me. The expressions on the faces of the others told me how deeply the loss of Dave Morris was felt, especially by the members of the Scout Platoon.

November 24th was a dark day. John Burt was put into the Scout Platoon. The ops officer had discovered his OH-6 qualification while reviewing flight records. I told John that I was glad I had removed those papers from my flight records. John Burt didn't think it was very funny at all. Somebody must have overheard our conversation. On the 26th, I was told by Lieutenant Albright, the incoming Scout Platoon leader, that I would report to his platoon the next morning. I woke up the next day with no flights scheduled and began to think that my conversation with Lieutenant Albright was just a drunken nightmare. I was out on the flight line helping the mechanics when Major Colley asked me to fly copilot with him on a mission. I began to think everything was going to be okay.

On the edge of a rubber plantation about three klicks north of Loc Ninh, one of our helicopters had spotted a large group of military-aged males with military haircuts. They were dressed in civilian clothing. They seemed to be foraging in a small Montagnard village. Two Pink Teams were on station. The scout helicopters down low were being flown by Mr. Art Murray and Lieutenant Albright. Major Colley made an immediate decision to insert the Blues.

As we waited for them to arrive, the scout choppers were busy keeping the suspects in the village. From my vantage point of 1,500 feet up, they reminded me of cowboys on cutting horses, rounding up cattle for a drive. Each time one of these men would try to sneak out of the village toward the rubber plantation, the Loach would herd him back. I was coordinating with a unit of the 11th Armored Cav that was operating in the vicinity of a small Special Forces camp nearby.

The 11th ACR sent one of their squadrons of tanks and APCs toward our contact site. Just as the Blue lift ships began the insertion, all hell broke out in the rubber trees. The 11th Armored Cav had run into an NVA battalion that had just infiltrated across the border to attack the Special Forces camp. We had accidentally discovered some of their soldiers foraging for food. The NVA didn't have much of a chance. They were in hasty fighting positions among the rubber trees, and those trees really didn't provide much protection from the heavy machine guns mounted on the armored vehicles. A .50 caliber will shoot right through a rubber tree. It was a classic combined arms attack that included air strikes and supporting artillery fire. The scouts could have killed the troops in the village, but they disappeared into the houses and we didn't want to kill innocent civilians.

At nightfall, the NVA broke contact and exfiltrated back across the border. They had suffered heavy losses. The 11th ACR losses were light, and we suffered no losses at all. Major Colley, myself and the scout pilots were written up for citations. I received a DFC for flying with the troop commander. Of course, the real heroes were the two scout crews. I never found out if they received their awards.

We were discussing the action back at Quan Loi when Lieutenant Albright walked over and reminded me that I was now a scout pilot. I told him that somebody would really have to twist my arm before I would ever fly a scout helicopter. Major Colley overheard the conversation and told me in no uncertain terms, "Son, you can consider your arm twisted." I was now a scout pilot. I was totally depressed. How was I going to explain that to my wife after what I had told her? Back at the tent, I could tell by John Burt's smile that he was really concerned about my dilemma.

My check-out in the OH-6 began the next morning. Nobody who arrived in Vietnam was ever trained in the States as a scout pilot. To be assigned to the scouts was usually the luck of the draw. The training in Vietnam was 10 to 15 hours of transition training—learning to take off and land and fly traffic patterns. The Cav's policy was for a new scout pilot to complete 50 hours of flying on missions with an experienced pilot before going off on his own. Since I was already qualified on the aircraft, my transition training consisted of a couple of short flights with Tommy Kinkovich, a scout pilot who was now our supply officer. Tommy had survived with the troop through the Tet Offensive, Khe Sanh and the invasion of the A Shau Valley. Supply duty was well-earned rest for him.

My actual scout mission training was mostly with Capt. John Hardy. The training I received from Cobra pilot Capt. Frank Miller, and my observations of scout operations from the Cobra, also taught me a great deal. The techniques they taught me kept me alive. At first, everything was a green blur. Captain Hardy and the Gunner, Doug Glover, were pointing out bunkers, trails and hootches, but I couldn't see a thing.

I sat in the front seat on the left, a red smoke grenade with the pin pulled in my left hand and an M-16 rifle in my right hand, while the Loach made right turns so that the pilot and gunner could look down.

My left seat position was usually flown by the helicopter crew chief or a Blue volunteer. The gunner sat in back on the floor with his feet dangling out of the aircraft. He was held in place by a thin seat belt or a "monkey strap" that allowed him to stand out on the skids and fire. The monkey strap was connected to a tie-down ring on the floor of the helicopter. Upon taking fire, the observer would release his smoke and the Cobra would set up for a run. If the scout pilot yelled, "Taking fire!" the Cobra pilot would put rockets in behind him as he nosed down and accelerated out of the area.

On a mission, the helicopter was constantly making right-hand turns, bouncing up and down over trees, and clearing them by inches. This made a very uncomfortable ride for the observer on the left side who was usually looking up at the sky. I had never been motion-sick before. Now I learned what it was like to puke my guts out all over the side of a helicopter. Getting the new scout pilots sick during their training became a rite of passage.

As each day went by, I got better at seeing things. The Loach would fly at forty to sixty knots until you were pretty sure the area was safe, then you slowed down and worked your way back in toward the sighting or target. A fatal mistake made by many scout pilots was to spot something and come to an immediate hover to check it out. Captain Hardy showed me how to work an area around an initial sighting, moving toward the center of the circle, checking the area thoroughly before slowing down.

Another thing that helped me as a scout pilot was working with the combat trackers. They were a small group of three or four men who used a black Labrador retriever to help track NVA by working the scent trails. I spent a lot of time in the evening discussing tracking techniques with them. I also discovered that a lot of the old Boy Scout Manual tracking techniques worked. I learned how to start reading trails, broken limbs and bent grass, how to estimate the number of people going down a trail, what direction they were traveling, and how long ago they had passed.

I learned how to make potato chip can bunker-busters from Matt Brennan, a sergeant in the Blues. It was quite easy—fill a can with C-4 explosive and insert a Willy-Pete fuse. But if you were not very careful, you could blow yourself out of the sky.

On 3 December, my training came to an abrupt halt after fifteen hours of riding as the observer. I was flying with John Hardy along the Song Be River east of Quan Loi. We were working an area of a B-52 strike that had gone in about two weeks before. Shortly after noon, at about fifty feet off the ground, I spotted a small group of North Vietnamese in green uniforms, walking south on a trail. The OH-6 was a pretty quiet helicopter, and if you approached people from a downwind direction, they often would not know you were there until you were right on top of them. All of my actions were instinctive. I released the smoke grenade and emptied twenty rounds of M-16 fire on full automatic. Everything went in slow motion. I watched my tracer rounds going out. The third man in the file was hit in the head. I watched his head explode. A couple of the others fell backwards. Hardy nosed the helicopter over and quickly accelerated out of the area while Doug Glover stepped out on the skids and fired his machine gun behind us. As we flew over the trees, I looked back and saw the Cobra's rockets exploding.

I'm sure that I was responsible for killing individuals on my first tour, but I was fifty feet off the ground this time. I had never looked into their faces, or seen the terror in somebody's eyes, and then know you killed him. I still remember his face today. That was my first experience with that sick feeling in your stomach from knowing that you have just killed someone, and the rush as adrenaline fills your body. He couldn't have been older than eighteen or nineteen. After we arrived back at Quan Loi, I got out of the aircraft, and John Hardy told me that my training was over. I took the call sign "Saber One-Four."

It's hard to explain scout flying. Your purpose is to find the enemy. You start a mission with extreme anxiety, then the fear starts to rise as you wait to shoot or get shot at, then you start taking fire and the adrenaline rush takes over. All your senses are heightened and everything clicks into place. The bravado builds up as the gunner tells you what he saw and how many he got, as the observer talks. Everyone's voice has gone up two or three octaves. The gunner and observer are shouting, "Did you see 'em? There's gooks everywhere! Let's go back and get 'em! Let's go back and get 'em!" Then you get back to the troop area and the realization of what has happened sinks in.

Some people got addicted to the adrenaline high. They flew scouts until they went home or got killed. Doug Glover was one of those people. He had already been gunning in the scouts for eighteen or twenty-four months. I often think about him and wonder how he is doing today. Doug always impressed me as a tough professional doing his job. Others were affected differently, and some even enjoyed the killing.

On 4 December 1968, the scout crew of WO George Hamilton, and

Specialists Bolton and Stalhnacher were flying over a bunker complex that Hardy, Glover and I had found two days before. We had found fresh tracks and bunkers east of Quan Loi, near an abandoned firebase called Sue. We hadn't seen people, but we could smell them. Their base camps gave off a strong odor of fish sauce and wood smoke. Hamilton's crew found an NVA command group moving toward the bunker complex. The NVA didn't hear the Loach approaching and Stalhnacher said it was like shooting fish in a barrel. In the middle of the confusion and shooting and the Cobra making its rocket runs, they spotted a 57mm recoilless rifle. They landed in the middle of bodies and running soldiers and grabbed the weapon. One of my after action reports suggested that the amount of activity in the area called for a B-52 strike. George Hamilton concurred. There were just too many people and bunkers out there.

Somebody up the line decided to put D/2/7 Cav, call sign "Heavy Bones," in there instead. The citations for the grunts probably state that they turned back the enemy with a gallant defense. In reality, they didn't have a chance. The LZ was completely surrounded by heavy machine guns, bunkers and troops. Our action the day before had alerted them. Heavy Bones took over seventy-five percent casualties from enemy fire and a raging grass fire. The grunts were trapped there all afternoon, and never got off the LZ. They were extracted only after rocket runs, heavy artillery fire and air strikes. That night, a B-52 strike hit the area.

We reconned the area the next day. On one of those flights, Fred Nunes spotted what he thought was an NVA in the bottom of a bomb crater. Doug Glover opened up, and bullets started hitting all around this person, then Fred shouted to cease fire. He felt something wasn't right. He hovered closer over the bomb crater and saw that this was an American soldier, dressed only in his underwear and covered with dirt and soot. He had survived bullets, artillery and a B-52 strike, and had now survived being shot at by a scout gunner from very close range. It was a miracle in many ways, because I never saw Doug Glover miss a shot. To this day, I would like to know who made the decision to put the infantry into that LZ, instead of calling for a B-52 strike.

The rest of the month was business as usual. Sometimes we found the NVA and sometimes we didn't. At Christmas, the 1st Cav sent everybody a box of Christmas cards with a great big Cav patch on the front and "Merry Christmas" on the inside. People started throwing them away, then I got the idea to have our Kit Carson scout, a former

NVA himself, write greetings on them from Bravo Troop. I soon had a couple hundred of them. We flew several missions on Christmas Day, with the truce in effect, dropping those cards on the North Vietnamese.

The mission I best remember was along a road near Song Be Mountain. We found a column of NVA walking nonchalantly until they saw us, then I saw the same fear in their eyes, the same that I had seen on the man's face on 3 December. I told Glover not to fire as he screamed, "I've got 'em! I've got 'em! Let me shoot!" He was a disciplined soldier and held his fire. We came back around and dropped Christmas cards to them. I might have done things differently if I had known that Fred Nunes was getting the hell shot out of his aircraft a few kilometers away.

In early January, we were working around an abandoned airstrip northeast of the Bu Dop Special Forces camp. Neither Americans nor South Vietnamese had been in the area since the 173rd Airborne briefly operated there a few years earlier. I noticed that the runway either had aircraft landing there or had been used by vehicles. One of the tricks that Captain Hardy had taught me was to hover over an area and look behind the aircraft where the rotor wash opened up the foliage. We made a major find while using that technique.

As I hovered just to the south end of the runway, we found a wide trail that looked like it had been cut by a bulldozer. Bamboo and tree limbs had been brought over the top and tied together. It looked like two large military trucks could travel down part of this road side by side. We worked that road both to the north and south of the airstrip. Our road was later named after one of our troop commanders who was credited with discovering it. As Captain James Brown (Saber Red) and I both know, we were the first.

On 6 January, we followed the trail so far north that we "accidentally" went about fifteen kilometers into Cambodia. There we found a large camp built above ground, just like ours. There were tin-roofed huts, sewing machines, ammunition points, stacked weapons, truck shelters, radio antennas and platform areas for instruction, but few bunkers.

The Vietnamese soldiers stared up at us in amazement. I told my gunner not to fire. I instinctively knew that, as soon as we opened fire, they would start shooting back. We were outside of artillery range and no one would come to our rescue if we were shot down. As we flew through the area just before I left, Captain Brown, flying above me in his old C-Model Huey gunship, got on the radio and told me to get the hell out of there. We were running low on fuel, so we made a final pass with my crew dropping white phosphorous grenades on everything that was burnable while Captain Brown recorded the map location.

On 8 January, we spent about nine hours flying the trail, this time to the south. At one point I lost track of the trail in two-hundred-foot double and triple canopy in mountainous country. Then I spotted a really beautiful waterfall that dropped about 120 feet to a small pool. As we flew over the waterfall, something seemed to shine off the surface of the pool. As I hovered down over the pool, we discovered an oil slick. I flew to the top of the ridge where the waterfall originated and tried to follow the stream back through the jungle.

There was something in the darkness below us. I could see shapes if I flew at a slow airspeed past a certain tree from a certain direction. The shapes were small buildings with tin roofs that had been painted black. I saw tire tracks in another location, and reported a suspected truck park to Captain Brown, who requested an air strike. The next team on station directed the strike. The scout pilot, Bruce Churan, later told me that he couldn't see a thing until the bombs blew away some of the foliage which then allowed him to pinpoint the targets I had reported.

As we moved south along the trail, we marveled at the engineering and military planning that had gone into it. I was amazed by the large, well-camouflaged teak log bridges on both sides of the border. The trail ran precisely between two Special Forces camps in an area that was not covered by artillery from either one. We followed it far into South Vietnam, into an area north of Saigon and east of Phouc Vinh, which showed us that the trail was one of the major infiltration routes into the Saigon area.

Another incident involved Mr. Marvin G. Metcalf—"Marvelous Marvin." He always had a big smile on his face and always seemed to get into bad situations. Not long after the other scout crew captured the 57mm recoilless rifle, Marvin had the idea of doing the same thing. He was flying with Doug Glover and Jesse Hill when they came across an old bunker complex. They spotted a 57mm recoilless rifle on top of a bunker. Marvin insisted that there were no signs of activity, and over the protests of the Cobra commander, landed in a horseshoe-shaped clearing. Glover and Hill scrambled out of the Loach and headed into the trees after the 57mm. The idea was for Marvin to wait for their return just outside the treeline.

Just as they got on top of the bunker to grab the recoilless rifle, a North Vietnamese stuck his head out of the bunker to see what was going on. Doug shot him with his .45. Then people started coming out of bunkers all around them. Jesse blasted away with his M-16, Doug fired his .45, and they made it back to the edge of the treeline.

As they tried to run back to the helicopter where Marvin sat, they had to run and drop, with bullets kicking up all around them. Each time they got close to the Loach, the NVA fire would start landing next to the helicopter, and Marvin would move it to another spot. So, here were two crewmen running for their lives and the aircraft jumping from place to place to avoid being hit. Finally the Cobra's rockets gave enough suppression to allow them all to get out of the area.

A rivalry developed in the last part of January between Art Murray and George Hamilton. They were counting bodies and taking chances that some believe later killed them both. George Hamilton had a patch made up that read "Fifty Kills." They were competing to see who could get a hundred kills first. Their bravado was starting to affect me, as well as others. Towards the middle of January, I was on a "last light" mission close to Quan Loi when we came across a trail with elephant tracks. I was flying with Stahlnacher as my gunner and Saint Laurent as my observer.

I started hovering slowly down the trail, following elephant tracks through heavy bamboo growth, totally ignoring every lesson I had been taught about scout flying. As we hovered across a small clearing, I saw the bright yellow flashes of AK-47s light up in front of me. I tried to turn left and all I could see was more yellow muzzle flashes. I started to turn to the right but saw what looked like a solid line of muzzle flashes there.

The only escape route was nose-down and straight ahead, pulling in power. I cleared a small tree on the edge of the clearing by inches. Looking back over my shoulder, I watched the area explode as the Cobra's rockets detonated. I asked Stahlnacher if he had seen anything, and he said, "No." It was only then that I realized that my gunner had always worn glasses with lenses as thick as the bottom of Coke bottles. Saint Laurent was shaking as badly as I was. He said that the whole left side of the helicopter had been glowing orange from muzzle flashes.

As we flew back to Quan Loi I got a cold chill that ran through my body. A bullet had come up through the floor between my seat and the cyclic stick. If I had been sitting in my normal position, instead of leaning a bit to the side, the round would have hit me in the lower jaw and come out through the top of my head.

Amazingly, we had taken only about six hits. Later in February, Major Colley told me they had enough scout pilots now and I could go back to flying Cobras. It was not a very hard decision to make. I loved the Cobras, but didn't want to appear to my friends in the scouts to be bugging out. But some of what Hamilton and Murray were doing was rubbing off, and I was beginning to make some stupid mistakes. I asked to go back to the Cobras.

All hell broke loose about noon on 12 February. We scrambled to the sound of the klaxon. By the time I arrived at the flight line, my Cobra was gone. I jumped in the front seat of a Cobra piloted by Robert Stamm. He was wearing my helmet. Shortly after taking off, I discovered that the helmet I was given could monitor radio traffic and Stamm's intercom, but had an inoperable microphone. We were left without communications inside the helicopter.

Northeast of Quan Loi, on the other side of the Song Be River, was an abandoned rubber plantation that still contained many of the colonial buildings. George Hamilton had been shot down over a bunker complex in the rubber trees. The scout helicopters of Fred Nunes and John Burt were darting over the crash site, using their door guns to hold off the NVA. When things got too hot, they would back off and their Cobras would roll in with suppressive fire.

The place had a short, north-south runway with rubber trees on the west side. This was where Hamilton had been shot down. Along the southeast end of the strip was a group of deserted plantation buildings. The plan was to insert the Blues, but as the slicks flared on final, hundreds of NVA opened fire on them. The trees were full of North Vietnamese who were lying along the shallow fire breaks between rows of trees. They were also in trenches inside the rubber trees. On the other side of the landing zone, the NVA occupied the plantation buildings.

Somebody yelled, "Taking fire! Abort! Abort!" Then the flight leader called back and said four Blues were left on the ground. The LZ was so hot that we couldn't go in to get them and we couldn't land anyone else to help them. All four lift ships had been damaged and only one remained flyable.

On the ground, Blues Sgt. Matt Brennan spotted a machine gun in one of the buildings that was placing heavy fire directly on their position.

Bob Stamm yelled over the radio, ''They're going to get their shit blown away! We've got to help!'' And down we went.

The next thing I knew, we were hovering over the end of the runway as I fired the minigun into the treeline and Stamm fired rockets directly into the buildings. It didn't take long before my minigun jammed. I felt helpless as he hovered down the row of buildings, shooting rockets into each one. Bob was in the back, yelling for me to shoot and I couldn't even respond. At one point, I had the cockpit plexiglass top cracked back and had my .38 in my hand, firing into the trees.

I believe the only reason we weren't hit was that the NVA were doing what they had been trained to do—leading a helicopter with fire. We were stopped or slowly hovering and they missed. All I could do was try to signal that the minigun was jammed, and for Stamm to get the hell out of there. We lifted out over the rubber trees and I saw John Burt and Fred Nunes still circling over Hamilton, with M-60s blazing away. I saw bits and pieces of John's helicopter falling off as he received hits from the heavy ground fire.

Then Fred Nunes started taking hits and had to leave the area. His cyclic control was shot out, but he was able to fly the helicopter, using only the tail rotor and the collective pitch control, about one and a half miles to safe clearing. We were out of rockets and the minigun was jammed. So Bob followed Nunes' Loach with the intent of picking up the crew. Behind the minigun were two long ammo bay doors that folded down. We had installed seat belts there in case we ever had to rescue downed crewmen. Another Cobra recovery method was for downed crewmen to straddle the rocket pods and face toward the rear.

As we landed beside Nunes' Loach, I could see the bullet holes all over the aircraft. It was amazing that he had made it this far. Stahlnacher had been shot through the foot and was in a lot of pain. He was in shock and pulled his .45 on Fred Nunes as he walked back to help him. Fred talked softly to him until he lowered the pistol. A Blue lift slick, shot up and leaking fuel, landed and took out the crew.

We refueled and rearmed at Quan Loi. I cleared the jammed minigun and got a different helmet. Then we flew back to the contact. John Burt had been shot down by then, but the crew had been rescued by another slick. Other Cobras were out of ammo and running low on fuel, so Bob Stamm and I took control of the situation. I used some of the skills Frank Miller had taught me, including laying on artillery fire, from Quan Loi and Song Be, while Bob Stamm coordinated air strikes and the other Cobras.

The problem now was to recover the four Blues, who were still under heavy fire, and the bodies of the Loach crew. We eventually got the Blues out. One of the slick pilots and his crew volunteered for the rescue. My Cobra and Saber Two-Two took positions behind each side of the slick as it went in. We were on the left side. I was firing the minigun into the treeline and watching the Blues run toward the helicopter as it landed with bullets kicking up the dust all around them and the helicopter. As the slick lifted out, the pilot yelled, "Taking fire!" and Bob pumped everything we had into the treeline.

We flew eleven hours that day, sitting down at Quan Loi with the engine running, only long enough to refuel and rearm. Then we were quickly back into the air and back out to the contact. We got a Loach low-level down over the wreckage at last light and they informed us that Hamilton and his crew were dead. Because of the size of the NVA unit we were fighting, we decided to wait until the next day to attempt to recover the bodies. We were the last helicopter to leave the area that evening. I had continued directing artillery fire. I saw six NVA run into a large building on the south side of the runway and destroyed it with eight-inch howitzer rounds. Even from our high altitude we could count about thirty bodies lying around the contact area.

A Cav battalion was inserted the next morning, and the bodies of our friends were recovered. We landed in a Loach, a Huey and a Cobra to take them back. While we were waiting there, a unit of what appeared to be NVA came out of the rubber trees. We started to respond, but it was apparent that the infantry was expecting them. They were part of an unconventional warfare unit called the "Green Lizards." They had been inserted on the Ho Chi Minh Trail up near Laos. They were dressed in NVA khaki uniforms and carrying AKs. They told us that we had run into an NVA regiment which they had maintained contact with all the way down the trail to our area.

Art Murray took George Hamilton's death extremely hard. He got all hopped up on some kind of pills and Binoctal and kept saying something about having to tell George goodbye. At one point, one of the slick pilots tried to calm him down and he pulled an M-16 on us. Finally, one of the guys was able to calm him down by saying he would take him over to see George. They walked together to the mortuary unit to view the body. George had been such an outgoing guy that the loss affected us all. At one point that evening, Fred Nunes, John Burt and myself sat there sobbing, with tears running down our faces. Art Murray seemed to get a death wish after that. His kills soon reached over one hundred.

George Hamilton and Art Murray were pretty much the same type of pilot—pretty sharp, but quick to take unnecessary chances. One day, I had been flying cover for George when he made contact. I told him to get out of the area so I could fire, but he hovered over the treetops, engaging groups of NVA. His reply had been, "If I fly any faster, I won't be able to dodge the bullets." Art Murray often refused to disengage. One day I was flying cover for him as he chased groups of NVA through a deserted village. The contact had been going on so long that Art's gunner was out of ammo. Art pulled out his pistol and proceeded to chase a guy around a tree with his helicopter until he was able to kill him.

During February and March, we started flying missions for Alpha Troop over by Tay Ninh. On 14 March, Bruce Churan was flying a Loach, followed by Dave Popp in a Cobra. They were at about 2,000 feet, straight and level, heading back to Quan Loi, when Bruce noticed that he had not heard from Dave Popp for a while. He called Dave Popp on the radio, but the Cobra was gone. Despite intensive searches by Alpha and Bravo Troops, the helicopter appeared to have disappeared from the face of the earth. It was almost a year later that an infantry company discovered it. Apparently, the pilot in the front seat had been hit by ground fire. The other pilot was killed by a tree limb as they hit the jungle canopy. There was no chance to make a Mayday call.

One evening, I was heading back to Quan Loi at last light after spending the day working with the gun platoon of Alpha Troop. I picked up tracers coming up behind us with my peripheral vision. As soon as the 12.7mm crew saw that I was turning back, they quit firing. My eyes hadn't left the target, and I hit them with seven pairs of flechette rockets. It was the same area where Dave Popp's helicopter was later found. I believe the NVA waited until Popp had overflown their position, and then shot him down from behind, just as they had tried to do with me.

Toward the end of March, the 3rd Brigade was pulled back to form part of the defensive shield around Saigon for the expected 1969 Tet Offensive. The Quan Loi area was supposed to be taken over by the 1st Infantry Division and ARVN units, but until that happened, Bravo

Troop remained behind by itself as a show of force. Then most of the troop departed for "Redcatcher," the base camp of the 199th Light Infantry Brigade.

Those of us who were left behind soon found ourselves running out of food and water. We couldn't change clothes, shave or shower. We finally loaded up the last couple of Cobras and Loachs and headed south. I flew in a snake with Frank Miller and our dog, Hamburger. The dog sat up in the front seat with me. After we got up to altitude, Hamburger went crazy and tried to crawl into the back seat with Frank. He got stuck between the back seat and instrument panel with his hind legs and butt over my shoulder, and his front legs and face staring at Frank for the next two hours.

We landed at Redcatcher, got Hamburger out of his predicament, and headed for the nearest PX to find some food. We walked into the PX with our steel helmets on, .38s on our hips and Hamburger between us, and went to the shelves with food. We ended up standing on both sides of this enlisted man in spit-shined boots and starched fatigues. He looked at myself and Frank, sniffed the air, got this God-awful look on his face and quickly left the area. Shortly after that, the PX manager came over and told us to take our dog and leave. We grabbed some food and left.

That place was a new experience for us. It was a court-martial offense in the Cav to get caught anywhere without your weapon and your steel pot, but nobody carried weapons at Redcatcher. We were challenged by MPs several times for carrying weapons, and at one time, the local commander tried to have us lock them in a conex shipping container and check them out for missions. That was shortly after one of the Blues tried to blow up a mess hall with a white phosphorous grenade, and shortly after one of my crew chiefs shot a couple of people with his .45.

The crew chief was a tall, slender young black man, one of the best Cobra crew chiefs we ever had. Some units in the rear were having racial problems. One day we were playing volleyball and some rear-echelon blacks came over and hassled the crew chief for associating with white boys. They told him they would take care of him if he kept it up. He got his automatic and took care of them first. This brave young man went to Long Binh jail. We left Redcatcher a few days after that, before I got to testify in his defense, or find out what happened to him.

The only officers' club at Redcatcher was the Second Field Force Club. It was located next to the quarters for the Red Cross girls and female nurses. We walked into the club with our steel pots and sidearms on, as per Cav policy, and they tried to force us to leave. Finally a colonel with a 1st Cav combat patch came over and told us that as long as he was the ranking officer there, we could stay. A Filipino band was playing for a couple of go-go girls. When we found out that the American women wouldn't have anything to do with us, we decided to drink and have a good time.

One of the Cobra pilots, WO Russell P. Smith, jumped up on the stage and started to dance with a go-go girl. One of the support troops jumped up on the stage and joined them. With the coolness of Dirty Harry, R. P. stopped dancing, pulled out his .38 revolver and told the young, spit-shined lieutenant to get the hell off the stage. He did. R. P. put his gun in its holster and went back to dancing.

Shortly thereafter, MPs arrived to escort us from the club. We went back to the troop, got a couple of CS grenades and gassed the club. We were escorted out of the club several times after that. The Blues had similar experiences when they arrived at the EM club with M-16s and steel pots per 1st Cav policy. They tore up that club several times. Needless to say, Bravo Troop wasn't very welcome at Redcatcher after hours. I guess those rear-echelon guys just didn't know how to have a good time.

Before we left Redcatcher we lost another scout helicopter. This time it was a good friend, WO Ken James, and Specialist Loften who were killed. Loften had held off the NVA with his machine gun until the Blues arrived on the scene. He was a blond-haired kid who always had a smile on his face. I had flown with him frequently in the scouts and hoped he would make it. The loss of Ken James and Loften affected me as deeply as Art Murray's death later on.

As I said before, the Army's policy of rotating officers to give them prized command time often resulted in disaster and men being killed. I served under good commanders and bad commanders. Two of them were after personal glory and medals, one without regard to the lives he was endangering. One was rejected by the troop and quickly replaced, and the other two were professionals.

Soon after returning to Quan Loi, we received Maj. Frank Stewart. He was one of the best. If he had any fault, it was that he cared too much for his men. Major Stewart was a good leader, but as his tour progressed, our losses and the combat affected him, and he appeared to age in his command. Each loss was like losing a member of his own family. Despite his sensitivity and decency, he was able to make quick command decisions. He took care of his men and we respected him.

In contrast, another commander liked to go on solo missions to hunt the enemy. He was after a Silver Star. In fact, when he arrived at a contact site, people would disguise their voices with an imitation of a trumpet call and shout, "Silver Star! Silver Star!" I had not done so, but he accused me of doing it.

On one occasion, while he was reconning by fire on a solo mission, he almost shot down a scout helicopter flown by Paul Barnhorst, and came close to shooting up an infantry unit moving up behind it. When I discovered the source of the tracers chasing our Loach down a trail, I had to make a quick decision to either shoot down the Cobra or see our Loach destroyed.

I flipped my radio to the emergency channel and screamed for the Cobra in the vicinity of Quan Loi to cease fire. I released my gun trigger cover and was in a dive at the other Cobra when it stopped firing. I pulled up over the top of the other gunship and saw that it was Saber Six, the new troop commander, shooting up the countryside without checking on the locations of friendly units and operations. That day I came close to ruining the rest of my life to save a scout crew.

James Dunn was a close friend in the scouts. He had followed my advice not to take unnecessary chances, but his death proved that sometimes you can do everything right and it's still not enough. We left Quan Loi on a mission around LZ Dot on the Cambodian border. I learned that artillery was firing out of An Loc, so we made a detour south, away from the gun-target line and just outside our troop's area of responsibility. We avoided open areas where the enemy could easily shoot at us. We crossed over a dense jungle area and headed north. We crossed a series of treelines and fields. Then a smoke grenade was tossed out of Jim's aircraft. It nosed down to accelerate out of the area. There was no radio call. I set up for a rocket run and watched in horror as the Loach flew nose first into the ground and burst into flames.

We hit the area to the north and south with rockets and miniguns, then came under heavy fire from AKs and 12.7mm machine guns. I saw somebody moving on the ground and turned my VHF radio to emergency frequency and called for help in the blind. We normally just called the troop, but Jim was close to me. I quickly had air strikes going in, ARA Cobras making rocket runs and a Pink Team from Charlie Troop on station.

A Huey lift ship came up on frequency and asked if he could be of help. I told him we had heavy fire from the area. The aircraft commander said that he was going in. My Cobra and the C Troop Cobra covered him. He sat down close to where the Loach was burning in the trees and rescued the survivor—the scout gunner—all the while under heavy fire. The pilot radioed that he had a badly injured man on board and was heading for the nearest field hospital. I never did find out who that lift ship belonged to. So many acts of bravery went unnoticed.

Next we inserted the Blue Platoon. They had a man killed by a machine gun as they ran across the field in a skirmish line. We had no idea that the NVA were on two sides of them. We later inserted a quick reaction force, recovered the bodies and extracted the Blues. I was going to view Dunn's body, but knew what kind of wounds men received from burning Loachs. I wanted to remember him as he was.

Only the day before, I had been informed of the birth of my son. I grabbed some cigars from my hootch. Everybody was gone on operations, and I wandered around the troop area, looking for someone to celebrate with. Then I ran into Jim Dunn and told him my good news. He hugged me and helped me celebrate. Now he was dead. To this day, I carry guilt about Jim's death. If I hadn't flown him so far south to avoid the artillery fire, maybe he would have lived.

May was a busy month for us. Quan Loi was hit twice by ground attacks and Art Murray died a few days later. I had a premonition that Art was going to die a day or so before he was killed. I knew that he was going to be next. He died shortly after we had flown support missions against the NVA assaults on LZ Jamie and LZ Grant where Art had raised his kills to well over one hundred enemy soldiers.

In June, one of our Pink Teams spotted a convoy of trucks inside Vietnam. They beat feet back across the border and parked in a Cambodian village. Most of the Cobras in the troop arrived on station. Major Stewart tried to get permission to shoot, but we had to wait a while. I was flying cover for Bruce Cheran and told him to make a pass over the village at altitude and drop a couple of white phosphorous grenades, hoping that maybe the NVA would think that they were artillery marking rounds and leave the village. Bruce dropped down to about two thousand feet on an east-west run. The grenades exploded at five-second intervals, about three hundred feet underneath his Loach.

An Air Force FAC bird saw the bursting white clouds of smoke. He called over the guard channel, warned Bruce that he was taking AA fire and told him to get the hell out of the area. Bruce didn't know what was going on and immediately dove for the deck. When word of the antiaircraft fire got back to division, we were given authority to strike at the trucks in the village. When we hit those trucks, it was like watching a film from World War II where the fighters strike vehicles and large secondary explosions come up at the camera. Shortly after that the International Control Commission showed up at B Troop to investigate our armed attack on neutral Cambodia.

It wasn't the first time we went into Cambodia, and it wasn't the last. I once was trying to put in an air strike just over the border on North Vietnamese in the open. The Air Force FAC pilot refused to cooperate because the target was 500 yards inside Cambodia. I asked him to explain to me what those B-52 bomb craters were about a mile further inside the country. He told me he didn't see a thing. The dipstick still wouldn't put in the strike.

On another occasion, we were working the trail I had found in January. There was a low cloud cover over the trees which was high enough for the scout to work, but obscured the Loach from us. My Loach was up to altitude with me and we were about ten kilometers into Cambodia. We spotted a column of trucks escorted by PT-76 amphibious tanks. My copilot, Bruce Babyack, told me I didn't have a hair on my ass if I didn't take them on. We dived from behind from 4,000 feet with me firing rockets and Bruce working both sides of the road with his minigun. Again, it was like watching film from World War II as NVA troops jumped off the trucks and the trucks exploded. We killed a lot of them. I continued shooting my rockets and hit one tank. It may not have been damaged, but it sure made me feel good. We climbed to altitude, headed for the border and notified the Bu Dop Special Forces camp that a column of trucks and tanks was heading toward them. I identified myself only as a friend. That and similar missions went unreported.

During June and July, we had a lot of convoy action on the highway between Saigon and Loc Ninh. Quan Loi was one of the stopping points, and the road south of the Chan Tanh Special Forces camp was a favorite ambush point. One night we evacuated most of the Pink Teams to Phouc

Vinh in anticipation of a ground attack on Quan Loi. We were flying at low-level back the next morning with our crew chiefs flying in the front seats. We were over Highway 13, and shortly before reaching the Special Forces camp, we saw a convoy being ambushed from the right side of the road. I was the lead aircraft and informed the others. We attacked with six Cobras and about five Loachs. The Cobras got into a daisy chain and emptied our rockets and miniguns on the ambush. I'm sure both the convoy troops and the NVA were taken by surprise by such a quick reaction. Our crew chiefs had a hell of a good time working out on the miniguns.

On 9 August, my Pink Team on a "last light" mission came upon a group of NVA who were setting up rocket positions for the night in the vicinity of Loc Ninh. We reported killing twenty-four of them. We were debriefed by Frank Stewart's replacement who tried to get us to up our reported kills. We refused to do so.

The next day, we received a commendation from division headquarters on the accuracy of our report. A Special Forces patrol out of Loc Ninh had captured a survivor. He told them that we had killed 24 men and wounded many more from a company that was preparing ambush and rocket positions.

On 12 August, we received the worst ground attack I can remember at Quan Loi. Sappers attacked and broke through the perimeter between our helicopter pad and the troop area. We would get a ground attack and people on perimeter guard would straighten up for a while, but they were getting complacent after two months without being hit. The Blues and the infantry killed forty-two NVA sappers. The closest ones were killed behind our mess hall as the battle raged through the area. It's amazing that none of us shot each other that night. We had no plans for defense of the troop area and never practiced any.

I was walking out to perimeter with another pilot the next morning to check the damage. I had a .38 on my hip and a camera in my hand. A North Vietnamese in full sapper gear, satchel charges and carrying an AK stood up in front of us and held out his AK-47. All I could think of doing was to take his picture. Our Kit Carson scout soon arrived and relieved him of his other equipment. I wish I knew where that picture was. I think that it was probably confiscated in processing, since I also had a picture of a dead NVA on that roll of film.

Just south of the flight line was a hole in the wire big enough to drive a jeep through. On the flight line itself were dead Vietnamese around the aircraft where the Blues had killed them. They had already put cigarettes in their mouths and beer cans in their hands. I walked by the 15th Med Aid Station. There were about seven North Vietnamese on cots, lying in the hot sun and guarded by ARVNs. I felt sorry for them. They were all shot up and appeared to be in a great deal of pain. Guys were standing around joking or asking why they were being given medical aid.

It was one of the first times that it hit me that North Vietnamese were people, just like us. I tried to solicit a poncho or some medical aid from the medics. They told me that they were too busy working on American wounded. It made me sick. They weren't really any different from us.

On 13 August, another young warrant officer, Funderburke, was shot down in his scout bird and killed just west of Quan Loi. Captain Niles, our maintenance officer turned scout pilot, hovered down in a Loach and rescued the crew chief. Funderburke left behind an unfinished letter to his wife in which he said that he was not going to survive in the scouts.

About that time in August, the mortar and rocket attacks were becoming more frequent. On 30 August, in a light drizzle, we received a mortar attack that is hard to recover from. Most of the time it was pretty easy to pick up the *"Pop!"* of a mortar or rocket being fired. That night we heard nothing until 60mm mortars started landing in the troop area. We were used to 82mm and 120mm mortars. I was the first one into our slit trench. It had an overhead cover constructed from half a steel conduit covered with sandbags. As more people piled in, I was shoved down to the other end of the trench until I was wedged in the other entrance and no longer under cover. Somebody yelled that Bruce Churan had been hit by a mortar. He had been in the shower when the attack came. He had wrapped a towel around himself and headed for a bunker when a mortar shell exploded in front of him and drove a piece of shrapnel into his chest.

He was quickly dragged into a slit trench. Somebody started yelling for a medic and help to get him to an aid station. Like everybody else, I wanted to help Bruce, but the rain of mortars made it a death wish to leave the safety of the trench. Just then, a mortar hit on the other side of some sandbags, about half a foot from my head. The blinding flash and concussion deafened me, knocked me back down into the trench and covered me with dirt. They got Bruce to the aid station before the attack ended, but he died from his wounds. One of the fragments had cut his aorta. I had cut open a knee and an elbow when I dove into the trench. The medics gave me a form for a Purple Heart the next morning. I tore it up and threw it in a trash can. Bruce and many others had earned their Purple Hearts the hard way. I didn't want to cheapen it.

As the year went into September, we noticed a change in the way the 1st Cav operated. It was no longer find, fix and destroy the enemy. Now it was find, fix and destroy the enemy with fire, but take no casualties. Troops would immediately sit back and wait for air strikes and artillery, wait another day and then enter the area, giving the enemy plenty of time to escape. Unfortunately, this new tactic caused more casualties than it saved, because the NVA knew we were no longer as aggressive. They felt freer to move throughout the area. It didn't change the way we were doing business. During this time, the 9th Cav accounted for probably 75 percent of all the enemy casualties inflicted by the division.

On 10 October, I was flying cover for a scout bird that was screening in front of an infantry company in contact just east of the Song Be River. The scout bird crossed to the west side of the river while I put in artillery. He was quickly shot down in tall trees. I had North Vietnamese troops to the north and south of the downed Loach. We hovered over the crash site and fired rockets and miniguns into them. When the Blues arrived, only one bird had long ropes for rappelling. We put that squad on the ground about one hundred meters from the downed Loach. They quickly blew down a few trees to make a landing zone for the other two birds.

As the second slick descended into the LZ, it drifted to one side and the main rotor hit a big tree. One of the Blues actually jumped before it hit the ground. The helicopter rolled in his direction, but his timing was perfect. He landed on the ground, having passed through the spinning main rotor. The Blues came under attack, and again I hovered down to hold back the NVA. Captain Niles dumped the excess equipment from his Loach and managed to pick up all three crewmen from the downed Loach. With the support of artillery and other Cobras, we were later able to extract our Blues. Our Pink Teams attacked the enemy in the area until after dark.

Later in October, at Song Be, we received a mortar attack aimed at our helicopters. We were a couple of hundred feet away and ran toward them. The rounds walked down the flight line but were a little long. As my gunner and I ran toward the helicopters, we had to hit the dirt at one point to avoid explosions. When we jumped into our Cobra, I felt a sharp pain in my foot, just above the heel. A piece of shrapnel had gone through three layers of leather on the back of my boot and lodged there. It left a bruise without breaking the skin. I still have that piece of metal. We found the mortar position too late. It was already empty.

I led a charmed life in Vietnam. That luck held until I climbed on a Freedom Bird at the end of October for the long trip home.

20. BLUE

(Infantry Platoon Leader, Alpha Troop, 1969)
*When Lt. **R. B. Alexander** was assigned to brigade headquarters as a demolitions officer, he didn't expect to go on missions with a recon platoon, and never would have guessed that he would soon be leading it on dangerous missions.*

My story begins in the jungles of Panama where I attended the Army's Jungle Warfare and Survival School. The Special Forces instructors there taught us that we had two enemies: the NVA and the jungle. Both were dangerous, but you could fight only one. Experience had shown that American soldiers were brave and well equipped, but noisy and clumsy when compared to our enemy. One of the many lessons that I learned in Jungle Warfare School was to have a dramatic impact after I arrived in Vietnam.

We had set up a squad-sized ambush along a trail, put out rear security and dug in for the night. Just as we detected movement that indicated that the aggressors were coming down the trail, an artillery simulator dropped into my position from the rear. It went off with a whistle and a blast that almost blew my pants off. Two Special Forces instructors had been inside my so-called perimeter the entire time. They stood up, laughed at my pants and said, "You'd better wake up, lieutenant! Don't take anything for granted!" I never forgot that lesson. We learned many things in those short weeks, but the real education was yet to come.

After arriving in Vietnam, I was assigned to the Cav. I will never forget the feeling of pride when I saw my name next to that yellow patch. I finished "charm school" at An Khe and was assigned to Headquarters, 1st Brigade, as a base defense coordinator and demolitions advisor. Tay Ninh was big, and it kept me busy upgrading our sector of the perimeter. I would attend the intelligence briefings at night, and they were all about the same. The straight leg battalions were slowly working through their AOs and trying to make contact with the NVA. Alpha Troop, 1/9th, was in contact and calling in more "step on's" than the rest of the units in the 1st Brigade combined. Alpha Troop was an enigma to us. They had a compound just down from us, but were totally independent. They asked us for nothing. In fact, the headquarters intelligence officer stayed glued to the 1/9th for his information.

One day in January 1969, I was told to report to Alpha Troop. They had found some hard targets and wanted me to blow them up. This was a shock to me. Up until then, my life in Vietnam had been simple. There had been a few rocket attacks, but they were no big deal. Going to the field was bad enough, but going to the field with the crazy 9th Cav was something else again. Arriving at the 9th Cav compound was like entering another world. They had their own strip with slicks and LOHs on one side, and Cobras and Huey gunships on the other. Some Cobras were waiting to rearm at the ammo dump while Pink Teams headed out on missions in the direction of the Nui Ba Den, the Black Virgin Mountain. That giant black mountain was the only prominent terrain feature above a patchwork of rice paddies and jungle.

I walked into the sandbagged TOC (Tactical Operations Center) and met Lt. Tony Buholtz, the Blue Platoon leader. He was an armor OCS graduate in his early twenties, with a big, confident smile. He was wearing a bright blue bandanna and carrying a sawed-off M-16, and I was impressed. Tony led me to a big map inside the Blues' operations hootch and described our mission and targets. He also introduced me to "Blue Mike," Platoon Sergeant King, who would turn out to be a real-life version of the comic book hero, "Sergeant Rock of Easy Company." The rest of the platoon CP consisted of the RTO (radioman), Ron Amain, and the medic, Doc Adams. Doc was a battle-scarred soldier who still refused to go home after being wounded three times.

The Blues wore mostly soft caps and those blue bandannas, and carried no packs, but had an unbelievable array of weapons and ammo. I counted at least four M-60 machine guns. We loaded aboard five slicks for the mission, and two snakes (Cobra gunships) fell in beside us after takeoff.

When we arrived over the target and headed in for a landing, the snakes worked over the treelines around the LZ with rockets. The Blues rode the skids in for the landing, and jumped off with rebel yells as we touched down. The target that day was bunkers with reinforced cement ceilings. I set charges against the ceilings with branches, linked them with det cord and set a ten-minute time fuse. As we moved to the PZ (Pickup Zone), the charges went off with a roar. They completely destroyed the bunker complex and a good deal of the surrounding jungle, and one of the machine gunners turned to me with a smile and said, "Nice bang, L.T." This was the beginning of a career marked by a generous use of C-4 (plastic explosive).

The extraction was perfect. LOHs zipped around the PZ, the high birds (Cobras) kept a watchful eye out, and the lift birds came in low and fast, flaring at the last moment. We were up and gone in a minute. It was the first time that I had seen such teamwork since joining the army.

I was called out with the Blues often in the next few weeks, each time for a different mission and target. On one of those missions, jet bombers had attacked heavy equipment and possible tanks near the Cambodian border, so each Blue carried a LAW (Light Antitank Weapon). That was a bad area. On the previous mission there, a firefight had resulted in four dead NVA, one of whom was carrying a radio. We blew up some logging trucks that had been carrying anything but logs down from North Vietnam. Just as we entered the PZ, the scouts began taking fire to our north. Three giant trees blocked a landing by the slicks, but I told Lieutenant Buholtz to keep the choppers coming in. I would deal with the trees. I taped blocks of C-4 to each tree, jammed in fragmentation grenade fuses, pulled the pins and ran. Count four, hit the ground and *"Wham!"* The Blues loved it.

One day I heard that the Blues had really hit the shit. After covering a downed bird near Nui Ba Den, they had been setting up a PZ when one of the squads saw movement. It wasn't properly checked out. When the four extraction slicks had picked up to a hover, all hell broke loose. The slicks came under intense RPG and machine-gun fire, and two of them were hit and crashed into each other. It killed six or seven Blues, plus the helicopter crews. Andy Anderson and his Cobras blasted the shit out of the area while Kit Beatton took his incredibly overloaded slick back into the hot PZ, time and time again, to pull men out. They kept the losses from being worse than they already were.

The next week, I was called again to the 1/9th, this time to stay. Tony Buholtz met me, took off his blue bandanna, put it around my neck and said, "I've had it. I'm going back to flying. It's safer. The men trust you, and I've recommended that you take over the platoon." I was now Apache Blue, ready or not! Tony Buholtz was shot down and killed two weeks later, and his loss was felt deeply by all of us. So much for relative safety in the 9th Cav.

Taking over the Blues was the biggest and most dangerous responsibility of my life. They were hot when I got them, but I felt that some changes were needed. Without Tony to confer with, I had to follow my gut instincts. I sat down with Sergeant King and the squad leaders and gave them the new rules. We weren't LRRPs, so helmets would be worn instead of soft caps. There would be no more blue bandannas in the field because they made too good a target. Equipment would be taped and muffled to reduce noise, and there would be no more exotic weapons. If we got into an extended contact, I wasn't about to try and scare up AK or Tommy-gun ammo. We practiced silent patrol techniques and trained hard at rappelling. The men got better and quicker at doing both.

Before I rotated home almost eight months later, I had logged almost one hundred combat assaults, on all kinds of missions, in hot LZs and cold LZs, with and without contact. We had destroyed almost two hundred tons of rice and other equipment, had killed many NVA, and had lost several Blues and flight crew members. Each mission was different, and yet each was the same. Some blend together now, but the ones I will share are those that I will never forget.

One of the Cobra pilots was a good friend. I will never forget the day his gunship was shot down near the Cambodian border. The platoon could be alerted and off the ground in a couple of minutes, on the way to rescue air crews in enemy territory. We did a lot of those scrambles for downed birds, and took the LOH crews out in body bags as often as not. One day, we were scrambled for a downed bird in late afternoon. We headed out with about thirty men on five slicks.

When we arrived over the crash site, all I could see was a solid jungle canopy that seemed to be burning. Cobra gunships were firing white phosphorous rockets, and there was no LZ this time. My slick hovered over the jungle above thick, white smoke and fire in the treetops. Bullets were cracking all around us, and standing on that skid and rappelling was like dropping backwards into hell. Burning embers hit my neck and left big welts for days afterwards. I had told the guys in training to only brake once during a combat rappel, about ten feet off the ground, but we couldn't see the ground. There were only burning tree limbs.

A few of my guys got injured on the way in. I hit the ground while a slick hovered above us, whacking into tree limbs with its main rotor as more Blues rappelled down. The racket from miniguns and rockets was incredible. I organized some control over that chaos, then we moved toward the wreckage down well-traveled NVA trails.

The whole area reeked of a heavy enemy presence. The Cobra had flown right into the ground, burned and exploded. It was a horrible, disgusting experience. We pulled out two torsos that were too hot to touch, put one in a body bag and it melted clean through it. We had to roll the torsos in the dirt until they cooled down, then put them in more body bags. We took them with us as we headed for a PZ over more of those scary trails. When we punched through the undergrowth to the small clearing for extraction, Swede Erickson was hovering his old B-Model Huey gunship about a foot off the ground and hosing down the trees with his miniguns. I heard him shouting over the radio, "Come on, Blue! We're gonna get you out of here!"

I found out when I got back that one of those dead Cobra pilots was my friend. I knew that the area was hot, but I wanted to go back in there and mix it up with those assholes. It was the only time that I ever wanted to get revenge. Operations had gotten clearance for an "arc light" (B-52 strike), but first they wanted to see what we could find on another landing. Two days later, we went in with a full strength of about forty men and plenty of air support.

The first thing we discovered was a well-built wicker-bamboo bridge. I set a time charge on the bridge, then we started moving through a complex of typical two-chambered fighting bunkers. We were well into triple canopy jungle, and these bunkers were fresh and previously unknown to us. I realized that we were walking into a big base camp and sent a message to alert our QRF (Quick Reaction Force). Next we discovered a bicycle factory that was set up along a big trail, in the middle of connected bunkers with interlocking fields of fire. I set a good charge under all the parts and equipment, pulled back the perimeter and, *"Bam!"* set that sucker off. We marked our position with smoke and the platoon moved out.

Sergeant Gill's squad was off on the flank when they made contact. The rest of us were on a dogleg of the big trail and could place three machine guns in support. Bullets were zinging everywhere by then.

We killed three NVA before they could hit any Blues, then my radioman was shot twice. I saw muzzle flashes and a line of bullets kicking up dirt as they walked toward me. I was throwing a grenade at the same time, but it seemed to hit ten branches before it got where I wanted it to go. It exploded close by the muzzle flashes. I don't know who got the guy, but the line of bullets stopped four or five inches in front of my face. We were still exchanging fire with the NVA when I moved us off the trail in a flanking movement that would take us ninety degrees into the jungle, then ninety degrees back to the PZ.

By taking those nineties, we were able to come in behind a platoon of NVA who were setting up along the trail to ambush us. It was just beautiful. Two machine guns criss-crossed the area and knocked them down all along the trail, and I don't know how many we killed. The Blues picked up two more wounded in the firefight. One of the old salts lost it right there and kept firing his machine gun after I called a cease fire. He had shot a gook coming out of a bunker, and just kept shooting the same guy. The body must have had 150 holes in it. The squad leader finally broke the butt of the soldier's M-60 to stop the firing. The machine gunner had gotten a "Dear John" letter and just flipped out. It was his last mission.

The bridge went off behind us at about the same time that we entered the PZ and secured the place as best we could. There were fresh bunkers everywhere around us, and we just didn't have enough men to hold the place very well. We kept coming across those big, ugly twenty-five-pound NVA claymores and kicking them over. They are usually command detonated, and if you're close enough to see one, it's too late. Andy Anderson's Cobras rocketed the treelines, and we came under some light sniper fire.

My guys were cool that day. We were quickly able to evacuate the wounded men, and then we came out shooting in a quick, five-ship extraction. They leveled the whole area with an arc light later that same night. The BDA (Bomb Damage Assessment) reported a lot of wrecked equipment, caved-in bunkers and body parts in trees. It had been a great mission for us, ambushing the enemy for once, instead of being ambushed by them.

On another day, we secured a downed Psy Ops (Psychological Operations) Huey that had the shit shot out of it while broadcasting surrender appeals and dropping propaganda leaflets. It was sitting in the middle of a clearing with the speakers hanging out and all these American leaflets stacked inside. As the Chinook slung it out, the rotor wash blew pamphlets everywhere over the jungle. Just as this was happening, one of my squads saw movement. We went in column toward that area, flanked it and came in on line. We shot up an NVA courier with a satchel full of leaflets telling the Cav to give up. There he was within fifty meters of one of our birds full of our surrender pamphlets. It was a strange sequence of events, and we all got a laugh out of it.

The first time we found a rice cache, it consisted of a beautiful stack of two-hundred-pound bags that was about eight feet tall and ten feet long. We were under small arms fire as I set the charges, and the major called and told me to wait in place for an NBC News team. I told him that waiting was crazy. We couldn't even hold the perimeter for much longer. The Cobras rolled in to suppress fire and an LOH dropped off a case with fifty more pounds of C-4. I had tunneled under the rice bags, circled them with det cord and set up a ladder charge where each block of explosive touched the other and would set it off. The first explosion would be from the bottom of the hole.

The film crew came in with a lot of clambering and noise, and I was pissed off that we had to play host. I wasn't paying attention to how much explosive was in the hole, and finally said "fuck it" and threw in the whole case of explosive. I had been having trouble with time fuse, so I set it up to fire electrically. We moved everyone back, and I told the film crew to get down, film before the explosion and right afterwards, but not during it. They were behind me, but I was crouching behind a rock outcropping.

When I twisted that thing off, I knew I had screwed up. I heard the high bird yell, "Holy shit!" I was flung backwards, and the next thing I heard was the camera crew being blown off their feet. The camera went flying through the jungle in a million pieces, the sky turned grey, and there were little pieces of rice falling on us for the next twenty minutes. Major Olsen was pissed at me, because he thought I had done it on purpose. Looking back, it couldn't have happened more perfectly. No one was hurt.

Toward the middle of April, the air force had been hitting an area near the Cambodian border. The jet pilots had commented that they had been bombing layers of plastic, and what looked like a hospital recovery room. The scouts crews that flew BDAs over the area kept smelling what they thought was ammonia. We were inserted to check it out.

I was blessed with great squad leaders—Sgts. Gill, Stuart, Espino and Gibson. They were tough, compact men who moved silently through the jungle, like cats. They led us through medium jungle into heavy jungle, until we arrived in the target area in about an hour and a half. We had received some fire earlier, but moved off the trail and encountered nothing more until we started finding fighting bunkers and more of those big, ugly claymore mines. The plastic was covering 155 two-hundred-pound bags of rice. It was all stacked, nice and neat, beside a large kitchen area. We were still on the edge of the place, and my squads were finding more and more equipment. I told the major to alert the QRF.

I set some charges under the rice cache while my squads called in more findings. First we found an operating room with IVs hanging on stands, then a recovery room with plastic-lined sinks and cases of medicine. They even had running water throughout the complex from a series of bamboo pipes. We were only on the edge of an enormous complex, so the QRF was scrambled. We pulled back under increasing NVA fire and waited for the arrival of the line company. When they got there, the captain reported to me and assumed operational control. I noticed that my men were much better armed, and carried a lot more ammo than those Cav grunts. It was getting dark by then, and we obviously weren't going to be pulled out, so our combined force moved into a clearing and set up an NDP (Night Defensive Position). The whole place was ringed with more bunkers, probably extending back into the jungle for miles around us.

My platoon dug in and sent out an LP (Listening Post), then Major Olsen flew over and dropped more rations to us. That was okay, but I could have killed for a couple more cases of machine-gun ammo before the night was over. All of a sudden came that *"Crack!"* They opened up with AKs at the chopper from two directions, and the major got out of there. Soon there was movement and fire from three sides. Just at dusk, my LP greased two NVA who walked down a trail right into them. One of the enemy soldiers was so close that he bled all over one of my guys. He was wearing fresh, clean fatigues, carrying a new Russian AK, and packing a radio that was better than ours. It was tuned to our air-ground frequency. The probes started shortly after that.

They moved through the trees like ghosts or shadows. The attack would ebb and flow in intensity, probe and pull back, probe and pull back again. I figured what they were doing was sucking the ammo out of our machine guns, and mapping their locations. I put a stop to the machine gun fire. About ten minutes after midnight, *"Thum-thum-thum-thum!"* the mortars pounded from the jungle in front of us. The mortar shells walked across the NDP in a series of loud crashes, and anybody outside his fighting hole was screwed. There were quite a few wounded in the line company, because they weren't dug in as well as the Blues. We got two wounded. They hit us with a heavy ground attack, then pulled back and mortared us again. We were outside of artillery range, and our fire support was coming from ARA Cobras, but the gunships couldn't see all that many targets through the canopy.

A "dust off" chopper came in for the wounded, and just as it touched down, the green tracers started slamming into it. The tracers seemed to be coming from a funny angle. I watched pieces of the helicopter being shot away until the crew aborted the mission and left the wounded lying in a pile. That chopper crashed on the way back to its base. A 9th Cav bird tried to rescue the wounded, and more tracers drove it away.

By then I realized that the tracers were coming from up in the trees. I had an XM-148 grenade launcher under my M-16, and when I saw a muzzle flash, I jumped out of my fighting hole and pumped two rounds at it. A shadow fell through the branches. I dove back into my hole and felt something running down my leg. Somebody out there had put a bullet hole through my canteen, but his aim was off by about an inch.

They hit us again in mass at two o'clock. "Puff the Magic Dragon" (C-130 gunship) stopped them this time. We marked the perimeter with strobes and that four-engined monster just tore up the jungle with its miniguns. Watching those tracer streams was like seeing a giant, red lava flow pouring down from the sky. The Dragonship hosed down the trees with a giant *"Ruurraamp!"* The growling, ripping noise and that strange, flowing light were just unbelievable.

The wounded were evacuated at dawn. We found a gook inside the NDP and a scattering of bodies outside our line, but most of them were gone. It had been an attack by two North Vietnamese companies. My platoon had held a small sector of the perimeter, but we accounted for more than a third of the dead NVA at a cost to us of only three wounded. I stepped over the body of an NVA killed the night before, and was ready to tear my Cav patch off and put it on him, but one of the guys had already pinned a note to his shirt. It read, "NVAs are sissies." It was signed, "1st Air Cav."

We later found a lot of equipment and new SKS rifles in that hospital complex and searched it all morning and into the afternoon. When we eventually moved into another part of the complex and set up a perimeter for a little rest, I remembered my lesson from Panama. Instead of just sitting back and taking it easy, I took one more glance around us. Right in the middle of us, a bush stood up. He was facing outward and started to turn to fire, but I already had my weapon up and shooting. I think that the man had been just as startled to see us as we were to see him. The lesson from Panama, to never take anything for granted, had saved some lives. A few minutes later, we finished our break and moved on.

After the line company was extracted, the slicks pulled us out under fire. When we got back to Tay Ninh, Kit Beatton and I went over to the small, sandbagged officers club. We were on our second drink when his crew chief came in with a sick look on his face and said, "Captain, you've got to look at this." His main rotor blade had six bullet holes. Kit's only comment was, "Well, Blue. I brought my wounded bird in again." We laughed and had another drink. That's the way it was. The platoon was back out on missions the next day.

One of my men from those days called me a short time ago and asked, "Blue, why did you care so much?" I think he expected some kind of heroic answer. I told him, "You know? You were my ticket home." If my guys did okay, I did okay. If I let them down, I was letting myself down. They were alert, good troops, and that kept most of them alive.

I don't know what to think about the war, or whether we should even have been there, but I served with a group of brave men. There was no comparison between them and some of the other soldiers I saw over there. I will always be proud of my platoon.

21. MID-AIR

(Scout Gunner, Charlie Troop, 1969)
*Specialist **Daniel Wardzala** was trained as an LOH mechanic and didn't know he was going to be a scout gunner until he was sent to draw his weapons. This is the story of his scout flying and an accident of war—a mid-air collision in the darkness over a LRRP team in contact.*

It has always been hard for me to talk about my Vietnam experiences. I came home with two rows of ribbons and a lifetime worth of memories that I never elaborated upon to anyone, but now I will share with you a brief chapter of my participation in the war. I will always treasure the time I spent in Vietnam, serving my country and being proud to be a trooper on the "First Team." I wouldn't have had it any other way, and being in the 1st Cav meant that I served with the best.

I entered the army on 30 September 1968 with a two-year enlistment. I received my basic training at Fort Gordon, Georgia, and was promoted to E-2. Orders sent me to Fort Eustis, Virginia, where I trained to be a mechanic on an OH-6A Light Observation Helicopter, otherwise known as an LOH. I graduated number one in my class and received an honors diploma. In February 1969 I reported to Fort Dix, New Jersey. It was there, in the middle of winter, that they took away our winter uniforms and gave us jungle fatigues. We were getting ready for our expected tour of duty in South Vietnam.

In-country processing put me on a flight to An Khe, where the training center for the 1st Cav, known as "Charm School," was located. After An Khe, I was put on a C-141 Starlifter to Phuoc Vinh, where I was assigned to C Troop, 1/9th Cav. Because I was trained to be a helicopter mechanic, I asked where I could pick up my tools. The first sergeant laughed and sent me to a maintenance shack where I was given an M-60 machine gun and an M-79 grenade launcher as a sidearm. I couldn't imagine having a grenade launcher as a sidearm, but they were all out of M-16 rifles and .45 caliber pistols. It was at that moment that I knew I was going to be a scout gunner.

Flying became my total escape, as ironic as it may seem. You must understand that Vietnam on the ground was unbearable—the heat, the bugs, the sunburn, the chow, the smell, the army bullshit. But flying was heaven. You rose above the heat and the war, and soared over the beautiful green landscape in the cool breezes. I would write to my best friend, Wayne Brzostko, who was a machine gunner with the 3rd Marine Division in I Corps. He thought that I was crazy for being a scout gunner, and I thought that he was crazy being a grunt on the ground.

One of the jobs a new guy got was cleaning the blood out of other peoples' birds when they got hit, and slinging out birds when they went down in the AO (Area of Operations). The blood wasn't too bad, but the slinging was scary. My LOH pilot would take me out to the downed bird, and while he hovered high above the ground, I would jump out with the sling harness and a sidearm in hand and climb atop the rotor blades of the downed Huey or LOH. Then I would attach the harness to the downed bird and hold the other end up so it could be attached to the Huey doing the tow. It was so scary because I was one man, alone on the ground, in the middle of enemy territory.

My training was finished, and I had learned how to fly an LOH, fire my M-60, lead my targets in reverse, and drop smokes and frags. I learned how to follow a trail through the grass. I could tell how many people walked the trail single file, which way they were going, and how many were on bicycles. I was becoming an effective scout. Finding underground bunkers became second nature when you learned what to look for.

We had two basic missions in South Vietnam—flying around our base camp at Phuoc Vinh, which was a piece of cake, because nothing ever happened, or flying the AO where we encountered some shit every time.

A Pink Team would go out to the AO, contact any friendlies (our infantry), and they would direct us to where they were getting any hostile fire. We would go off in that direction to draw fire. If we were lucky, we would entice the enemy to shoot at us, and we would return fire. If it was too much for a scout to handle, the Reds would radio for us to get out of the way and they would come down with rockets, miniguns, and chunkers (automatic M-79 grenade launchers) firing. If that didn't handle the problem, we would call in the Air Force to lay the area with napalm. Nothing survived napalm.

I had started flying AO missions regularly when my disastrous flight occurred on 14 July 1969. I had flown "first light" that day and got about a dozen kills. We landed and refueled in the evening, like any ordinary day, and my pilot and observer left to get something to eat. I was exhausted from flying all day and decided to rearm the ship in the morning, knowing that we would not be flying in the AO again. We never flew the AO two days in a row. I was walking down the flight line with my machine gun on my shoulder, enjoying the evening after a job well done and hoping the mess hall had something decent to eat, when I saw almost everyone from the unit heading my way.

Pilots, observers, and door gunners, the crews for Hueys, Cobras and LOHs, were running toward me, screaming that the gooks were at the wire. Everyone was looking for air-worthy aircraft and telling me that the enemy was at the concertina wire, and trying to overrun our LZ. Since I had just come back from the AO, my bird was not armed with enough ammo to be effective, so a pilot, a gunner and I jumped into a fully armed aircraft and took off in the dark. Once we were in the air, I looked around and realized that the bird had no safety belts, no armor to sit on and no fire extinguishers. Some guys liked flying "light," as we called it.

We tried to contact the ground troops, so we wouldn't be firing on any friendlies. After being in the air for only about fifteen minutes, our radio began screaming. The CO ordered us to go north a couple of clicks and pull 360s (fly in circles) while he did a recon in his Huey. I remember laughing to my pilot that the major was goofy enough to fly a night recon in a Huey. We did what he ordered and started flying 360s in pitch blackness, seeing only the flares from the battlefield below. We didn't know who was friendly and who wasn't, so we were ordered not to fire. It was total chaos.

As we were going around for the second time, a powerful force hit my ship. I had never experienced anything like it. I had been shot down before, but this was like being hit by a bus. Not having any seat belts, I was thrown from the aircraft and hung on to one of the skids for dear life. The next thing I remember was lying in the beautiful green grass of the jungle. I was lying there, overtaken by such a feeling of contentment and joy, as I looked at a bright light at the end of a tunnel. I vaguely remember looking down at myself on the beautiful green lawn when my dream was interrupted by a voice saying that I was going to be all right.

I was medevaced out and taken to Long Binh where I was in a coma for four days. During that time, I relived my whole life. I dreamt of being six years old, of being an altar boy, of graduating from grammar school and high school, and when I came to the present day, I awoke.

I woke up in a Quonset hut with wounded soldiers all around me. My body was full of tubes and stitches. I had tubes in my nose, drainage tubes in both sides of my stomach, and tubes to my throat for a tracheotomy. I also had a fractured back, three broken ribs, a concussion, and a ruptured spleen, which was removed. The doctors told me that I was lucky to be alive after falling 90 feet into the heavily wooded jungle and having the trees break my fall.

Every morning another vacant bed made me ask what had happened to the guy who was there. Each one had died. I figured that this was where they put the wounded to die. One day, a three-star general came to visit me and awarded me a Purple Heart and a Bronze Star. At about this time, I realized that I might not die after all, and was soon transported to a hospital in Japan. Once I realized that I could call home from Japan, I called my parents and ran up a $400 phone bill. My parents were so happy to hear from me that they didn't care about the cost. In another month, I was transferred to Great Lakes Medical Hospital where I remained until I was fully recovered.

22. HOOTERS

(Scout Gunner, Bravo Troop, 1969–70)
*Sergeant **Charles Hooten** re-enlisted for Army aviation, then was sent to a support unit when he arrived in Vietnam. He volunteered to see some action, and got all that he bargained for.*

I had already done my time in the service, four years in the Air Force, when I volunteered for army aviation. I was sent to Fort Polk for basic training, then on to Fort Wolters and Fort Rucker for flight training. I was eliminated from flight school three weeks before receiving my wings because of a broken eardrum. After that, I volunteered for Vietnam. I arrived in Vietnam in June 1969, and my first week there was spent in the Cav jungle school at Bien Hoa. It was quite a reception, because Viet Cong sappers blew up the ammo dump while I was there. After jungle school, I was sent to the 15th S&S (Support & Service) Battalion. The battalion was responsible for resupplying the soldiers at the forward firebases.

After two weeks at battalion rear in Bien Hoa, I was sent forward to Song Be to set up a refueling point for Cav choppers. Bravo Troop was working out of the area, and I got to talking with one of the guys in scouts. They flew LOHs (Little Ole Helicopters). It sounded like they were having all the fun, and were doing what I had come back into the service to do. Three months later, I volunteered for Bravo Troop, 1/9th Cav, because I wanted to get back to the helicopters. All my friends in the 15th S&S said I was nuts, and I probably was at the time.

I was assigned to the scout platoon at Quan Loi, which was ninety miles northwest of Saigon and about six miles from the Fishhook region of Cambodia. Our area of operations extended north past Song Be and west to the Cambodian border. Some of the area north of Song Be was very mountainous and very deadly. That was where Charlie was getting resupplied for assaults on Song Be, Quan Loi and much of that portion of South Vietnam, so that was where the scouts flew most of their missions.

When the pilots found out that I could actually fly the LOH, I was made an observer for a while, because of the dual set of controls on my side. Then I got my own bird as crew chief and gunner.

One of the weapons we carried was what everyone called "Hooters." I would take a one-quart oil can and put one pound of C-4 explosive in the bottom, then a concussion grenade to act as a primer, then two more pounds of C-4 around the grenade, along with metal links from M-60 machine gun belts for fragmentation. We dropped these bombs on bunkers or enemy troops. From what a POW captured on the Jolly Jungle Highway later told us, they were nasty. I would like to tell you about a mission where my bombs started a battle.

We were working over the Jolly Jungle Highway, which was named after our troop CO, Major Charles Jolly. This was an extensive system of camouflaged trails and roads, leading into South Vietnam from Laos and Cambodia. The roads were floored with bamboo, and some had bridges that could accommodate trucks. It had underground hospitals, bunker complexes and triple canopy jungle. The main areas were a few kilometers north of Song Be and a large mountain called Nui Ba Ra. The entire troop would leave Quan Loi at first light—scouts in their LOHs, Blues in their Hueys, and Cobra gunships. Our standby and refueling area was the Duc Phong Special Forces camp, about halfway between Song Be and the Jolly Jungle Highway. In that area, we used "Heavy Pink Teams" of two LOHs and two Cobras, or one LOH and two Cobras. If the Pink Teams spotted anything, the Blues, or infantry platoon would be inserted to investigate.

Major Jolly and his platoon leaders had an instinct about where the VC and NVA would be. A good gunner could tell if there had been activity along a trail the previous night, no matter how hard Charlie tried to hide it. The leaves would be dry from people moving by, or you might see a few footprints (we flew that low).

On this particular day, my Pink Team was working a mountain valley north of Duc Phong. I picked up a trail that looked good and the pilot followed it, using the rotor blades to blow away top cover so that we could look down. We found about four bunkers next to the trail. I dropped a "Hooter" into one bunker and it almost blew us up with it. They had stored fuel inside. We came back around after the secondary explosions and saw a Charlie kicking and jerking around inside the ruins of the bunker. He was on fire.

We had made them mad and started receiving fire from all directions. There were green tracers flying all around the LOH. We marked the place with smoke and got the hell out, then our two Cobras rolled in with 17-pound rockets and miniguns. An Air Force OV-10 bird dog (spotter plane) was monitoring the air channel. He had two "Fast Movers" (jet bombers) on station with napalm and 500-pound bombs. About this time, one of the scout LOHs working two or three kilometers away went down from hostile fire. We had planned to put the Blues into that bunker complex, but now we dropped everything and headed for the downed crew. We pulled everyone out of the crash site, one by one, riding on the skids of my LOH.

After the air strike was finished and we had refueled at Duc Phong, we headed back to the bunker complex in a "heavy Pink Team" of two LOHs and two Cobras. When we got back there, VC in black pajamas and NVA in green uniforms were running everywhere. They must have been dazed by the 500-pound bombs, or thought that we were gone for good. They just looked up at us with blood running out of their ears and noses. I shot ten or twelve of them before we figured we had better move on before those dudes realized what was happening. All eight Cobras came a-running (made gun runs), and after that, the Fast Movers came back for more air strikes. It was a bad day for Charlie.

We got over sixty enemy KIA, with no telling how many more were wounded. By then, it was almost dark and the CO would not risk putting the Blues in for the night, not with just the one platoon. The next morning, the 2/5th Cav went in with company strength and found a big cache of ammo and weapons, and captured ten NVA. There had been sixty to seventy bunkers along the trail.

On 30 April 1970, at the Bravo Troop TOC at Quan Loi, Maj. Charles Jolly made the following announcement: "Gentlemen, I want all aircraft and personnel ready at first light in the morning. We're going into the Fishhook to kick Charlie's ass."

That statement was the best Christmas present in the world. We were going to get some payback for all of our fallen comrades. I was the

Blue Lift Platoon sergeant by then, and my job was to put the right door gunner with the right crew chief, and be sure the aircraft were armed and ready to fly. There was no problem that night. Morale in the unit had always been high, but when we found out about the operation everyone pitched in to be sure that there were no red-lined (down for maintenance) Hueys the next day.

About one o'clock in the morning, the rumbling started—B-52s pounding the Fishhook and the Parrot's Beak. The bombs and the artillery went on all night. Quan Loi was about ten kilometers from Cambodia, and we could hear the explosions clearly. Everyone was restless to get started. Guys were sitting on top of bunkers or standing by in the aircraft, listening and thinking about the future. There were supposed to be radar-controlled .51 caliber machine guns in the Fishhook.

At five o'clock, we were all ready—scout gunners, scout observers, pilots, Blues—all waiting for the order to "saddle up." The heavy Pink Teams were the first to go, then two Huey lift ships for command and control. I was on one of them. The Fishhook looked like something out of a World War II movie—the Blitzkrieg, the Normandy invasion. Everywhere you looked were Ch-47 Shithooks (Chinooks), Cobras, Hueys and LOHs. Below us, the 11th ACR was moving on line into Cambodia with their Sheridan tanks and APCs. Ahead of them were B-52 craters and LZs blasted out of the jungle with 15,000-pound Commando Vault bombs. The firepower was awesome.

We had a Pink Team scouting in front of the 11th ACR and my Huey was above them at 1,500 feet. The gunners were stationed right behind the pilots to cover them better, and we free-fired our M-60 machine guns. They were hand held, not mounted to anything. This probably saved my life the next day. As the 11th ACR approached a small village on the outskirts of Mimot, they started taking fire. The first two Americans to be killed in the Cambodian incursion died there. The tanks came on line, puffs of smoke appeared from the muzzles of their 152mm cannon, and the village just disappeared. They received no more fire from there. My crew flew twelve hours that day and killed five enemy soldiers.

We were too excited to be tired on 2 May, the second day of the incursion. Again, the Huey lift ships tagged along behind the heavy Pink Teams. One of the Pink Teams, "22" with CWO Don Chandler, spotted a deserted bunker complex with papers scattered all over the place. My pilot, Captain Kaufman, decided that we should check it out. There were two treelines below us with a big clearing in between them, and we sat down next to the jungle. The crew chief and I got out to investigate. He had a machine gun and I was carrying an M-16.

The bunkers we searched were abandoned, thank God, and we collected everything we could carry, including a new Honda motorcycle that we later gave to Major Jolly. The NVA must have gotten mad when they saw me grab the motorcycle, because they opened up with automatic weapons. We took ten rounds in and about the fuel cell on my side of the chopper. Had I been sitting in the normal position for a gunner, instead of free-firing the M-60, I would have had about six rounds of .30 caliber in me, instead of in the fuel cell. The pilot flew the Huey to a clearing, where a Cobra had landed after it got shot up, and we transferred ourselves and the Honda to another ship. Major Jolly was soon tooling all over Quan Loi on his new motorcycle.

On 3 May, our emotions were still running high. We were getting close to something, but didn't know what it would be. Major Jolly called me into his office, and I thought it was about the direct commission he had put me in for in March. Instead, he joked about the Honda and said the NVA wouldn't have shot at me if I had paid them for it. Then he informed me that I was taking over the scout platoon as platoon sergeant. My first love had always been LOHs, anyway. The scouts had the best and the craziest pilots in Vietnam, like Chandler from Alabama and Jim Cyrus from up north. The gunners were tough men like Mike Hanlon and "The Greek." That day we worked between Mimot and Snoul, and the Blues found a cache with 2,000 semiautomatic rifles.

By 4 May, every time we went out we took fire. I was flying as scout gunner, but was also trying to keep everyone in ammo and WP grenades, etc. Then we found "The City." One of the Pink Teams spotted bunkers just as it was getting dark. The Blues went in early the next morning with backup from a line unit. The place was big—paved bicycle paths, eighteen mess halls, lumber yards, street signs, truck repair parks, switchboards, and pig and chicken farms. There were over four hundred huts, and bunkers big enough to park trucks inside. They even had a swimming pool. At first we thought that this was the legendary COSVN headquarters. On 6 May, we found "Rock Island East," northeast of Mimot. It was even bigger than "The City" and had many GM and Mercedes trucks. We were really hurting Charlie.

The war in Cambodia rocked on until 17 June. That day my chopper crashed at Quan Loi. I had broken ribs and a concussion and was evacuated to Japan. It was the third time that I had been wounded in one year, so it was probably best to go home while I still could. One thing upsets me. I never officially heard about my direct commission, although my friends told me that it came through after I was medevaced. The army should have let me know.

23. GROWING UP

(Cobra Pilot, Charlie Troop, 1970–71)
*Warrant Officer **Randy Zahn** arrived in Vietnam at age nineteen. Events and the loss of friends over the next year made him grow up too fast.*

I always knew that at some point in my life I would serve in the military. It was something my father had done, and his father before him. My father was in the Army in World War II, and having done that, he advised my brother and me to join the Navy or the Air Force. My brother heeded his advice and joined the Navy, but I wanted to be a pilot. I went into army aviation.

Going to Vietnam was an experience charged with many emotions. I had played Army as a kid. *"Bang-bang! Pow-pow!"* Two minutes later, you're up and playing John Wayne again. I was seeking a challenge, as many young men do, and this would be mine. At the same time I was scared to death. On the flight over, I wondered if I would ever go home. It was about two o'clock in the morning when the pilot announced that we were over the Republic of Vietnam. We came out of our slumber, and there were about three faces glued to every window to see what was going on below us. It was like flying over a bottle of ink. We saw an occasional tracer or explosion, and that was about it. When the door of the aircraft opened, we were engulfed in the odor unique to Vietnam. We were soon drenched in sweat. One of the coldest things was the jeers and cruel comments from the guys lined up to take our places in the plane and fly home. A year later, I understood.

At the 90th Replacement Battalion, we were asked where we wanted to go. We had to fill out a dream sheet. I had heard all these horror stories about the 1st Cav Division. I put down every unit I could think of, other than the 1st Cav. I was assigned there the next morning. I did some research upon arrival at the Cav replacement center, and found out that the 1/9th Cav were a bunch of swashbucklers who were too good to call in the troops, and liked to handle all the action on their own. I wanted something safer and saner. I filled out another dream sheet with every unit I could think of, instead of the 9th Cav. That day I was assigned to the 1/9th Cav.

I was flown to Phuoc Vinh on a Chinook. I walked down the ramp, a scared nineteen-year-old, and saw the Cobras armed to the teeth with rockets and miniguns. They reminded me of the World War II Flying Tigers of General Chennault, because most of them had tiger's teeth painted on them. I was sent to the gun hootch and told to find a place to sleep, and was immediately befriended by Kevin Frye. He had been there a couple of weeks. We became close friends.

I was flying missions within a week. One of the things that still gives me bad dreams happened then. We were operating at Song Be, about ninety miles from the base camp. At the very end of the day's flying, we were told that a Long Range Reconnaissance Patrol (LRRP) was in contact up by Bu Gia Map on the Cambodian border. Could we shoot for them?

We sent the scout bird home, because it would be dark by the time we got there and visual reconnaissance would be out of the question. We made radio contact with the LRRPs. The fear and fatigue in the team leader's voice, his pleading with us to please hurry, were horrible. He had already lost one of his men and had two others wounded. In the background was a continuous crackle of small arms fire. We pulled as much power as we could to get as much speed out of the aircraft as possible.

We called him again a few miles later. The first thing I noticed was that the crescendo of the small arms fire had gotten much louder. The fear in the team leader's voice was more apparent. His pleading with us to get there was beyond description. We tried to keep talking with him on the radio as much as we could. We were probably only ten miles away when he finally said, "I really appreciate you guys trying, but there just wasn't enough time. Thanks guys, but we're goners."

The only thing I heard after that was an extremely loud volley of small arms fire. The radio went dead. My platoon leader in the back seat said, "Oh, fuck!" We tried to get into the area, but we had no one to contact and couldn't see anything in the jungle below us. Tears streamed down my face on the way back. I was thinking about the team members' families and loved ones.

Things progressed normally after that. Our mission was visual reconnaissance for the 1st Cav, looking for targets that ground troops could move in on—bunker complexes, trails, live sightings. We had a reputation for not really calling in the rest of the Cav and basically taking care of things ourselves. Then we went into Cambodia.

My folks sent me newspaper and magazine articles and cassettes of newscasts. It was interesting how our experiences contrasted with what the news media was saying about us. They were putting out such bullshit. I hardly recognized the descriptions of contacts in which I was personally involved. The media was saying that there was almost a rebellion among the troops in Vietnam, because they didn't want to go into Cambodia. In our unit, pilots were actually threatening to fight each other to get places on the available aircraft to fly on Cambodian missions. This was the first opportunity to hit the enemy in their sanctuaries, instead of waiting for them to come across and hit us. Other guys got similar news clippings from their homes all over the United States, and they did hurt our morale. We felt betrayed.

The squadron found almost every major cache site in the division's sector of Cambodia. Ones that I remember were "Shakey's Hill," "Rock Island East," and "The City." They were filled with armaments, weapons, powder, bullets, etc. We found "Walter Reed East," a huge hospital complex, and "The Hardware Store," a huge depot for building materials. We also killed more NVA than the rest of the division combined. It hurt the enemy so badly that the effects of depriving the enemy of weapons and personnel lasted for almost two years. It was a good campaign and we were all very proud of it. Our only regret was that we couldn't stay in there longer.

Two things stick in my mind about that campaign. The first of my close friends to be killed was a scout pilot. I was off that day when I heard that an aircraft was down. I immediately ran to the Tactical Operations Center to find out what was going on and listen to the action over the radio. When I found out that my friend was dead, the emotion I felt was new and puzzling to me. I knew that it was bound to happen, but as hard as I tried to make myself believe that he had just gone home, it was difficult. But life and the war went on.

We used to be given an east-west grid line that we couldn't go beyond.

Most of our pilots would stray farther into Cambodia to find something. My team crossed the grid one day and found a large city with antiaircraft emplacements on a range of hills to the north. There was a long runway with masses of warehouses on both sides. We were very high, out of small arms range, and were looking down at this complex, wondering what the hell was going on. I spotted a small, black aircraft taking off from this runway.

We dove down to a position about five hundred meters behind him and about five hundred meters above him. It was a small reconnaissance-type plane that was definitely not made in the United States. There were no markings of any kind, except for the red star on the side of the pilot's jet black helmet.

I called "Paris Control," who controlled air ops up there, and let them know that we had a suspected enemy aircraft heading north. We dogged him for a while and finally asked for clearance to shoot. They came back that he was a confirmed friendly. I asked them how he could be friendly if he had no markings and was heading north. They came back, "Negative! Break off the contact." We did so reluctantly. In a matter of seconds, a flight of F-4s went screaming past me, did one or two orbits around this guy and blew him out of the sky. I radioed back to operations that this was our big opportunity to shoot down an enemy aircraft and we were deprived of it. I was really pissed.

After Cambodia, the amount of enemy activity in South Vietnam diminished. Our base wasn't shelled so often at night and we had the opportunity to work the area and inflict pain on those who had been harassing and shelling us. Kevin and I continued our friendship. We fixed up our room, installed closets, cabinets and a sink, stained everything and built our own furniture. It was a place where everyone liked to visit. It was our refuge away from the war.

Kevin talked a lot about his girlfriend and often showed me her picture, but I never saw him write her a letter or receive a letter from her. One night I told him that it was really none of my business, but he could talk about it if he wanted to. He told me that she was his fiancée, but while he was in flight school, she had been involved in a horse-riding accident and had died. I didn't know what to say to comfort him. He told me that he really didn't give a damn what happened to him in Vietnam because of what had happened to her.

About two days later, I was out working the Duc Phong area when we got a call that there was an aircraft down. We didn't know who it was. I was still flying copilot at the time and I asked the aircraft commander if we were going over there. He told me, no, there were already two other teams in the area and there was nothing else that we could do. We were to continue our mission. It's difficult trying to fly around and carry on a routine when you know that someone's down. We got back to base camp a couple of hours later, and before the aircraft was even shut down I jumped out and ran to the TOC. The operations officer was writing something on a board with grease pencil and had his back to me.

"Mike, who was it?" He didn't respond. "Mike, who's down?" Again there was nothing but silence. Finally I said, "Goddammit, Mike! Where's Kevin?"

He turned around with tears in his eyes, then walked over to me and put his hands on my shoulder. "Randy, Kevin's not coming back."

Going to Vietnam was filled with many emotions, but this was one I was not ready for. I had been all of twenty years old for one week. I walked over to our hootch, locked myself in, and cried all night long, until the morning.

Kevin had become like a brother to me. I had been looking forward to being his lifelong friend, but now I was asked to pack up his belongings. My platoon leader had the wit and maturity to keep me on the ground the next day. He told me that I needed to grieve, needed to cope with it. He didn't want me ending up the same way as Kevin. I wrote a letter to my folks and said, "I know life and death are a part of growing up, but why didn't you tell me that growing up is so damned hard?" I still have cassette tapes with Kevin's voice on them. I still think about him. I still cry.

We started getting hit at night again in the first part of September. The mortar and rocket fire all seemed to be directed at the C Troop area. They usually fired two shells, followed by two more and so on. My new roommate was the Blue platoon leader. The Blues were an elite infantry unit that had their own helicopters to tote them around, had gunship cover over them the entire time they were on the ground, and basically got to come back and sleep in a warm, clean bed at night. We inserted them on a downed Chinook near the base camp one afternoon and Blue decided that it would be good training to keep the platoon out there overnight. Help was close at hand if they needed it.

We took a round of incoming rocket fire about midnight, relatively close to my hootch. The second round hit. I got up and began to head toward the bunker. Something, a sixth sense, told me to stop running and hit the ground. I remember seeing smoke and debris and feeling something in my head and face. The explosion was excruciatingly loud. I got up and walked into a bunker and could tell from the looks on the guys' faces that something was wrong. The White platoon leader grabbed me and laid me over a foot locker. Every time I moved my head I felt this thing there—a strange feeling. A two-foot long sliver of wood from one of the walls was stuck just above my right temple. It flapped up and down when I walked. Somebody pulled it out, then I reached down to touch a sensation of pain or tingling in my leg. My hand came away covered in blood. At that point, I realized that I had been wounded. We got between fifty and seventy-five rounds of incoming that night, all concentrated in the 1/9th area.

I was taken to the aid station and evacuated by helicopter as soon as it was safe to fly. They operated on my shrapnel wounds at the 93rd Evac Hospital. The next day, some of my friends came down to see me. They told me that the EOD (Explosive Ordinance Demolitions) people had discovered that the rocket that wounded myself and three other guys had landed almost dead center on Blue's pillow. If he hadn't been in the field that night, he would now be dead. Had I not hit the ground when I did, I would have been dead. Our hootch had burned to the ground. Between Kevin's death and my being wounded, I learned a lot about myself and about growing up, about life and the meaning of death.

I didn't know if the Army was going to contact my folks about the wounds, so I called them from the hospital. My dad was a very emotional person, and I felt that if they had the opportunity to hear my voice, I could tell them myself that I was all right. I had called once before and both of them were almost instantaneously on the phone. But not this time.

I asked mom where my dad was. She told me that he was in the hospital. Two days before, he had the feeling that something had happened to me and the doctor, our cousin, put him in the hospital for observation. He had suffered a mild nervous breakdown. I told my mother as gently as possible that I wasn't just visiting someone in the hospital. I had been wounded, but would be okay. After that, it was important to take an R&R to Hawaii to let my folks see me in person and see that I was still in one piece. My dad had tears in his eyes when he saw me. His first words were, "Your mother just told me on the plane over here.

Are you all right?'' We later worked out that he had this feeling within five minutes of my being wounded.

It was a great reunion, but I had mixed emotions about going back. I wasn't as keen on the war, the way we were fighting it, or our goals and objectives. It seemed to me now to be more of a political circus than a real war. We continued to work around Phuoc Vinh until around Christmas of 1970, then we moved to Tay Ninh. We moved from our comfortable hootches to GP medium tents. All but one other American unit had been pulled out, and it was virtually an abandoned base camp. ARVNs provided perimeter security. We worked out of there around the Dog's Head and Parrot's Beak regions of Cambodia.

In early January, we got a report that a battalion of NVA regulars was going to be coming across the border to hit the base camp. Being a bunch of pilots and mechanics, we had forgotten most of our infantry training from basic and weren't too keen on doing hand-to-hand combat. We sent all our Pink Teams up along the border to wait for them to come across. On 10 January, my scout ship was on the deck when I looked back toward Tay Ninh and saw a towering column of black smoke rising straight into the air about three or four kilometers from the base camp. I called back to operations and asked what was going on. They didn't know.

I ordered my scout ship back to altitude and we headed toward the smoke column. An ARVN convoy had been hit on a road running from Tay Ninh to Cambodia. About four APCs and three trucks were burning and it looked like utter chaos below us. I really didn't see any firing going on and couldn't decide who was where, then I saw some soldiers by a truck pointing to a treeline on the west side of the road. I came down along the side of the road and punched off a pair of rockets. All of a sudden, it looked like this entire field pulled the grass up around their waists and started running. I had never seen more enemy soldiers in the open. More teams arrived and we worked over the area for about two hours.

The NVA battalion had slipped down a couple of days before we got the intelligence report on them, which was almost always the case, and they were posturing to hit the base camp. The convoy was just too tempting a target for them and they couldn't resist attacking it. My roommate, Larry, and I were credited with 256 kills. We both received Distinguished Flying Crosses. Tay Ninh never did get hit.

Nothing else really significant happened during my tour. I yelled along with the others when we boarded the airplane for home. Now I understood why we were doing it. In the cabin were some familiar faces. The lack of some others was painfully obvious. I thought about Kevin and all the others who wouldn't be going home, and I couldn't help but think of what the parents had gone through. I know a lot of us were saying that we would go to heaven, because we had spent our time in hell, but our hell couldn't have been as bad as the hell we put our parents through while they waited for us to come home.

Larry would be coming home three weeks after me, and I couldn't rest until he got back. Part of me would still be there until he got home safely. Shortly after I got back, I received a tape from him. I listened to it with mom and dad. He was on his way home, but he told me our other roommate, who had just made Cobra aircraft commander, was killed along the border in my old aircraft. It had disintegrated in mid-air. We don't know to this day whether it was ground fire, sabotage or catastrophic failure. My folks heard that and walked out of the room to give me some time alone.

There are so many unanswered questions. What if I had been on that mission instead of Kevin? What if Blue had not decided to spend the night in the field? What if I hadn't had that premonition to hit the ground during the rocket attack?

I'm not sure that I would want to go through it again, but I wouldn't trade the experience for anything in the world.

24. THE POINT

(Infantry Squad Leader, Alpha Troop, 1970)
*Sergeant **Ed Beal** transferred to A Troop Blues from the LRRPs after six months in Vietnam. There he learned to love the danger and excitement of walking point.*

March 19, 1970, started out as just a normal mission for the Blues of Alpha Troop, but we came very close to being wiped out before the day was over. We had been briefed on a mission the evening before. Division intelligence told us that the area we would be working in looked empty. Flying above triple canopy and looking to see what you could see on the ground was a good tactic, but the most effective one was to actually set foot on the ground and look for the enemy. That's why we were going to be inserted into the area, which was better known as the Dog's Head.

After the briefing, we broke up into squads to check out all our equipment and weapons for the insertion. I made sure that the guys in my squad had plenty of ammo, smoke grenades and water—just anything they could use in a firefight. It was tough humping all that gear around the jungle, but when the situation arose and you needed it, you were all set. I was a sergeant and a former member of Company H, 75th Rangers (LRRPs), and I had developed a sense of survival. I was out to save my life and the lives of my buddies.

At first light on the 19th, we boarded three Hueys for an insertion close to the Cambodian border. The mission began as usual. We arrived at the LZ, jumped off the helicopters, and immediately set up a perimeter. After a few minutes of just sitting and waiting, we set off toward our main objective—some high-speed trails that had been spotted from the air. My squad was the point squad, and one of the jobs I liked best was walking point. Kregg "P. J." Jorgenson and myself used to fight over the position. There were times when we would even walk point together. Lt. Jack Hugele used to talk to us about it, and we tried to do better, but it was in our blood. Kregg and I had both been in the LRRPs together, and now we were in the Blues.

That particular morning, I was teaching an FNG (Fucking New Guy) how to walk point. It was his first mission. We started walking down this high-speed trail and came across some bunkers after a couple of hundred meters. I stopped the patrol and carefully checked them out. There were signs of movement all over the place, and we decided to go down the trail a little bit more and see what we could find. As the platoon walked deeper into a very large bunker complex, we began thinking about turning around and getting the hell out of Indian Country while we had the chance. But before any plan was made, the bunkers to my left flank, about ten-fifteen meters off the trail, opened up at us with heavy automatic weapons fire. Gooks were coming from everywhere and all hell had broken loose.

A couple of NVA soldiers charged down the trail about thirty meters ahead, firing at me with a .30 caliber machine gun. I didn't think I had much of a chance, but I fired back and killed one of them. It broke their stride when he fell. I brought my M-60 machine gunner, Duane Bloor (Porky), up on point with me, and he laid down a very impressive pattern of fire. The NVA were throwing everything they had at us by this time. We were taking heavy automatic fire and some B-40 rockets from all around us, so they had the platoon surrounded. We popped smoke and marked our position, and the Cobras came in firing within a few meters of us. That's how close the gooks were. The gunships kept working for us like that all day long. Before it was over, the combat lasted from early morning until evening.

We tried to set up a better perimeter, but we couldn't move. Porky and I were pinned down by machine-gun fire, and both of us tried to get behind a tree that was only two feet in diameter. It worked. You'd be surprised where you can get when you have hot lead flying over you. We were even being shot at from the trees, but we couldn't see their positions.

I looked around and saw Kregg Jorgenson, and he had his hands full. I finally managed to crawl over to help him. The two of us were killing gooks six feet away. You could see the ones we weren't able to shoot, running from bunker to bunker.

One of the heroes that day was a squad leader, Sgt. Tony Cortez. His bravery saved a lot of lives, and the survivors of that battle will always remember him. The gooks repeatedly tried to break our perimeter, but all of our firepower, and the gunships above us, stopped them.

After marking our positions so many times, we had run out of smoke grenades and were getting short on ammunition. One of the choppers dropped a case of smoke, but the NVA got to it first. The gooks then started popping the smoke and throwing the grenades at us, trying to get the gunships to roll in on us. A chopper pilot saw the smoke and asked us to describe our situation to him and verify that we had popped smoke. Our RTO (Radio-Telephone Operator), Jim Braun, told him that the gooks were popping the smoke, and to roll in on them, so many meters away from our position. We were dropped more smoke to mark our positions.

All of a sudden, we had a guy shot in the upper thigh. I was wounded also. I received shrapnel to the side of my head from a B-40 rocket. I didn't even know I was hit until someone saw blood running down the side of my face. The adrenaline was really flowing now. The brutal excitement of combat, the explosions from rockets and grenades, and the sounds of automatic fire were playing an ear-piercing kind of music that I would never forget.

When Porky and I were pinned down by machine-gun fire, I knew that I wasn't going to make it out of that part of the jungle alive, so I was going to try to take as many of them with me as possible. I believe that's the way we all felt. There's no way to find out how many gooks I personally killed, or how many we killed together that day. The guys and I had a click going on. We had teamwork, and that got us through the day. You depended on each other, and you had to, because your life was in your buddies' hands.

We were in such heavy contact that we had to get reinforcements to help us out of the jam. A quick reaction force from Bravo Company, 2/8th Cav, was inserted, and they came under heavy automatic fire. Bravo Company was pinned down too. Gunships worked out for both forces now, and later on the company began moving our way under sporadic sniper fire. Our platoon started moving around the base camp, throwing concussion grenades into bunkers. But there were so many bunkers we didn't have time to clear all of them.

When we got through with that area, there were dead gooks lying all over the place, and the rest of the NVA had run off somewhere in the jungle. We made a partial count of thirty-nine bodies around the bunkers and along the trail, but there were many more. You could see them dragging off their dead and wounded. We were exhausted to the max. Combat will completely drain you.

After we regrouped, we had to get out so artillery could shell the area. I was the one who got those guys there, so I was going to be the one to get them out. That's how strongly I felt about it. I started walking point, leading us to the same LZ that we had used that morning. I was really taking my time as I walked down another high-speed trail, because there were still a lot of gooks in the area.

I was walking down the trail, very slowly, when an NVA soldier stuck his head out of the bushes to see where we were. He had made a bad mistake. I stopped the patrol, knelt down on one knee, took careful aim and shot. The S.O.B. fell out onto the trail, dead.

They had set up another ambush for us, and we were back into the thick of it again. All hell broke out after I shot the gook, and for a while there, I didn't think that it would ever end. We were taking fire from all down the trail, and the gunships made a few more runs on the NVA. We finally made it to the extraction point, and the choppers came in to take us back to Tay Ninh. Bravo Company stayed behind. They had a lot of movement, and took small arms and sniper fire throughout the night.

Now, that's one thing I've always wondered about. If that gook hadn't stuck his head out when he did, or if I hadn't seen him, we would probably have walked into that ambush. What would have happened then? We would have had some KIAs, and I might have been one of them. I can't forget that day, but there have been times when I wished that I could have. When I hear a helicopter pass over, the sound of it will put me right back there.

I will never forget the chopper ride back to Tay Ninh. Not a word was spoken. The aftershock of something like that is tremendous, and everyone of us was in a daze. Those young boys had a look in their eyes that could cut right through you. If those eyes could talk, they could probably tell some stories like you see in movies, but it was real life, and I was part of it. You have to realize that we were a recon platoon and we worked in small numbers, eighteen or twenty guys. We were the eyes and ears of the 1st Cavalry Division, and I was very proud to have served with them.

We dismounted after the choppers landed at Tay Ninh, and started walking back to our hootches. To tell the truth, we all looked like a bunch of zombies. We were in such a state of shock that it would take a while to get over it. It had been an experience that you couldn't just shake off. Now it was time to clean up, get our gear and weapons clean and just unwind. There would be a debriefing soon, while things were still fresh in our minds.

During the debriefing, it was estimated that we had run into a couple of NVA companies. We had walked right into a battalion base camp, which was used as a training area as well. We knew that because of the training aids that were found there. Intelligence told us later that this base camp was being used as a gathering point for a massive attack around the city of Tay Ninh.

I was so mentally and physically exhausted after the debriefing that I didn't have any trouble getting to sleep. When I woke up the next morning, it all seemed like a bad dream, but then I came to my senses and knew that it was for real. I missed breakfast, because I still didn't have the stomach for it. About thirty minutes later, we were back on the choppers, heading for another insertion on the Cambodian border, "Rock and Roll."

A few days later, Duane Bloor and myself were given Silver Stars. Major General Roberts flew in to pin the medals on Porky and me. I received a Purple Heart at the same time.

25. WILD BILL

(Scout Pilot, Alpha & Charlie Troops, 1970–71)

Warrant Officer **Bill Frazer** *didn't want to fly scouts and was quickly told he was going to die there. He ended up flying the limit in one troop and volunteering to do it again with another. The incident with the black aircraft described in this story is not the same one as described by Randy Zahn. Bill Frazer states that encounters with unmarked Communist reconnaissance aircraft happened on several occasions during the Cambodian incursion.*

I entered flight school at age nineteen and turned twenty just prior to going to Vietnam in February 1970. I had heard Stateside that the 1st Cav was the unit to serve with in combat. When I arrived in Vietnam, I was assigned to the 9th Cav, and eventually served with both Charlie and Alpha Troops as a scout pilot. I flew an OH-6 Light Observation Helicopter. My job was to get up every morning, attend a briefing, fly up to the AO (Area of Operations) along the Cambodian border and shoot people.

We would hover over the treetops at about twenty knots, staying just inside transitional lift to keep from falling out of the sky. We worked in an area that was primarily triple canopy jungle, and a slow hover would put us looking down through the trees from about 120 feet off the jungle floor. We watched for trails, hootches, equipment, people or any other signs of enemy activity. We often fought our battles to music over the intercom from Armed Forces Radio, bobbing and weaving over the jungle to the sound of Jimmy Hendrix or the Doors.

A Cobra, the cover ship or "high bird," flew circles above me at

217

3,500 feet. This was the famous Pink Team. The high bird's job was to provide fire support and to record and relay my spot reports. We would maintain a constant dialogue, and the Cobra pilot would record sightings with a grease pencil on the inside of his Plexiglas bubble. He would later relay them to headquarters.

We generally flew for twelve to sixteen hours each day, seven days a week. Because we covered the hot areas, we were constantly in action. There were only eight or ten days during my entire tour in Vietnam when I did not come under fire, or initiate an enemy contact.

We would fly to the AO at an altitude of about 3,500 feet, then I would put the LOH into a slip and basically drop like a rock down to the treetops to minimize exposure to small arms fire during the descent. I would begin working in tight right-hand circles which would put myself, and the crew chief (called the gunner or torque) in the back section looking down. In my unit, the torque sat on the floor in the rear with a hand-held machine gun. All seats and excess equipment had been removed to lighten the load and allow us to carry more ammo, grenades and homemade bombs. The observer sat in the left front seat beside me with an M-16 in his lap and a smoke grenade in his hand. When we spotted something, the observer would mark it with smoke for the high bird.

If I spotted enemy soldiers, I would shout "I got gooks!" The torque would immediately pull the trigger on his machine gun, even if he couldn't see the target, and I would adjust his tracers by maneuvering the aircraft. For the first two or three months, the pilot was about worthless. We hadn't developed the highly skilled vision that was needed to spot enemy activity, and we were wrapped up in just flying the helicopter, trying to keep from running into trees or crashing into mountainsides. During that time, we relied on the gunners to train us. Once the pilot was trained, the pilot did most of the directing.

I was terribly afraid when I arrived in-country and never believed that I could kill someone, but it's amazing what the human mind can adjust to. We lived a form of insanity, but it was an insanity that helped us survive. The mortality rate among scout pilots was incredibly high. Scout pilots just didn't last long. You literally had to become the meanest son of a bitch out there to survive, but if you did, you became so charged up with the excitement of it that you were worthless at anything else. There is nothing that can get you as high as that kind of life and death intensity on a daily basis. Neither drugs nor booze could possibly reproduce that kind of adrenaline high.

I was one of two pilots from my era to survive for six months, was pulled out of scout flying against my will and made a gunship pilot, and ended up volunteering for another six months in the job with another troop. The other pilot, Chuck Frazier, did the same thing. Shooting rockets at smoke drifting up through the treetops was not as personal as scout combat. This takes nothing away from the brave Cobra pilots who covered our asses so many times. We got addicted to combat, and the people who couldn't reach that level of intensity just didn't make it.

It got to the point where I would be running low on fuel and ammo, and have the helicopter shot to pieces, and would rather crash it on top of enemy soldiers, rather than let them get away. That kind of insanity radiates itself to the enemy. It kept him running, it kept him scared, and it kept me alive through twelve months of scout flying.

My first unit was Charlie Troop. Nothing impressed me more than walking into my first scout meeting and seeing these grungy, haggard men with a wild look in their eyes that I just can't describe. I later noticed that everyone in the scouts had that look about them. They were about my age, but looked much older, and had the presence of being older. At the same time, they were still high from the day's combat. My platoon leader, Lieutenant Harmond, had been shot down once that day, had gone back out and been shot up again with two crew members seriously injured. They had lost seven scout pilots in the previous five days. They went over the day's events, and it scared the hell out of me that somebody could do that and look forward to going the next day and doing it again.

After the meeting, a couple of crew chiefs came in, politely introduced themselves and asked for my initials. One of them asked me if I would mind standing next to the wall for a minute. He pulled out a tape measure and measured me. I asked him what he was doing. He looked me in the eye and said, "I'm measuring you for a body bag, motherfucker! You ain't going to make it!"

The first time that you kill somebody stands out in your memory for life. They would send new scout pilots on what were called "rat fuck missions." These were flights into areas where you weren't expected to find much and couldn't get into too much trouble. On this particular day we were working an area southeast of Song Be that had been quiet for a while. My high bird pilot was a CW-3 who had been in the Army for close to twenty years and was on his second tour with the 1st Cav. I give him credit for his past experiences, but by the time he got to the 9th Cav, he was not much more than an alcoholic. Nobody wanted to fly real combat missions with him, so they usually sent him on the rat fucks.

We were working alongside a river, and had come across a rocket pod or a minigun pod that had been jettisoned off a Cobra. We were flying around, trying to figure out what it was, when I looked across the river and saw a sampan tied to some trees. I told the high bird about it and went over to take a look. He told me, "If you see gooks, shoot 'em." I assumed that he was covering me, but he was still messing around over that Cobra pod. I was brand new and hadn't shot anybody, and didn't want to indiscriminately shoot some fishermen.

I suddenly realized that we were overflying a cultivated cornfield and spotted two guys, squatting down on their haunches beside two pottery kilns. One of them was dressed in white. They had their AKs between their knees and I couldn't see the weapons from my vantage point of twenty or thirty feet above them. I notified the Cobra that I had gooks. He told me to shoot them. As I started to say, "No. They might be friendlies," both men stood up and aimed their rifles at the front of my helicopter.

We took about fifteen hits along the underside of the aircraft, and the bullets just ripped the helicopter to pieces. My torque opened fire, got off about three rounds and his machine gun jammed. The observer got shook and dropped his smoke grenade inside the aircraft. It filled the cabin and reduced visibility to zero. While he fished for the smoke, I kicked the aircraft out of trim, so the air would flow through my side and out the other and clear some of the smoke.

We were flying around, shot all to hell and trailing red smoke. You can imagine the confusion inside that LOH. I was hollering at the high bird, trying to give directions to where the gooks were on the ground. The Cobra pilot had not been watching us, which was an unforgivable sin in that business, but now he spotted the red smoke.

Because of his drinking problem, the fact that the red smoke was moving at 150 miles per hour didn't register. He started firing rockets at it. I was racing over the trees, trying to outrun his rockets while others exploded on both sides of me. It didn't help that the radio was working only intermittently as a result of battle damage. We finally got the radio working, got the red smoke kicked out, and got him to stop shooting at us.

He made a couple of firing passes over where the two enemy soldiers had been, then I told him to hold up and I would go back over the cornfield. I was scared to death this time, because I knew that they were well armed and that there was sparse cover. We immediately noticed a man on the ground with an M-16 rifle. My torque opened up and walked a path of bullets across the top of him. It was the first time that I had ever seen anyone killed, and they don't die like they do on TV. He kept crawling and looking up and crawling again. The torque had been in Nam for two years and knew he was done for. I shouted for him to shoot again, and he said, "He's dead, sir!"

"Bullshit! The guy's still moving!" When the torque tried to protest, I said "Dammit! Just open up on him!" He put about thirty more rounds in him, and the guy just kept crawling and pulling himself along. But I was convinced by then that he had to be dead.

We ended up killing ten people in the open area that day. We were low on fuel and ammo, and the Cobra was about expended, but I remembered the guy in white by the pottery kiln. There were two ARA gunships circling overhead and a Pink Team to relieve us on station, but I wouldn't leave until I found him. We flew over the top of a tall clump of vegetation and saw the guy standing in the middle of it. He was invisible unless you were directly over the top of him. We hovered back over him, and as he raised his rifle to shoot at us, we dropped our last two grenades and blew him to pieces.

I was a big hero that night back at base camp. People congratulated me and bragged about how badly shot up the helicopter was, but I couldn't sleep for the next three or four nights. I kept fighting that entire battle over and over again in my dreams, then waking up. It was okay after that. I became one of the top pilots in my unit, and the killing didn't bother me any more.

We went into Cambodia in May 1970. Many people don't care for Richard Nixon, but the men in my unit whom I have been able to contact still think a lot of him. He eliminated some of the stupid restrictions and allowed us to fight the war and try to win it. The problem was that we would fight them all day along the border, then they would slip back across, recoup and come back at us again. We couldn't touch them in Cambodia. I can still remember how excited we were when we found out that we were going to be able to hit their base camps and big supply lines.

I was the first 9th Cav scout pilot to go into Cambodia, a day before the incursion officially started. We came in to refuel about noon. It had been kind of slow in the AO, and we decided to shut down and eat some lunch for once. As soon as we landed, we got a call on the radio to come over to the TOC (Tactical Operations Center) and bring our maps along. They exchanged them for maps of Cambodia, and sent the Red Platoon leader and me across the border to look for LZs (Landing Zones) for the next day.

Something interesting happened on that first mission before we even crossed the river that marked the border. I was flying low level when an 0-1 Bird Dog type aircraft pulled up alongside me. We had received no warnings about other aircraft in the area, and this 0-1 was solid black with no markings, and had rocket pods under the wings. The pilot was Vietnamese. We stared across at each other as we flew along, side by side. He was on my right side and the torque was locked and loaded, so we called the high bird for permission to shoot him down. The location and the lack of markings had convinced me that this was an enemy aircraft, and it would be a feather in my cap to be able to shoot him down.

Just across the border in that region was a NVA R&R center and airbase at a place called O Rang. The Russians made some aircraft that look just like ours, such as the 0-1 Bird Dog and the DC-3. We had seen DC-3s flying at altitude across the border, and I had seen a Russian Hound helicopter which looked like a much larger version of our H-19. To get permission to shoot this enemy aircraft down, the high bird called our operations officer, who in turn called MACV. By the time thirty minutes had passed, and we were finally given permission to engage the black 0-1, the pilot had peeled off and headed for O Rang.

Cambodia was amazing. After being in Vietnam, where the hootches and bunkers and spider holes were all hidden under triple canopy jungle, we found everything built in the open. Repair crews in trucks were working on the roads. The big NVA base camps had buildings in plain sight, zig-zag trenches, and large gun emplacements. Some of these places were deserted. The NVA had already gotten the word about the coming invasion, and many of them were gone, but they had left behind groups of their Montagnard slaves.

We went into Cambodia with eleven scout pilots. We were down to two pilots within three days, Chuck Frazier and myself. There were ten aircraft available to us, and each day, we would go through between seven and ten of them. We would get one shot up, fly in to maintenance and drop it off, then grab another fueled and armed LOH and head back out.

We flew "Purple Teams"—a White bird, a Red bird, and a Blue lift bird with a squad of Blues on board to rescue you when, not if, you got shot down. We would go down, the Cobra would shoot up the surrounding area, then the Blues would rappel in and get you out of there. If it was too hot for the one squad of Blues, they held their ground until reinforced with a platoon, a company, or even a battalion, whatever it took to end the fight.

On the first day in, we dropped down on the deck as soon as we reached the river that marked the border. As we approached a mountain, the Cobra pilot, Steve Bean, radioed that he would bring me up over the top of it, and that there was a village up there. "As you come up over the top of the mountain, you'll be flying right down the main street, so watch your ass!" I hovered down the main street, almost dragging skids in the dirt, and looked in at what appeared to be barracks windows. I could see polished floors, bunk beds and foot lockers. People were sitting on some of the bunks. Steve told me to shoot them, but I still did not want to indiscriminately kill somebody, so we held our fire. He could see what I couldn't—trenches, 37mm antiaircraft emplacements, and a flagpole with an NVA flag flying from it.

As I got to the end of the street, I pulled up over a long barracks and caught sight of a clothesline full of NVA uniforms. I hollered, "We got gooks!" the torque opened fire, and they started shooting at us from all sides. We immediately took eight or ten hits, and I just bent the nose over, took off and dropped down the other side of the mountain. I bounced back up in time to see the Cobra blow three rooms off the end of the long barracks with his rockets. Steve told me that the area was so hot that I should climb to altitude. There was nothing we could do with just small arms. We climbed up to 3,500 feet and spent our time dropping hand grenades on the main street.

There was one mountain in Cambodia that took its toll very early in the campaign. I had been directed in at low level to what looked like a deserted village on top of a mountain. As we slowly cut across, tracers started coming from everywhere. The torque's gun jammed, the observer's M-16 jammed, Plexiglas and instruments were flying all over the cockpit, and I could feel the bullets impacting all over the aircraft. We took twenty or twenty-five hits, including two bullets that missed me by about an inch. We were able to get away before setting it down, but we lost that aircraft. The Air Force quickly hit it with 500-pound high drags and nape.

The next day, Tommy Widden went in to do a BDA (bomb damage assessment) and took many hits from what remained of the burned-out village. He and his torque were both shot in the stomach, and the observer was wounded in the leg. The transmission had been hit and it was slinging hot oil all over the crew. He tried to get back to Bu Dop in South Vietnam to avoid going down and being captured in Cambodia.

About five klicks out from Bu Dop, he began screaming that his instruments were going crazy on him and the helicopter was falling apart. He had been flying low level. The helicopter went inverted and crashed into solid, triple canopy jungle. The torque was thrown free and managed to crawl back to the aircraft and pull the observer to safety. The torque then crawled back to the aircraft to rescue Tommy, even though the observer was yelling that he was already dead. The chopper exploded as he tried to free Tommy Widden.

I went into that village three or four more times, each time losing an aircraft. You wouldn't see a thing in the rubble, but as soon as you tried to cut across it, the whole world would open up at you. We put in air strike after air strike with no apparent results, and finally thought about it and decided on a joint operation against the mountaintop.

Four teams of F-4 Phantoms hit it with napalm and 500-pound bombs, then Chinooks with bulldozers and engineers landed as the jets pulled up and the perimeter was rocketed by three teams of "Blue Max" (Aerial Rocket Artillery gunships, carrying seventy-six rockets per Cobra). The engineers jumped on the bulldozers and began pushing everything off the side of the mountain and constructing an earth berm. Next came Chinooks with infantry and artillery crews. They finally just bulldozed all the tunnel openings and put a firebase in their place in about an hour and a half. The whole mountain was honeycombed with tunnels. There had been approximately 2,000 NVA regulars on the mountain. They retreated into the mountain during air strikes, and would come back out to attack our LOHs.

We had guys who had been over there eighteen months or two years. Sometimes we'd get a real misfit, and one of them was a guy I'll call Tom. He was a pretty good torque, but he had an attitude problem. One day, he really hung his fanny out in a battle and I wrote him up for a Distinguished Flying Cross that he well deserved. The A&D (Awards and Decorations) Committee told me that they could not put him in for a DFC, because I had been recommended for a Silver Star for the same fight, and you couldn't have two high-powered awards in the same aircraft. I told them to forget my Silver Star. I figured there would be a lot more opportunities to get one of them. I received three DFCs and other awards over there, but the only other time I was recommended for a Silver Star, they gave it to the new CO instead.

Anyway, Tom liked to wait until there was a group of enlisted men around and then bum a cigarette from me, "Bill, have you got a cigarette on you?" I let it happen a couple of times, then called him aside when everybody was gone and told him that the first name familiarity would have to stop. I was an officer and he was an enlisted man, and he could call me "Sir" or "Mr. Frazer" or by my call sign, "One-Five." He was pissed off about it, and it was a symptom of the problem he had with authority. We rearmed the aircraft and went back out to Cambodia to aid two reinforced companies that were getting their asses kicked, bad. I was putting an air strike in for one unit and Cobra gunships in for the other.

One unit had its perimeter breached, and the only way to help was to hover above them. The gooks would quit shooting at them and open up on us. We lost a lot of helicopters and people at different times, playing target to save the infantry. In the midst all this, Tom hollered over the intercom to get out of there and keep moving. I told him to shut up and do his job. He threw down his machine gun and pulled a .357 out of his holster, put it to the back of my head and told me to leave the area or he'd blow my brains out. I told him to pull the trigger, if he thought that he could fly the LOH from the back seat. He holstered the gun, pulled the pin on a hand grenade, stepped out on the skid, popped the spoon on it, and let it cook off in my face. He threw it just before it blew up, and the explosion peppered the underside of the aircraft. We finished the mission, went back to base, and I kicked him off the LOH right there. I told him that he had two choices—never step into a helicopter again, or go to Long Binh Jail the next time I caught him in one.

That prepared me for a similar situation that happened about two weeks later. My torque had been there for two years and had seen more than he should have, including a couple of helicopter crashes where he was the only survivor. It was amazing how tough this guy was, but everyone has his breaking point, and he reached his while we were flying together. We were in Cambodia, and had lost a lot of people in a short time. A good friend of his had been gutshot the day before, and even though he was badly wounded, he had fired his machine gun one-handed from the skid to cover the pilot's break away from the target. The first word was that he was badly hurt, but would live. As we refueled and rearmed after a mission the next day, my torque learned that he had died. I should have seen it and should have left him off right there, but we were just too busy, and it got by me.

He started wandering around, finding chicken plates and lining the whole back section of the helicopter with them. It was a good idea, but we never did that, because it increased the weight and meant that we couldn't carry as much armament. I didn't say anything to him. Too many good people had already been killed in Cambodia. We went out to the field to cover another unit that was getting its ass kicked. The company commander told me that one man had a serious head wound, and he thought the soldier was going to die. I volunteered to make an immediate medevac by throwing off all our armament and taking the guy out.

The torque just flipped. He stuck the machine gun in the back of my head and told me to get out of there or he'd blow me away. I told him the same thing I had told Tom—fly from the back seat, if you can. He dropped the machine gun and started crying hysterically. His nerves were just gone.

The company commander told me then that the soldier's wound wasn't that bad, and there was no reason to come in under that intense fire. I immediately broke off the mission and flew back to base. I had a long talk with the man and told him that he had proved himself for two years flying scouts. He didn't have anything to prove to me or anybody else, and that nobody would know about the incident, except him and me. I wanted him to get a job in maintenance before he got hurt. That's what he did, and we remained good friends.

After two months in Cambodia, we couldn't get a good fight going in our area. The few gooks we came across were pretty easy to pick off. We had ransacked their supply lines, and all these soldiers usually had was a handful of bullets and another handful of rice. Body count was still the name of the game.

On one mission up around Bu Krek, I came across a group of about 250 Montagnards. This had been a bad area at one time, but we had pretty well cleaned it out. These people had apparently been slaves of the NVA, and when we moved into Cambodia, they had taken the opportunity to escape across the river into Vietnam. Montagnards are fierce fighters, but their nature is that of a nomadic, farming people.

We found a small village under construction by this group of mostly old men, women and children. There were no fighting positions being built, and the people were just tilling the soil and raising cattle. They gave us their peace sign when we flew over. I called in a spot report, primarily to get the location on record and keep other pilots from coming in and shooting those people.

It surprised me about a week later when I was called into the TOC and told to recon the area and get a good body count from 250 suspected NVA in the area. I described the situation and told the operations officer that these were noncombatants, but his orders had come down from higher up. We flew back to the area, and there were still no fighting positions at the village. The people were still farming and giving their peace sign. I gave the high bird a complete spot report, and he reminded me that I was supposed to get a good body count in the area. I told him that there was no way that I would shoot those people, and asked him to call my spot report back to the TOC. The TOC repeated its orders. I repeated my refusal to shoot. About this time, a voice came over the radio that I recognized as the brigade commander.

He didn't use a call sign, but told me that I knew what my orders were and asked if I recognized his voice. I replied that I knew him and used his call sign, so that anyone monitoring the transmission would have no doubt about who was ordering whom to do what. I told him that there were no fighting positions and that the only weapons these people might have were knives and an occasional crossbow. I told him, "I'm not refusing orders, but I want you to know what's down here. If you're going to slaughter these people, I want you to know that they are strictly civilians and noncombatants.'' Having been exposed by his call sign, he told me to turn in another spot report and report to his office back at base as soon as we landed.

When I entered his office, he locked my heels and began dressing me down about being a soldier and following orders. After less than a minute of that, I told him, "Sir, with all due respect, if you have a problem with my actions in the field, you need to contact Colonel Burnett. I don't answer to you. I answer to him. By God, I don't kill civilians. You are not going to put me in a prison cell next to Calley. You have the ability to do it. You can go back up there, but I am not a mass murderer.'' Because somebody had heard our conversation over the air, this man was personally put in charge of evacuating those people and their cattle from the area about a week later.

About 3:30 one morning, we were told to load our ammo, equipment and homemade bombs into the aircraft and take off, then we would be given a heading to follow. We followed the altitude and heading we were given until we got low on fuel, then landed at an improvised area and refueled from fuel bladders already in place. We took off again, and followed another heading until we landed at an old French plantation. The best I can tell from the headings and the amount of time in the air, we were somewhere in Laos by then. It wasn't until we were on the ground that we saw how big the operation was. There was probably a battalion of ground troops there, all of Charlie Troop's aircraft and Blues, and other aircraft.

The deputy commander of the 1st Air Cav and my CO came over to my aircraft and instructed us to unload all the weapons and ammo and drop off the crew. These two men got on board, and we took off to look for a POW compound that was supposed to be in the area. We found it after ten minutes of flying. We saw the POW cages through the trees, but couldn't tell if they were occupied. There were NVA everywhere, dressed in khakis and green pith helmets and carrying AKs. All we had were sidearms, and they could have blown us out of the air, but they didn't fire. I think they were just surprised to see us. They held their AKs in one hand and waved at us with the other.

We went back to the plantation, briefed the ground troops about what we had, and started inserting them about an hour and a half later. The NVA were ready this time. The first infantry company on the ground immediately started taking heavy casualties. Another company was inserted to reinforce, and both were soon getting their butts kicked, big time.

The third company was inserted with the same result. In less than an hour, they had seventy or eighty casualties and were about to be overrun. They estimated an engagement between about 375 Americans (with only helicopter support) and at least 2,000 NVA. All we could do was extract them. The NVA gave fancy medals to soldiers who shot down helicopters, so all you needed to do to give the infantry time to disengage was to hover over them. They would stop shooting at the ground troops and open up on you. We drew the enemy fire while the infantry disengaged, then rolled in Cobras behind them as the Blue lift ships picked them up. All we succeeded in doing was getting them out of there. We never did get another chance to go back into the area.

When I volunteered to fly with Alpha Troop, I immediately became the most experienced scout pilot in the unit because of the six months that I had already spent with Charlie Troop. As a present for volunteering, Major Harris gave me the unit's mascot to fly, an LOH called "Queer John." Nobody seemed to know how it got its name, but it had a picture painted on the side of a frog sitting on top of a Purple Heart Medal. "Queer John" was written under that.

The LOH was kind of a good luck piece. It had about 55 or 60 yellow patches where bullet hits had been patched up, and it had gone through seven or eight tail boom replacements after crashes. It was pretty scruffy and nasty looking, but it was the most powerful aircraft in the scouts. "Queer John" had been in maintenance for almost a month. When any aircraft was down for maintenance for over four days, there was tremendous pressure on a CO to get it flying again, but this one had just taken thirty days to repair.

There's probably no pilot who flew scouts the way we did in the 1/9th who didn't hit something at one time or another. Because you're new at the job, you usually hit a tree or something in the first month. There's so much going on, and you aren't a very good pilot yet.

Those damaged ships were flown in to maintenance and logged in as bird strikes. Maintenance knew what had happened, but nothing was ever said. I hadn't hit anything yet, but that changed on my first mission with "Queer John." We were working an area of good-sized hills with a light jungle and bamboo cover. I was working the slope of a hill, going uphill with the wind at my tail. A scout pilot depends heavily on his peripheral vision to see ahead of the aircraft as he flies right-hand turns and constantly scans out the door and below him. I was working up the side of the slope when I spotted a gook and hollered, "I got gooks!"

I started to do a hammerhead to come back down the hill on top of him, and all of a sudden, I saw this mass of green in my peripheral vision. I was headed straight into the center of the biggest, bushiest part of a huge tree with the wind at my tail. The strike busted out all the Plexiglas. Luckily, I was in the midst of a hammerhead and flew back out of the tree, back downslope with the RPM dropping off to nothing. Rotor RPM came back up just as I was settling over an area of bamboo. When I flew into maintenance back at FSB Buttons, I noticed that everybody stopped working and gathered around. The maintenance sergeant ran over to the aircraft and asked what had happened. Like everybody else, I told him we had hit a bird. He stepped back, looked at the aircraft and said, "That motherfucker must have been nesting, because you brought half the tree back with you!"

I was put in for a second Silver Star later on in my service with A Troop. I had already turned down the award in C Troop to get my torque a DFC. This time it started when I flew a new CO down to An Loc for a meeting with Special Forces, some CIA types and a Frenchman. It was interesting to hear about some of the things going on that we didn't know about. After the meeting, we headed back towards FSB Buttons, and I picked up a call on the radio that a Special Forces team was in contact and had a gut-shot ARVN striker. We were right over the top of them at the time. There were no open spots, but the double canopy would allow you to slide down under the treetops and fly above the next canopy, then drop down again and fly between that canopy and the vegetation on the jungle floor. To get there, you had to back up, drop down, back up, drop down again, and then land.

We didn't have a torque, and the new CO was along as the copilot, so I told him what I was going to try. He told me to get the hell out of there. At that point, I explained to him that I was the PIC (Pilot in Command). He wasn't even "in-country" qualified yet. I can understand that he was brand new in-country and scared to death. We finally got down to ground level with tracers going off all around us. A tree had been blown down, and I had to hold the LOH at a hover over the stump, while the CO was screaming and hollering that he was going to court-martial me. We got the wounded guy out of there.

The ARVN commander put me in for a Cross of Gallantry and the Special Forces put me in for the Silver Star. About a week later, they called me in out of the field and sent me to An Loc for an impact award of the Silver Star. The III Corps deputy commander was going to present it.

Just before the ceremony, his aide came into the room and asked if I heard that I was going to receive the medal. I said yes. He told me, "I hate to tell you this, but the general feels like it would look better for the senior captain, promotable, to have the Silver Star, and for you to have a DFC." That's how it happened. The captain was really embarrassed about it, and he apologized to me a few days later. He did what he could to make up for it. That's the way it was in Vietnam.

One terrible incident happened in base camp. We used a lot of Willy Pete grenades. They were excellent for starting fires, marking targets or for antipersonnel use. They were horrible grenades with about a thirty-meter bursting radius. Phosphorous ignites upon exposure to air, and the only way to put it out is to cut off the air supply. I've thrown it on gooks in a field and watched them run to a river and jump in to stop the burning, come back out and start burning and smoking again. At the time, in a war like that, it didn't bother me. It bothers me today.

Willy Petes came in little canisters with a key, like the old-fashioned coffee cans. You opened the canister and slid the grenade out so that it would be ready for use. Early one day, one of the crewman opened up a can and noticed a grenade without a pin before he slid it out. He was able to find an extra pin and insert it into the safety. I have thought about this for nineteen years, and I can't imagine how it could be loaded without a pin at the factory by accident.

Later that evening, we got word that we were going back into Cambodia. One of the crewmen went out into the darkness to prepare ammunition. A WP grenade from the same lot slid out of its canister and exploded. The crewman was one of those people who always had a smile and a good word for everyone. He had a young wife and two children, one of whom he had never seen.

The grenade covered him with white phosphorous, burned off his arms, legs and genitals and blinded him. He screamed for five hours for somebody to kill him. People from Alpha Troop begged the medics to put him out of his misery or let them kill him for mercy's sake. The only reason that didn't happen was because the MPs ringed the aid station with armed guards. He screamed for five hours nonstop while the Army tried to save what was by then a stump.

I don't know what was right in that situation, but I would want to die if it happened to me. He mercifully died after his lungs stopped working, because of the damage to them from the white phosphorous. Even after all these years, I dream about that incident and shudder over it.

We believed in never leaving a man behind. Everyone would risk his life, rather than letting the gooks get hold of one of them. But we did lose one crew while I was there. "Jack" was a pilot from New York. He was a new pilot when we went into Cambodia and we wouldn't let him fly there, because it was so dangerous. He was allowed to fly missions inside South Vietnam. He had been married shortly after graduating from flight school to a girl who was impressed that he was a pilot. But when he went home on the thirty-day leave prior to going over to Vietnam, she tried to talk him into going to Canada. Jack just couldn't do it, so she filed for divorce a couple of days before he left to come over. We became close friends and stayed that way, even after I went to Alpha Troop.

He went down one day over by Song Be. It was during the monsoon season, nothing but a wall of rain and thunderstorms, and there was no way that we could fly through it. The old OH-6 had a weak tail rotor. You could only fly maybe thirty minutes in a light rain, fifteen minutes in a moderate rain and about five minutes in a heavy rain. The rain would just eat the tail rotor off, like melting sugar. There was a line of thunderstorms between Jack and us, and we were going nuts, trying to get around it, or find a "sucker hole" to fly through. We knew that it is usually only a matter of minutes before the gooks beat you to a downed bird. Jack's high bird stayed on station until he was critical on fuel and about ready to fall out of the sky himself.

When we did get there, the gooks had cut his head off, castrated him and stuck the genitals in his mouth. They had done the same thing to the crew chief. Apparently, they had captured the observer and marched him off. The Blues followed a trail of one pair of GI boots and lots of Ho Chi Minh sandal prints as far as they could, but we were too late.

My homecoming was similar to what happened to many others. An E-7 was waiting for us as we stepped off the jet at Oakland. He called for any warrants with less than two years of college. We raised our hands and were directed to the "Group W" bench with all the mama-jabbers and papa-stabbers and other weirdos who were waiting for out-processing. It was odd that we were qualified to fight the war, and most of us were in it because we were from working-class families and couldn't afford to go to college. Now they wanted us out because of our lack of college credits.

After I was discharged, I applied for six or seven jobs, many of them below my ability, and was always asked two questions. What kind of drugs was I now doing and what kind of mental problems was I having? When I explained that I had been an officer and didn't do drugs, they told me that was bullshit. They had read the papers.

When I told them that I had no mental problems, they told me anybody who had killed women and children for a year had to have some mental problems. The last time that happened, I grabbed a guy by the lapels and dragged him across his desk. If I hadn't worked for the phone company before going over, I wouldn't have found a job. They were obligated by law to hold a job for me.

Many returning vets had problems because of attitudes like this. Nobody wanted to be around them anymore. Former friends deserted them. The newspapers and TV portrayed us as an unsavory lot. Many people had to take substandard jobs when they came back home, and only then developed mental problems and slipped into drugs. I'm one of the lucky ones, but I'll never forgive the media. They really shit on us!

Note: I am indebted to Philip D. Chinnery, author of *Life on the Line*, for sharing one of the two tapes which form the basis of this story.

26. CHEMICALS AND PEOPLE SNIFFERS

(Commanding Officer, 184th Chemical Platoon, 1970–71)

Capt. **Bob Parker** *led a chemical platoon the size of a regular company. The platoon's unsung missions often brought them in contact with the 9th Cav, and were a secret and important part of the war.*

It was 1970 when we stood in the crowded aisle of a Flying Tiger DC-8 after a long trip from Fort Lewis, Washington. We had landed as the sun was rising over the South China Sea at Cam Ranh Bay. Most of those on the plane were draftees. I was a volunteer, but we all shared in the tension that filled the plane as we waited to disembark, ready for what could be the adventure of our lives. None of us would return to America as innocent as we had come.

I had requested assignment to Vietnam from Germany after a recent divorce. The request was denied, but my orders arrived a few weeks later. I guess that was typical of the army. In early February 1970, I left Germany and returned to my home in California. Spending time with family and friends was great, but the political climate had changed in the nearly two years I had been gone, so I felt a strange coldness, even in the warmth of the California sun. I proposed to my future wife, with whom I still share the future, and put my life in order in case this was my last visit home.

In April, I was off to Fort Lewis for the flight that brought me to where I now stood. I was a twenty-four-year-old first lieutenant who had always wanted to be a Cavalry officer, but the army felt that my scientific education should not be wasted, and had instead assigned me to the Chemical Corps.

After "Cherry School" at Bien Hoa, I was sent to 1st Cavalry Division Main at Phuoc Vinh, which was located about sixty kilometers to the northwest. It had been an old French colonial garrison, and many of the buildings in the heart of the base were from that colonial period. My first assignment was to the division chemical staff as part of G-3 (Operations). Our responsibility was to plan and conduct chemical support of tactical operations. That included smoke, flame, herbicide spraying and riot control agents. We would also send out teams to assist tactical units when they were putting in new firebases.

The use of flame weapons in the final defensive perimeter was very effective. "Foogas" and "Husch" flares were most commonly used in the final wire. Foogas was a 55-gallon barrel of napalm, equipped with an ignitor and burster, which would cover a twenty or thirty meter area in front of where it was emplaced. The Husch flare was made from a steel powder canister buried halfway in the ground and filled with diesel fuel mixed with gasoline. It was ignited by a trip flare. This would provide a plume of fire that would illuminate an area for up to six hours.

My first real assignment was to Task Force Shoemaker at Quan Loi, 3rd Brigade headquarters located in the Michelin rubber plantation northwest of Phuoc Vinh near the Cambodian border. Task Force Shoemaker was the forward command post for the 1st Cav's invasion of Cambodia in late April and early May of 1970. My orders were on short notice and consisted of, "Get your gear and be on the bird!" In less than an hour, I was crowded into a Huey and flying off into the night.

As we approached Quan Loi, aerial flares lit the night, and large, bright green "cotton balls" rose up toward us, while thin lines of red reached out toward the cotton balls. It was like a fireworks display and I was enjoying the view, until someone pointed out that the cotton balls were NVA antiaircraft tracers that were aimed at us. Pretty and deadly could be one and the same. The approach and landing were routine, and I soon found myself wandering amongst the mass confusion that is typical of such an event (the invasion). The next two weeks were an excellent introduction to the operational style of the 1st Cavalry and the politics of war.

While at Quan Loi, I made friends with several scout pilots from the 1/9th, and even had a few beers with one of my former traveling companions, who was now a Cobra pilot with the unit. It didn't take long to separate the risk takers from the bus drivers, and those 9th Cav guys spelled risk with a capital "R."

I was attached to the 184th Chemical Platoon (DS) at Phuoc Vinh after TF Shoemaker was disbanded. As a combat support unit, our Table of Organization and Equipment (TO&E) called for two officers and 115 enlisted men. In June of 1970, I was given command of the unit after my promotion to captain. A command was a rare event for a Chemical Corps officer as most were staff officers. I had a reputation among my troops as a risk taker, and they were not happy with my aggressive attitude. The mix of educational levels varied from high school dropouts to master's degrees, and trying to convince and motivate these guys was a constant challenge. I have always been content that all of my troops got home alive and in one piece. There were things that I would have done differently, but hindsight is always 20–20.

Our mission was to maintain chemical equipment, provide training in CBR warfare, and conduct other missions as ordered. What we did was to provide the Cavalry with direct support aerial napalm drops, and aerial drops of a terrain denial agent CS. This gave the Cavalry an on-call bomber force when it was needed.

People sniffers were another mission for the 184th, and these were usually controlled by G-2 (Intelligence). Each brigade had a sniffer team attached, and we had three more at Division Main. These teams were rotated back to Phuoc Vinh on a regular schedule to reduce the stress of flying at forty feet and forty knots, day in and day out.

A "Napalm Drop" was usually from a CH-47 Chinook cargo copter. The 184th prepared the napalm and hung twenty or so fifty-five-gallon drums in cargo nets under the bird. One corner of each net would be pulled through the three-foot-square hole over the cargo hook and tied down inside, while the other three corners attached to the cargo hook. The pilot would dive on the target until it lined up with the bolts in the rudder pedals, and then release the hook. As the drums cascaded downward, a four-man crew would snatch the nets in through the floor and stow them away. As the mission commander, I would lean out the right side and drop a white phosphorous or thermite grenade to try to land with the napalm and ignite it. That sounds really simple, except that a normal drop was at max airspeed and less than 400 feet above the ground. Chinooks are big and make excellent targets, so most pilots were wary when they were tagged for a nape drop. In some cases, when we were close to friendlies, we had to come to a hover to be sure that the nape was on target.

In most cases a scout ship would mark the target for us and ignite the nape with tracers if my grenade did not. A single drop could cover an area the length of a football field and one-half the width.

On one mission, this was a literal lifesaver to a grunt platoon on patrol near the Song Be River bridge. We were diverted to try to assist in the extraction of a platoon in heavy contact. They were in a bamboo thicket several hundred meters across. Heavy fire was coming from three sides, and snipers controlled the fourth. Two 9th Cav Pink Teams were working the area when we arrived. They had placed ordnance on the main part of the ambush and asked us for a load of napalm on the enemy position. The ground unit marked their position with smoke, and we came to a hover over the VC and punched off the load. My thermite grenade missed, so the infantry lieutenant offered to light it for us.

The lieutenant had his radio keyed when it lit, and you could hear the cheers as the fireball snaked up through the trees. The firing stopped and he reported that several VC had decided to surrender. They came bursting out of their positions covered in jellied gasoline and ran into the arms of the American troops screaming "Choi Hoi!" (in effect, "I surrender!"). The others stayed in their bunkers and cooked in place. The Pink Teams continued to pick off stragglers as they tried to escape from the ambush site. We made several more drops in the area that day, burning a path for the platoon to follow, so the lift ships could come in and take them out.

We also used the Chinook as a high-level bomber. Internal racks were installed in the cargo bay, and loaded with thirty fifty-five-gallon drums, each filled with eighty pounds of CS II. Each drum was fitted with a burster and an Air Force bomb fuse, so that it would arm as it fell and would detonate on impact, covering an area forty to fifty meters across. The drums were armed by two men, standing on the tail ramp and pulling the pins and safety wires as they were shoved out the back of the ship. The fall from a normal altitude of 10,000 feet usually armed the fuse, but if it didn't, the impact alone would disperse the CS from each drum over a twenty-meter or larger area.

CS II is a powdered riot control agent that will make the most disciplined soldier totally ineffective. During Chemical Warfare School, it was said that "one teaspoon of CS in the central air-conditioning system of a four-story building would make it uninhabitable for up to six weeks." When we dropped CS, it would cover the area with a continuous layer up to an inch thick. This worked like a solid wall for anyone trying to move through the area, and it would channel the enemy so that our troops could set up ambushes at the gaps we deliberately left. I'm sure that many of our own troops would have liked to ambush those who dropped it, especially if they had just walked into an area covered with CS. Because of its silicon coating, CS would continue to be active for up to six weeks, even during the rainy season.

On one occasion near the Cambodian border, an antiaircraft gun (37mm) opened up on us as we made a drop. A round went through the fuselage, but didn't detonate. The gunners were setting the fuses for the wrong altitude, and the shells were bursting several hundred feet above us. Officially, Division said that it was B-40s (a rocket-propelled antitank grenade) and not an antiaircraft gun. They had to report it that way, or they could not have gotten any helicopters back into the area for months to come. It didn't matter what was said, because a B-52 strike was put into the area the next morning to obliterate everything.

Probably the best example of the value of CS drops was when we made a series of CS runs on the outskirts of Quan Loi. There had been several mortar attacks in recent weeks, and it was decided that a line of CS might keep the mortar crews out of range. We dropped nearly 120 drums on the Michelin plantation, along a road that was the suspected firing point. The second night after that drop, the flight line began to take incoming mortar shells, which suddenly stopped. Normally the attack would last until our artillery began to return fire.

The next morning, scout ships were sent to try to locate the mortar firing points. What they found was a Land Rover wedged on its side between two large rubber trees. The driver had died in the crash, but an 82mm mortar was still bolted to the bed of the truck and several armed mortar rounds were scattered around the wreck. The VC had been driving down the road, firing the mortar as they went, but that night, they drove through our CS zone and panicked. The driver made a hard left, which caused the Rover to flip and wedge itself between the trees. That was the last time Quan Loi had a night attack from the plantation side.

Our most unusual mission was with the people sniffers. The sniffer was a complex air pump and sampling device that was mounted in a Huey or an LOH, and measured the content of the air for particles that were unique to men, water buffaloes, or any other large animals. The machine indicated the relative level of particles on a strip chart, and when a peak was recorded, it was called a "mark" and the operator would drop a smoke grenade. Each brigade headquarters was assigned a sniffer team from the 184th Chemical, and three more teams were available from the platoon at Phuoc Vinh.

It was in mid-January 1971 that we were called into the TOC (Tactical Operations Center) for a briefing by G-2. They had several reports of a major NVA concentration near the Parrot's Beak region on the Cambodian border near An Loc. These reports also indicated sightings of American prisoners in the same area. They wanted a sniffer mission to try to locate any concentrations of people. It was a voluntary mission, but the only thing voluntary was which lift company would fly it. There was total silence for several minutes as the S-3s (operations officers) shuffled maps and looked at their feet. Finally, the S-3 from the 1/9th spoke up and volunteered to personally fly the mission. The sound of relief was deafening as the other S-3s hurried out of the briefing area.

The young captain from the 9th Cav and I conferred with G-2 and G-3 (air) until we were comfortable with the details. We soon realized that we had walked into a mission that was possibly going to have a high pucker factor, and getting back would not be as easy as going out there. We were scheduled to lift the next morning to be on station at 0830 just as the warm air began to rise from the forest floor.

We completed the plans, briefed our NCOs and greased the skids for the next day, then headed for the wildest officers' club on the base. The 1/9th hangout had a rough reputation, and outsiders were not well tolerated. That night I was glad to be among friends. I met the rest of the pilots that would be flying with us, and gained a healthy respect for them. I went back to my hootch and crashed.

The sniffer crew consisted of myself, my best operator and an NCO. I don't have their names anymore, but those two men were willing to do what others would not. The decision was made that E158 aerial clusters would be carried to stir things up if needed. The E158 was a modified Air Force munition consisting of clusters of D-cell battery-sized canisters held in a plastic unit that was three feet long and one foot across. A timing fuse would detonate a bursting/igniting charge that would send the smaller munitions skittering over a fifty-meter area, spraying CS as they went.

We knew that E158s could be dangerous inside a helicopter, because a captain friend of mine had recently lost his life while trying to drop them. Somehow the arming wires had come loose, and the E158s began to detonate inside the Huey. He was badly burned by the black powder bursting charges, but was able to push all of them out of the bird before falling 1,500 feet to his death. His quick thinking saved the rest of the crew and the helicopter. He had less than a month to go, and a newborn daughter that he would never see. Capt. Fredrick P. Smith will always have a place in my memories. I still miss him. I guess that his death was one of the reasons we carried E158s, just to prove that they would work.

When the bird landed at our pad, we started installing the sniffer unit. First we laid salvaged armor plates on the floor. The armored back and side panels from damaged pilot seats would literally save your butt, as well as anything else between your legs. The sniffer was locked down to the floor and the sampling hose taped to the left side of the Huey. We loaded aboard weapons and the dozen E158s, and then lifted off to meet the rest of the flight. As we approached the target grid, we were joined by two Cobras and an OH-58 LOH. This was the Hughes LOH, and it was like an angry bumblebee that could get down under trees and really stir things up.

Our technique was to plot an area on the map, and starting downwind, fly at right angles to it, making successive back and forth runs across the grid, each time working farther upwind until the box was covered. The copilot and I kept a running map check, plotting each mark as it was called out.

This time we picked up a couple of small marks and dropped smoke for the LOH to stick its nose in and see if anyone would snap back at it. As we approached the middle of the box, we found several large and small bomb or shell craters. A young NVA was sitting on the lip of one of them, washing his socks and feet. My operator hollered, "Mark!" and dropped a white phosphorous grenade that detonated at face level in front of the NVA. The LOH gunner finished him off with a quick burst from his machine gun. We should have wondered why an NVA FNG would be casually doing his laundry out in the open.

On the next passes, we started seeing signs of more activity—fresh trails and bicycles lying up against the underbrush. These were supply bicycles, kind of like pack mules on two wheels. The area was dry woods with hardwood trees and scrub underbrush, somewhat like the backwoods of Virginia, but flatter. Every time we sent the LOH in to poke around, no one would bite, so we decided that the NVA had to be stirred up.

On the next pass, we used E158s, setting the fuses on "quick" which would detonate the munitions just below the ship. We kicked them out, four at a time, over the bicycles, and kicked out more on a second pass. As we turned to begin a third pass, it was like flying a helicopter through a bread slicer. We were just above the treetops when the instruments began blowing out of the panel, the maintenance manual was turned into confetti from bullet hits, and rounds impacted into the armor plates under our feet.

Everyone opened up with whatever they could find. Both door gunners were chewing up the area below as the bird fought to gain altitude. The adrenaline was really flowing as the pilot managed to pull us out, so the Pink Team could work out below us. Then we realized that the noise in our ears was not the sound of our hearts pounding, but the warning buzzer in the headphones, telling us that the engine was near stalling. The hydraulics were gone, among other things, and remaining air time was being counted in seconds.

We needed to set the chopper down in an open area. The pilot headed for the craters and set up for auto-rotation, flaring at the last second. Just as we were about to impact, we gave the area a burst of everything we had. I stepped out just as we crash-landed, and slid head-first down the side of a bomb crater. I heard gunfire and scrambled back up the side of the crater to see what was going on.

We had landed in the middle of the NVA's lunch. The door gunners had opened up at several Vietnamese as they ran out of sleeping bunkers at the edge of the clearing, leaving their tea on boil. All of this had taken place in only a few seconds, but it seemed to last forever. Besides the Huey, the only damage was a small nick in the sole of the copilot's right boot.

It was obvious that we had landed in the middle of an NVA replacement way station. The entire area was a warren of trails, hootches and bunkers. This was a resting point for NVA troops as they crossed into South Vietnam from Cambodia. The worst part was that it was swarming with people, and we were right in the middle of them. We set up a hasty perimeter, took a count of our people and weaponry, and contacted our friends above us. The LOH and Cobras were engaging anything that moved in the area. The LOH was short on fuel and had to break off, but before they left, they flew in fast and low, came to a hover over us and kicked out additional frags and ammo. As they lifted out, the seven of us dispersed into a stronger position around the downed bird. Our guys who set up in the sleeping bunkers actually enjoyed a hot lunch, courtesy of the NVA. We had three M-60 machine guns, an M-79 grenade launcher, five M-16 rifles and, we hoped, enough ammo to last until the Blues arrived.

To those who didn't know them, the Blues were a ready reaction, airmobile infantry platoon which was organic to the 1/9th. As soon as we went down, they were notified and scrambled. They were some of the best fighters in the Cavalry, but they were a nightmare for officers who were used to spit and polish. They wore blue bandannas and looked real rugged, and could be your best friends or your worst enemy, depending on which end you were on. They were professionals, and they had the highest body count in the area. Their reputation was outrageous, and it was earned in sweat and blood.

We expected to be overrun at any second, but had received only sporadic rifle fire that wasn't even aimed at us, just wild shots. Probably what saved us was that the NVA were FNGs and in a state of confusion about who and what we were. For all we knew, they could have thought that we meant to land in the middle of them. Anyway, the Cobra was keeping their heads down and keeping them away from us. The Cobra radioed for us to get down as deep as we could, because he needed to make a close pass.

We heard him line up as he came in, then the most God-awful sound. It was like someone had turned a million hornets loose over our heads. He fired two pairs of "nail" rockets! These were 2.75-inch rockets armed with warheads packed with thousands of flechettes. Flechettes were small nail-like projectiles made from hardened steel with fins. They were about two inches long and could go completely through a person. As the Cobra pulled out of its run, we stuck our heads up long enough to see that the area the rockets had hit was stripped bare of anything smaller than a four-inch tree, and the perimeter had been pushed back about fifteen meters. The Cobra made several more gun and rocket passes over our position before breaking off to rearm.

The LOH returned and began to work the woodland near us, then other Cobras came on station. The Blues arrived overhead, and we prepped the area around us while they made their approach. As the slicks settled in, the Blues stepped off like it was a bus ride or something. We were immediately thrown on one of their lift ships and flown out to Quan Loi, and then back to Phuoc Vinh. On our way out of there, we passed several more slicks inbound with more infantry. They made several sweeps and got a decent body count. After the damaged Huey was lifted out by a Chinook, and the dust had settled, the night rumbled as B-52s dropped their loads on the area we had sniffed, turning the ground like a farmer tills a field.

After that incident, the 9th Cav decided that my guys were just as crazy as they were and we were welcome in their clubs. My XO and I were invited to join the Operations and Intelligence staff and other key people from the unit for an evening of relaxation. What happened that night is still kept secret, but it did weld the units together. We had always been a bastard outfit within the Cav. Nobody knew what we did, and if they asked, we really couldn't say anything. If some of the correspondents had only known how sensitive a story they were sitting next to when we ferried them out to firebases. The Agent Orange controversy was already heating up, and we were dropping it by the netfull from the same birds they were riding on. If only they had known.

For the balance of my tour, we flew most of our sniffer missions with 1/9th support, but the 227th and 229th Assault Helicopter Battalions provided aircraft for our missions as well. The assault helicopter crews were excellent in every way and deserve to be proud of every minute they spent in the air, but the bond with the 9th was solid, because they wanted to do more than just fly. They had a blood fever that drove them all to seek out the enemy and destroy him. It may be unfashionable to say this, but I think that killing was as important as flying to them.

My chemical troops flew more missions that counted as combat assaults than the average grunt, often several a day. We were not an elite unit with the history or the pageantry that many of the battalions shared. We were just a bunch of guys from diverse backgrounds whose only wish was to get home in one piece. We didn't get CIBs like the grunts, but my guys sweated it out on firebases while the NVA tried to blow them away, just like the grunts.

In no way do I want to diminish the day-to-day suffering that the grunt units had to endure to survive. Ours was a life of luxury by comparison, and I've always felt guilty when I am with anyone that served in the infantry. But like each war, there are inequities that should not diminish the contributions that each soldier makes by just doing his duty as ordered. Our people were mostly doing a job that nobody could talk about or admit to. I've always been proud of the men I served with, and I hope that they are as proud of themselves.

When the Cav was being stood down for deployment back to Fort

Hood, the 184th Chemical was one of the first units to leave. Those who were eligible for reduction in their tours got drops, and the rest were reassigned to other units. This was in late March 1971. I was given a twenty-eight-day drop and was scheduled to leave, but a new major from MACV had been assigned as the Division Chemical Officer, and he would not let me leave as ordered.

For many officers, this period was the last chance to get their tickets punched for career purposes. Many were not competent, and they got people hurt while trying to make a name for themselves. The division chief of staff gave the major a direct order to get me to the rear or else. I was on the colonel's slick that afternoon.

When the chief of staff dropped me off at the out-processing center at Bien Hoa, I was quickly out-processed and sent over to the replacement battalion at Long Binh for a flight assignment. They thought Long Binh was safer than Bien Hoa. The morning before I arrived there, several 122mm rockets had landed on a formation of new arrivals. Many of those troops had very short tours and lives. Five were killed and 33 wounded, just for the sake of standing in the sun to listen to some administrative type give a lecture on the dangers of a combat zone.

After two days at Long Binh, I was taken to the Bien Hoa Air Force Base to wait for a "Freedom Bird" home. My Cobra pilot friend from the ride over was there. He had arrived looking like a child, but was going home looking like he had aged ten or fifteen years. Whatever weight he was carrying, I hope that he was able to shed it before it destroyed him.

Finally, it was time to line up to board the jet for home. As we stood there in our fresh tan uniforms, the new troops filed past us, and I thought of that same image nearly a year before, when it was me walking past the vets on their way home. Soon I was seated in the freshly cleaned jet, waiting for it to taxi for the takeoff. We pulled out for the takeoff, only to watch an ARVN Skyraider crash on the runway we were to use. Things weren't working out like they should have. We taxied back to the terminal area and sat in our seats as beads of sweat ran down our bodies. It was the kind of sweat that comes from fear and not heat, because we were sitting in cool, dry air for the first time in months.

Then the runway was clear and we taxied back out for takeoff. As the engines began to whine, the tension became fierce. I think that everyone aboard was silently trying to lift the jet as we rushed down the runway and finally got airborne. A collective sigh of relief was heard throughout the cabin, and a cheer went up as we turned toward the Pacific coast to begin our journey home. After stops in Japan and Guam, we settled in for the final leg of the trip to Travis Air Force Base near San Francisco.

We landed there as the sun was setting into the Pacific, and we stepped out into the cool, moist air of California. It was warmer than usual for a March evening, but most of us wished that we had jackets. We filed into the terminal area and began to clear Customs. I approached the Customs officer, dragging my bags, and began to open them for the check that would spread my life in front of everyone. The officer smiled, and with a wave of his hand, he thanked me for the job we had done and then shook my hand. I couldn't believe that I was calling my wife at her parents' home less than ten minutes after landing. I was actually home! Forty-five minutes later, she was running to meet me where I stood waiting on the curb. We made it as far as the first motel off the base and snuggled in for the night. Forty-eight hours and half a world away, I had been flying missions, and now I was in a soft bed with my wife, as if nothing had ever happened.

The next morning, we drove to the nearest shopping mall to buy me some civilian clothes. I went into a bank to cash a check. First of all, they wouldn't cash the check until my account was transferred from Bien Hoa. As I was waiting to discuss it with the bank manager, a college-aged fellow noticed my flame-thrower qualification badge and made some unflattering remarks about me being a baby-burner. I commented that he had a lot to learn. What I really wanted to do was rip his head off and dropkick it across the mall!

That was the first run-in with the people I had been fighting for, and how much they appreciated us. I never did get a check cashed as long as I was in uniform. I got used to people walking away when they figured that I was in the army. It was almost like we smelled bad. I was an outsider in my own country, and in many ways, have stayed that way ever since.

You can never explain the feeling of going into a hot LZ or the adrenaline rush of a firefight. Those who weren't there can never see the beauty in the aerial ballet of a Cobra or a LOH as they roll in from high cover. I tried to relate to the VFW or any of the other veterans' groups, but all they did was parrot the same old patriotic rhetoric from World War II and the Korean War. They had nothing in common with me or my feelings. I never got to be a Cavalry officer, but the 9th Cav brought me as close as I could get.

This last December, they dedicated the California Vietnam Memorial here in Sacramento. The city hosted each military unit at different watering holes in the Old Sacramento historical district. I was fortunate enough to have been able to visit with several Cav vets that evening. They were amazed that we had thought that sniffer missions were routine. As one 2/7th man commented, ''You either had balls as big as basketballs, or you were just crazy like those nuts from the 1/9th.'' I don't think that we were crazy, so . . .

This has been a story about men in that place at that time, but I could never do justice to all of those who changed my reality, nineteen years ago. For those of you who were part of the 184th Chemical Platoon, hold your heads up, pull your shoulders back and know that you did your job and did it well. And for those that thought we didn't know about those other things and were ''getting over,'' we knew and we did! Maybe we can meet again and swap tales some time. I would be thrilled to hear from those men.

It was a good tour for me, and I will always know that it was one of my best years. Those who chose not to go will never know, and it will always be their loss.

27. WELCOME TO WAR

(Scout and Cobra Pilot, Alpha and Echo Troops, 1970–71)
*Warrant Officer **Lou Rochat** heard about A Troop during training and volunteered to go there. His instructors warned him not to do such a foolish thing. He arrived in the troop on the evening before the Cambodian Incursion and the action never stopped after that.*

I was born on 20 July 1949 at Fort Knox, Kentucky. That tells you I was an Army brat. My father was an officer, and later on, an aviator. I graduated from high school in 1967, in Mineral Wells, Texas, home of good old Fort Wolters. We were faced with four choices upon high school graduation. We either had to get into a long-term college program, volunteer for the service, wait to get drafted, or leave the country. We really didn't know a damned thing about what was going on in Vietnam, but we did know that it would affect us. I completed a year in technical school and then entered a four-year college course before finding out that I was about to be drafted. I decided to enlist.

I told the recruiter that my home was in Mineral Wells and that I wanted to be a chopper pilot. I didn't even know what a warrant officer's insignia looked like. All I knew was that they flew helicopters. I had no idea what flight training involved, but I did know that I didn't want to hump a rifle and live in a foxhole. The ironic thing is that my father had always wanted me to join the Army, but my dream was to build, design and race cars; I do that to this very day as a hobby.

Flight School was a bastard, but it was the best training I ever got. I was going to graduate in the top ten percent of my class and qualified for a back-to-back transition. I asked for the LOH, but had to choose between the Cobra and the Chinook. In my opinion, the "Shithook" was a flying gas tank, waiting to blow up. I chose the Cobra, then wrote a letter requesting Alpha Troop.

By then I had discovered that the helicopter models in the stores all came with Alpha Troop's "Headhunters" decals and the crossed sabers. Some officers told me they were a mythical unit that didn't exist. They were supposed to wear black cavalry hats, Sam Browne belts and spurs, and fight each other, if they weren't fighting Charlie. My father knew about them from his tour in Nam and told me they were real, but they lived, and were treated, like animals. God, I couldn't wait to get there. He told me, "You don't want to go to the 1st Cav, especially the 1/9th. Go to the 1st Aviation Group in the Delta." Little did I know how true all that was.

My instructors at Cobra School warned me again about the 9th Cav, but we all thought we were hot shit, and I didn't listen very well to advice. I was only at Fort Hunter-Stewart, Georgia, near Savannah, for the seven-week Cobra Transition Course. It was TDY (Temporary Duty) at $32 a day, plus regular pay and allowances and flight pay. We had money to burn, and burn it we did. My buddies and I didn't bother with the usual TDY apartment hunt. We all rented motel rooms on Savannah Beach itself for eight weeks—two of us to a room. We were going to Snake School in style. Rock and roll Savannah Beach, twenty-four hours a day. We were the Army's "Top Guns" and we played the part to the hilt. I met my future wife, a "Georgia Peach," one day on the beach when I was waxing my wheels—a brand-new 1969 Javelin SST, Big Bad Orange, 390 v8, Borg Warner 4-speed position, posi-track with aftermarket carb, intake, cam and headers.

I was twenty years old and just married when I left for Vietnam, and I couldn't wait to get there. I didn't even think about the feelings of my folks or my new wife. After I got over there, I never once thought about what my bride was thinking or going through. She was strong enough to keep it inside her and not burden me with her thoughts or feelings. She watched a twenty-year-old, six-foot, 175-pound Army warrant officer gunship pilot, full of piss and vinegar and a will to live life to its fullest, leave for a place she had heard nothing but bad things about. She got back a 102-pound, dark hollow-eyed, morphine and demerol dependent, shrapnel and nine times gunshot-wounded, nine-month and two-day Vietnam veteran who barely knew where he was, much less that he was facing two years in the hospital and thirteen surgeries.

I arrived in Vietnam on 21 April, 1970. We landed at Long Binh Air Force Base and began seeing what the country looked like. It reminded me of the Panama Canal Zone. The heat and humidity hit us when they opened the doors, and most of us were drenched in sweat by the time we left the plane. We were picked up by Air Force buses with chicken wire over their windows. That told us that we weren't safe, even in the rear. A couple of other pilots and I were flown to squadron headquarters at Phuoc Vinh in a Chinook. There I saw my first "Head-hunter" chopper. It was called the "Family Car," and I believe it belonged to the colonel. We were briefed and told that we would only spend the night there. I wandered over to the officers' club. The club had been hit the night before by a 122mm rocket that had gone through three feet of steel and sandbags, and everything inside was smashed and broken. The sergeant who ran it looked heartbroken after all the time he had spent building it up.

The next day I was in-processed and taken by Huey to Alpha Troop at Tay Ninh. The 1/9th was hurting for pilots, so I was signed off on my in-country check ride on the one-hour trip there. The troop was located on the western end of the base, next to hot shit Blue Max (an all-Cobra unit). I wandered around the area that morning and got some of my gear, but in the afternoon I was told to hang around the officers' club for a meeting. Right after it got dark, we started hearing this rumbling, and felt the ground shaking and vibrating. That's when we learned that we were going into Cambodia, publicly. B-52 strikes were supposed to hit the border for three days, then we would cross the border en masse, with all the other units and the aircraft from the squadron.

As we stood around the briefing room with its red lights and maps, the CO asked Captain Kunz, the Cobra platoon leader, who he was going to ride with. There were some snickers in the background. It turned out that a lot of the other pilots didn't like Kunz's personality, despite the fact that he was a damned good Cobra pilot. Kunz looked at the CO and said, "I'll take the FNG." That was the first time I had been called a Fucking New Guy. He walked over and got ten pounds of maps, returned and handed them to me. "Put this shit together and be ready to fuckin' fly in the morning." The maps encompassed everything from the southernmost point on the Dog's Head to the Parrot's Beak and the Fishhook. I put together the set and folded them into a book.

I liked .45s, so I got one of those as a sidearm, an M-79 grenade launcher, shotgun rounds for the grenade launcher and an SRU-21 survival vest. After flying the next day, I found a guy going down to Long Binh. The Provost Marshall's office there had Thompson submachine guns for sale, so I asked him to get me one. I paid thirty dollars for it and six magazines. The first thing I did was remove the rear stock and tape the magazines together into two groups of three each. I carried that Thompson from then on. I got a puke-green flight helmet and painted the unit's yellow triangles and "Apache" on the sides. I later painted the whole front of my chicken plate breast armor Cav yellow. I figured if they were going to shoot at me, they might as well have a target. That stunt paid off later.

We got ready to go into Cambodia. We had equipment, ammo, maps and fire support bases at places called "East," "West," "Bravo One," "Bravo Two," and "Snuffy." On the first morning of the Cambodian invasion, one of our teams was crossing a huge field when they spotted something. The pilot called for us to join him at that particular location. Several of our teams were soon circling over the field. In the middle of it was a thirty-foot-high pole with a flag flying from it. It read, "Apache Troop. Welcome to War." That was strange. We knew then that they knew what we were doing on our supposedly top-secret mission. One of the guys still has the flag. Maybe someday it will end up in a museum.

Crossing the border was unreal. Within a month I had a regular AK-47, a folding stock AK-47, and a Kar-15 I took off dead gooks. I even had a brand-new French rifle that had been stored for many years, and a lot of other things that were FNG collectibles and trade items. When we took off for Cambodia on the first day of the invasion, the Cobras were so heavily armed that we had to bounce them off the ground to get them airborne. I had thought that I knew how to read maps. For three days, I didn't know where the hell we were. My maps were all neatly cut, folded and marked, scattered all over the front seat, and I was lost. Captain Kunz would ask questions like, "Where the fuck are we, New Guy? Are we in Cambodia yet, New Guy? Are we even in fucking Southeast Asia?" Every now and then he'd give me a four-digit grid of our location, without using the map. That's how well he knew the AO. The guy was damned good, but still a prick on personality.

We crossed the border, and for three days, we did nothing but shoot and shoot and shoot. We were getting three loads of ammo to one load of fuel. We were hitting trucks, jeeps, elephants, and hundreds of VC and NVA. Those guys were in full fatigues and heavily equipped. The

Cobras would kill them and the LOHs would land and pick up all the goodies—rifles, canteens, packs, ammo, anything they could get their hands on—then haul ass.

For three days we flew twelve to fourteen hours each day. Each evening we did fly-bys at Tay Ninh. The Cobras would come over the flight line, busting 160 knots, climb as far as they could climb, stand on their tails and do a wing-over hammerhead. The LOHs did basically the same thing. For three days, I was constantly harassed by Captain Kunz. I was his last FNG.

I walked into the O-club on the third night and asked one of the pilots who was going home, "Hey, what do you have to do and who do you have to see, to get into the scout platoon?" The place got deathly quiet.

One of the other pilots looked over at me. "You want to fly fuckin' scouts?"

"Yeah. That's what I wanted to fuckin' fly in the first place when I got here."

I already knew that you couldn't just walk into the scout platoon. The gunners, observers, and other pilots checked you out and decided if you were good enough to fly with them. All of the privates, specialists and sergeants in the platoon voted on you.

It was a special platoon. Their hootches were even in a separate part of the company area. They slept together, drank together, flew together and pulled maintenance together. They even screwed the same broads together. The scouts used a lot of neat stuff, like super bombs and modified weapons.

The next day, the platoon leader came to see me. There was a guy going home, so I could fly with him at first light the next morning, 9 May 1970. I started in the left seat as observer. We flew ten and a half hours, and I never felt so beat up and tired as I did after riding so long on the left outside of a helicopter doing right-hand turns. I got my first kill that day. We were in the Dog's Head when the pilot said, "I'll be damned. We got us a shithead gook." Not only did we have us a shithead gook, we had us a dumb fucking shithead gook. The pilot told the torque, "Don't kill him. We gonna let the Fucking New Guy have this asshole."

The gook was standing about two feet off a trail with a tree limb pulled down over his face, thinking he was hiding from us. You could see him from the collar bones down. I still didn't have the eyesight to see stuff down there, and it took me a few minutes to spot him. He was dressed in black pajamas and Ho Chi Minh sandals.

The pilot said, "Now, this dude is yours. I'm going to back off a little bit. You're going to take your M-79 grenade launcher and shoot that son of a bitch dead center in the chest with it." I didn't think anything about it. The pilot backed off and came to a hover, and I fired. What a *"Boom!"* The grenade cut him right in half. The pilot landed, and the torque ran over to grab his AK-47. I later found out that my flight that day was my check-out ride in the LOH. I was now a member of the Scout Platoon. Later that night, the torque congratulated me and gave me a real souvenir—the dead gook's ears. Welcome to war!

My roommate got blown away the next day. He had been in-country about a week. Crashed, burned and died. He was twenty-one, a year older than me. He was flying his LOH around in a supposedly safe area when a B-40 rocket zipped him. He never knew what hit him. I had to pack up his shit to send home to his fiancee. They were planning to be married on his first R&R to Hawaii.

The next day I got one hour of flight time. We got shot up, the first of fourteen times. I didn't even know we had taken hits. The initial shock of Cambodia was over by then, and our missions settled down to a routine. We were called out as needed. Some days we flew a couple of hours, and some days we flew fifteen hours.

Our LOHs arrived in-country stripped of everything but essential equipment, because we lost so many of them. They took out the transponder. It cost $4,000. We had some radios, but the fancy stuff was gone. The engine doors were safety wired shut, because rockets normally hit tree limbs first, and the concussion would blow them open. They would beat everything to pieces. We slung a piece of safety wire between the pilot's and observer's seats to hang smoke grenades, four of each color—four reds, four Cav yellow, four crazy grape (purple) and four white. There was a lot of other equipment.

The observer in the left-hand seat carried a handgun and a box of ammo for it, and either a Kar-15 or an AK-47. M-16s weren't allowed in the aircraft. They were too long, fired too fast, and were erratic. You couldn't hold them on target. I always wanted my observer to carry an AK. Nothing would piss off Charlie like having his own ammunition shot at him. It would bring him out in the open. The observer also carried a red smoke marking grenade in his left hand with the pin pulled.

If anything happened, or if he got hit, the smoke grenade would roll out and mark the target. After an observer was broken in, he carried a white phosphorous grenade with the pin pulled. That would get thick, white smoke up through sixty or ninety feet of trees fast. We wanted the target marked quickly and marked big.

I carried a .45 automatic, my Thompson and sometimes a Kar-15. The torque carried a highly modified M-60 machine gun and an extra barrel. Most torques could change barrels in the air in less than sixty seconds. The flash suppressor and sight were removed, and sometimes the barrel was sawed off. They got a different spring to make the gun fire stronger and faster. The gas safety plug was wired in to keep it from coming loose, and the chamber was sandblasted for a better feed.

None of the issue ammo feed trays worked, so the torques used C-ration cans that allowed a smooth feed into the chamber. A hole was drilled through the forearm and a $5/8$-inch bolt was inserted as a side handle to hold the machine gun level. We used minigun ammo because we believed the links were stronger. A torque carried 1,200 rounds in a wooden box. One thousand rounds were linked in a belt and the last two hundred were broken off, so he wouldn't shoot all his ammo. When we were down to 200 rounds, it was time to break station and rearm.

In my particular aircraft, we also carried forty HE, CS and buckshot M-79 grenade rounds, six white phosphorous grenades, six incendiary grenades, twenty concussion grenades and forty baseball frag grenades. In heavy bamboo, we would take a long piece of safety wire and string it through twenty or thirty baseball grenades in place of the safety pins. When we needed to recon by fire, we'd snip the wire and let them fly. The string of explosions was like a miniature cluster bomb attack.

We made super bombs out of C-4 and C-3 with blasting caps, time fuse and igniters. I even attended a demolition course down at Long Binh on how to make shit go bang. We would take an empty .45 ammo can, fill it with plastic explosive, punch two holes in the top and rig dual 30-second fuses. We carried them like briefcases by the metal carrying handles on the cans. They were devastating against big bunkers and caves. Sometimes we put metal, nails and rocks around the outside edges of the super bombs and made miniature daisy cutters. Ten or twenty pounds of C-4 could do a lot of damage.

On two occasions, I took a big 20mm minigun can and made super bombs with about sixty pounds of C-4. The first one was used in support of ground troops in bamboo who needed to get out. We kicked the bomb out of the chopper and it made an LZ big enough for two Hueys. The second time, we blew up a big bridge after an F-4 strike had missed the target with all its bombs. I landed, and the torque and observer put that thing between the bank and the span. The bridge went 300 feet in the air. How you constructed the bombs was limited only by your imagination. We used one-gallon cans of transmission fluid and taped a concussion grenade to them—instant napalm. If you were good enough at it, you could set them off about twenty feet off the ground, blow the stuff all over the place and set a big area on fire.

We'd drop anything that would go bang or burn. It's hard to describe the smells and the feelings involved in flying through cordite from rocket explosions, the smell of burning bamboo and hootches, the adrenaline rush when we hit a target and smelled Charlie burning down there and knew we had gotten some of them.

It wasn't unusual to take one, two, or three hits a day. The holes would be patched up and painted over. We had some of the ugliest, multicolored helicopters in Vietnam. I later flew a Cobra that had about eight shades of OD green. The tower would call, "The ugliest Cobra in Nam is cleared for take-off, if it'll make it." We painted names on our LOHs, such as "The Little Green Killing Machine." I got to fly the most famous 1/9th LOH in the world for a while. That was "Queer John." It always came back. It came back shot to pieces, it came back with dead crew, it came back with dead pilots, but it always came back.

One of the awards officers had written up Queer John for a Purple Heart, using the serial number on the side of the tail boom, and the Army issued the award. The paperwork was carried on board. It was painted with a picture of a frog with purple eyes over a Purple Heart Medal. A queer frog. I personally took over thirty hits in it, and lost a couple of tail booms, main blades and chin bubbles. It was the only LOH in A Troop that I remember making it past its first 300-hour PE. It lasted through several of them, and they later tried to bring it back to the States.

One thing about LOH crashes was that everyone walked away or no one walked away. One day we were low on Cobras, and two LOHs were flying the AO in a heavy White Team. One LOH was down low and another one with a minigun was covering it from higher up—about fifty feet, if you want to call that high. The high LOH took hits, went down and exploded on impact.

The OH-6 had a design flaw. Over the left rear strut, inside the engine compartment, was the main fuel line. One of the things we learned was that if you were going to crash a LOH, get it skid level or land on the toes of the skids. Don't hit on the heels of the skids. If you hit on the heels, it would shove the strut right through the main fuel line. The line would break, fuel would go everywhere, and you would turn into instant napalm. That's what happened to this guy. He took hits, went down, landed on the skid heels and exploded. Normally, all that was left of a LOH that crashed and burned was about the last three feet of the tail boom and blades.

Our Cobras were a mixture of the original G-Models, conversion G-Models with the air conditioning, and production G-Models with air conditioning and a 20mm Vulcan gun hanging off the left wing. Those 20mm Vulcans were devastating weapons. The nose turrets carried M-79 automatic grenade launchers and a 7.62mm minigun. The 20mm ships carried three seven-shot rocket pods. Most of the other ships carried two seven-shot pods and two nineteen-shot pods.

We carried 50 percent ordnance for the nose guns. Any more and we couldn't get the Cobras off the ground. The standard mix was flechette rockets or 17-pounders in the seven-shot pods, and 10-pound HE rockets in the nineteen-shot pods. We had one ship with two wing-mounted minigun pods. They were okay until you had a hang-fire and the miniguns kept shooting after your finger left the trigger. They later took that gun system away from us.

We also had a couple of heavy hogs with four nineteen-shot pods. Blue Max (the Aerial Rocket Artillery Cobras) normally carried thirty minutes of fuel. We had to carry enough fuel to conduct two-hour missions, stay over a target and fly back. That limited our ordnance. We flew in single teams of one LOH and one Cobra, and the troop put up five to seven teams a day, every day.

After we went into Cambodia, they moved the troop out of Tay Ninh and up to Song Be. We left wood hootches and moved into rat-infested GP tents. Shortly after we got there, Miss America came through. We were flying perimeter security to keep Charlie from hitting the place, but he hit it anyway, so we shot him up and went back to base to meet Miss America. Kill some Commies and then meet Miss America.

The war over that beautiful country continued. Cambodia made me think of what it would be like to take a huge botanical garden and incorporate the New York and Los Angeles zoos. Unfortunately, a water buffalo was an NVA jeep and an elephant was an NVA deuce-and-a-half (2.5-ton military truck). We killed a lot of those animals that were not in the immediate confines of villages.

South Vietnam had some of the most beautiful deer I have ever seen. They looked like Texas whitetail deer, but they were the size of big, fucking Colorado mule deer. Every two or three weeks, we would go deer hunting. They made great steaks. We also went fishing. There was an area in the Song Be River that was about one hundred yards long and only six inches deep. We'd fly up river and drop about ten frag grenades, fly back, land and collect fish in baskets as they floated by. That night we would have a fish fry. We also hunted wild pigs. It's amazing how many machine-gun bullets a wild pig can take and keep running. We'd fly back, stick the pig on a stick and have a barbecue. We killed huge monitor lizards every now and then, and delivered them to the mess sergeant. They made delicious stew. If the mess sergeant didn't get his lizard, he didn't feed us very well. So we made do for ourselves, and ate lots of C-rations. We traded captured stuff for air conditioners, cases of shrimp, steak and anything else that we didn't have.

The 9th Cav was always placed as near to the heavy shit as it could be. We lived in barbaric conditions compared to other units, but people adjust to the conditions in which they find themselves. We weren't anything special when we got there, but our experiences made us different.

We flew long hours, more than we were credited with. Operations took some of our hours and credited them to the ground crews so they could draw flight pay. In nine months, I flew 675 combat hours in Cobras, 725 hours in LOHs and twenty-some hours in Hueys. I didn't really like flying Cobras, circling around and waiting for the LOH pilots to find something. The LOH pilots were greedy. They didn't want to back off and give us a chance at something. They and the torques just loved to hang it out and take on Charlie by themselves. We got shot up daily. We got shot down. We crashed into things. Our days were just unbelievable.

Sometimes we had to buy boots, flight suits and gloves on the black market. When they started rationing ammunition, we would fly down to the ammo dump in Long Binh and steal pallets of ordnance by slinging it out with our Hueys. We needed the ammo. The troop shot the shit out of anything and everything. Infantry units wanted us to support them because we had developed the technique of pinpoint rocket shooting, even from 3,000 feet up. We had to know how to do that to support the LOHs and the infantry. The grunts meant a lot to us. We went back to our tents and hootches at night, while they stayed in the jungle.

Half of our missions were assigned from headquarters. The other half were what we did best—search and destroy. And when we found something, we destroyed it. When they sent us into areas where we had to request permission to fire, we would sometimes call in maintenance problems and head back to base. Command got the idea. Don't send those guys on bullshit, nonshooting missions.

We'd contact the bad guys and waste them. If we didn't get clearance to fire, we didn't report the bodies. We just flew on to another mission. These were bad areas—the Testicles, the Jolly Jungle Trail, the Bamboo Trail, the Dog's Head, and the Parrot's Beak. We were out to find Charlie, and politics didn't matter.

Normally, the NVA didn't mess with us. If we took fire from them, it was mostly because some dumb-ass FNG took a shot at us, because he was trying to be a hero for Ho Chi Minh. We'd go down and waste him and his buddies. If the NVA wanted to fight, they would stand there and duke it out with you, one on one, until only one side was left. The NVA regulars were tough.

Our experienced LOH drivers worked from a hover, using the rotor wash to find shit. Most of our scout pilots were farm boys, hunters, and etc. They were fairly experienced trackers. I've spent as much as three missions tracking one trail. We could tell what direction bicycles were traveling by the direction they swung out on bends in the trails. How do you tell what direction someone is walking? Wait for a log. Everybody walks right up to a log and steps over it. There's a gap on the other side, and that's the direction he's moving in. You can tell from footprints, grass, and bent branches how long ago people have used a trail. I tracked a gook one day for almost five klicks (kilometers). He was walking, then he was jogging, then he was running. I hovered sideways after him. When we got to the place where the tracks stopped, I backed up. There was Mr. Charles hiding off the trail. He was made a statistic.

We supported all kinds of units. The U.S. Marines were bold, brave and foolish. As far as the Marines were concerned, one of them was worth ten gooks, and tried to prove this time and time again. We would have intelligence that a regiment was in a valley and they'd send a company. We would find a platoon-sized element of NVA. They would send a squad. We would call in a sighting and tell them to be sure and send enough men. They would send two Marines, and we would end up having to get out the Marine bodies.

We told them, "Hey, guys. One Marine is not worth ten gooks. One Marine is worth one gook, maybe less. You're on their turf, and these guys have been fighting for years." They never listened. We lost several ships and crews because of their "few good men" concept of fighting.

The Navy would run missions with some sort of heat-seeking device hanging out the back of a Navy helicopter flying at 200 feet AGL (Above Ground Level)—the dead man's zone. It didn't take Charlie long to figure that one out. You could hit them with a rock, and they were regularly blasted out of the sky. When they asked for cover, we gave it to them with a LOH at treetop level and a Cobra at 2,000 feet. When they took fire, then we went into action.

The ROK Marines were so gung ho that they'd be hanging off the skids of the Hueys and jumping from fifteen or twenty feet in the air. They'd secure the LZ, wait until they saw our marking smoke, fix bayonets and haul ass toward the target. The ROKs kicked ass. The ARVNs weren't worth a shit. They would take hours to move up to a target. They'd move in circles and take rice breaks. Anything to avoid contact. They were the biggest bunch of chickenshit cowards ever, and we were dying for them.

Against policy, I sometimes flew gunner on a LOH, because I wanted to feel what it was like. I would trade off with the torque and let him ride front seat in a Cobra. With the extraordinary number of LOHs we were losing, it was an automatic Article 15 to be caught with two pilots in one LOH on a combat mission. I would tie myself to the floor with a monkey strap that allowed me to step out on the skid and fire without falling out of the aircraft.

On one of my first missions, we went to do what we did so often— BDA (Bomb Damage Assessment) an Arc Light (B-52 strike). It was the fourth BDA that day. Most torques looked forward to the twenty or so percent of arc lights that hit a target other than wildlife and trees. It was like shooting fish in a barrel. The bad guys would be stumbling around, bleeding out of their eyes and ears from the bomb concussion. Killing them was doing them a favor. On my mission we found a bunch of dead NVA and I killed two more. Fly-by time.

On another mission when I was flying gunner, we spotted two guys in NVA uniforms with pistol belts and equipment, hiding under a log. We described what we had and asked for clearance to fire. The Cobra pilot came back with that clearance and I pulled the trigger at the same time. Wasted both of them.

Sixty seconds later, he radioed that the clearance had been cancelled. We were now staring at two bodies under a fallen tree. I initiated Emergency Procedure Number Thirteen. When you don't have clearance to fire and you have fired, you have to take fire and hits to engage the enemy. I threw down a red smoke, leaned out with my .38 and punched a hole in the main blade with a bullet. Then the pilot transmitted, "Taking fire! Taking fire!" The Cobra knew we were trying to cover our asses. The Cobra made its rocket run, then we landed and collected their equipment and weapons. We had taken fire and hits and terminated the bad guys. End of mission.

We had to do that a lot when things started getting more chickenshit. We did that almost every day. The maintenance people always wanted to know why we went through so many main rotor blades. Things got so tight that we couldn't engage targets without clearance and somebody's initials to go with it. So, we stopped reporting many contacts. For every hundred kills the 1/9th reported in a month, there were probably 160 bodies on the ground.

One day at Song Be, I almost crashed because of my own torque. We were engaging a target when I saw a couple of gooks get up and run. I banked real hard, and one of the torque's rounds hit a rotor blade about eighteen inches from the end. No big deal. We flew ships all the time with bullet holes in the blades. All we did was put tape over them. But this bullet hit from the inside, going out at an angle. It blew the honeycomb completely out of the last eighteen inches of the blade. The blade puffed up and started flapping, and I was afraid it would cut off the tail boom.

I ended up flying back at full red line power at about twenty feet off the trees, which was as high as we could get. The aircraft was shaking so bad that it broke the glass out of some of the gauges and shook radios from their mounts. To lighten the load, we were shooting ammo and chunking out grenades as fast as we could pull the pins. We had to get rid of that weight, and I wasn't about to set down in Bad Guy Land. We made it back with the aircraft beat all to pieces. One bullet destroyed that LOH. It had to be retrograded back to the States for total rebuild.

Echo Troop, 1/9th, was formed on 1 September 1970 and stationed at Lai Khe. The wooden hootches were in pretty good shape, and that was about it. As far as equipment goes, we got every piece of shit, Slick, Cobra and LOH, that the other units could push off on us, anything that was a maintenance nightmare. We got the elite personnel from the other units—hot-rodders, hell-raisers, give-a-shit bad-asses. I was sent to E Troop.

Maj. Herbert Chole was put in charge of this conglomeration. He made Echo Troop work, and work better than any other 9th Cav troop. We decided that our unit emblem would be a yellow star. We painted them on the helicopters. We named all of the helicopters, painted them and made them look good. We had some crazy times, like low-leveling down highways in Cobras at about 160 knots, six feet off the deck.

While on R&R, I got some red whorehouse wallpaper for our hootches. We also used a lot of tit magazine fold-outs for wallpaper. I traded a captured rifle for a real porcelain toilet, and we drank beer out of it at the bar. We stole plywood from the engineers and soaked tarpaper from the rocket containers in aviation fuel. This discolored the JP-4 fuel. We then painted the plywood with the solution, lit it and let it quickly burn off. It gave walls a beautiful burnt-wood look. We insulated the walls of the hootches with styrofoam from the rocket boxes, and used rocket box wood and nails to build furniture. Use all available assets.

One of our diversions at Lai Khe was the intra-unit rat-killing competition. The platoon with the most kills got a couple of gallons of Jack Daniels at the end of the month. We would pull the bullets out of .38 rounds and replace them with soap or candle wax. This gave us all .38 caliber rat guns. Every revolver was loaded with these bullets. We'd sit in the room, turn the light off, hear a rat crawling around, switch on the lights and blast away. That shit went on all night long.

We also hunted rats in the officers' club. We had one rat there that was just super quick. We'd hear him rooting around in the walls, turn off the lights and wait for him to come out of his hole in the corner. Here's thirty pilots with revolvers, waiting to kill one fast rat.

We would switch on the light and catch him half out of his hole. A bunch of rounds would go off, but he always got away. One day I took an M-79 round and replaced the shell with soap. I had a 40mm rat shell. The next time we switched the lights back on, we caught that damned rat half out of his hole again. I fired. It killed the rat. It also deafened us, filled the place with cordite smoke and blew an eight-inch fucking hole clean through the wall of the O-club. Killed the big rat, though.

Another time, the contest was real close between the scout platoon and the weapons platoon, and it was almost the end of the month. About seventy-five yards behind the officers' club was a trash ditch about fifty feet long by ten feet wide by seven feet deep. It was about a third full of trash, and you wouldn't believe the rats that were in there at night.

Myself and another scout pilot got this grandiose idea. We poured JP-4 along three edges of the trash pit and left the ground level opening alone, then we threw more fuel on the trash. Another pilot, two torques and I each got M-60 machine guns and 1,000 rounds of ammunition for each of them. When we lit the fuel, it looked like the trash was moving. The rats all headed straight toward where we were standing at the ground level end. Four thousand rounds later, we had a raging fire, four burnt-up machine gun barrels and over four hundred fucking dead rats. We won the contest.

I loved to experiment with different types of weapons. When we lost a lot of the ground troops at Lai Khe, word came down that we would have to handle our own perimeter security. We set up five bunkers. Each end bunker had a .50 caliber machine gun. I traded some captured SKSs for a 90mm recoilless rifle for the center bunker and put an M-60 machine gun on each of the other two bunkers. We emplaced lots of trip flares, phoogas and claymores, plus additional spotlights.

I decided to supplement this firepower with a weapon I had heard about. I mounted a pole on a mule (flatbed cargo vehicle) and mounted a minigun on the pole with .50 caliber hand grips and wired it with two electrical switches—one to start the barrel spinning and one to fire the gun. We used four aircraft batteries to drive the gun and stored 12,000 rounds of minigun ammo for it.

The first time I fired it, the mule turned over. I was told that the bullets made a beautiful arc across the sky. I welded stops so that the gun could only traverse 45 degrees out the back of the mule. We rearranged all the ammo cans and batteries and backed it up to the berm to fire. That SOB was awesome.

We got hit one night. Charlie hit the trip flares, and the four machine guns opened up while the 90mm fired beehive rounds. We waited a couple of minutes, hit the spotlights and I opened up with that minigun. It was awesome, like mowing down grass. The next morning we had over sixty bodies in the wire, including the village chief of Lai Khe.

The rule around hootches was that you never opened a door without knocking and waiting for someone to open it. You just did not open a door, because someone would shoot you. One night I had returned from a night mission and was lying in bed with my back to the door when it opened. I rolled over with my .45 and punched off three rounds. It was a hootch maid who had stayed over or sneaked back on base. She had a sock full of ammunition that she was collecting. She was stealing a few rounds here and a few rounds there. I hit her right between the tits and killed her instantly. She had been a good maid.

We didn't fire on Charlie at night. If we found his fires or lights out around our perimeter on last light and fired at them, we would get mortared. If we left him alone, he would leave us alone. The understanding was that the night belonged to him and the day belonged to us. The rule also went that anything we found at night more than five klicks out was ours. Inside that zone, we lived and let live. If Charlie did mortar us, we would fuck up the area and blow everything away for three klicks in all directions. It usually took a couple of weeks before more Viet Cong assholes came through and mortared us. We'd do the same thing all over again.

We did fly night missions, cruising around in the dark looking for campfires or other targets. We usually flew the 20mm Vulcan ships. My hairiest night mission was when we scrambled out of Tay Ninh for an enemy aircraft crossing the border as GCA radar vectored us toward the target. There was no Air Force out there because the weather was so bad. I never saw the guy, but as soon as we reached the border, I pulled up the nose and opened up with the 20mm and filled the skies with those fuckers. GCA reported that as soon as we fired and it crossed the border, the unidentified aircraft disappeared from their screens.

We didn't lose many Cobras or Hueys, but scouts were another story. We lost a lot of scouts. Pilots had a different experience and perception of Nam from the ground troops at that time. We viewed it as a game. You played it hard and you played to win, but it was just a game. I turned in over 265 bodies as a scout pilot and have no remorse. That was just the way we played the game. A lot of the pilots didn't want to fly when they got back home. They just wanted to do the best job they could while they were there, get out of the Army, and go back to being a civilian. When we weren't flying and fighting, we were partying and fighting. We did so many crazy things to turn our misery into a game party.

Once we were up at Song Be and were waiting for our resupply convoy. One of the vehicles was a flatbed truck loaded with beer and soda. Charlie blew up every vehicle. The entire convoy was lost. We took every Cobra and LOH to the hit zone, marked it dead center on our maps and worked out for five kilometers around it. We killed water buffalo and elephants, blew up wood-cutters' trucks, destroyed bunker complexes, blasted trails. Then we put the word out to the Vietnamese civilians on base that the same thing would happen the next time our beer and soda flatbed was hit. The moral of that story? The next convoy got every vehicle hit, except the beer and soda truck. Drivers were fighting each other to drive that truck.

We also did some pretty hard things over there, especially when we lost a crew. Once, division questioned whether the body counts we were giving were real. They said we were turning in paper kills. The next day, we dropped a couple of bodies on the lawn at division headquarters with a note saying, "Count this shit as paper."

Lopsided brutality and kindness were everywhere. We tried to help villages that had been hit by Charlie by flying out C-rations to the people. There were villages we avoided, because every time we came in with C-rations in the daytime, Charlie would come in at night and torture the people.

In late December of 1970, I was flying over a field surrounded by tall trees in a free fire zone when I spotted some Vietnamese. I was getting ready to rock and roll on them, but they looked like civilians— one woman, one teenage girl and a man. We made a couple of passes around the area and they remained standing still, so I decided to take a chance. I hovered over them and moved in close, then told the Cobra that I was going to pick them up. He told me to wait. A Huey was on the way out to get them. We took them back to Song Be.

We landed, shut down and went over, and I saw the three Vietnamese walking away from the Huey. They were walking funny, wobbling back and forth like clowns would walk. They were taken inside a debriefing tent and I followed them in, then the smell hit me. They hadn't bathed in a long time.

I asked a Kit Carson Scout why they walked so funny. He told me that these people were VC slaves who had their toes cut off so they couldn't run, but could still walk. I said, "Bullshit!" went over and lifted the man's pant leg. He didn't have any toes. The women were the same way. They were a family of father, mother and daughter. I told the scout that I wanted to know where the VC were who had done this to them. He talked with the people for about a minute, then told me that there had been seven NVA, with AK-47s and a rocket launcher, forty meters away from us in the treeline. They had watched us pick them up. The NVA were on a special mission and could not take the risk of firing on us. It was the first feeling I ever had that I could have bought it and didn't. I had been a sitting duck, hovering over those people, instead of wasting them as we usually did in war zones.

It had already been getting dark when we picked them up, but I went back out there after those NVA. We couldn't find them that night. When we got back to Song Be, the debriefers had all the information they needed and were getting ready to take the ex-slaves over to the medical tent. The scout told me that they were going to be resettled. I had about sixty bucks in scrip on me. I handed it to the mother and told the scout to convert it to piasters. It was a small fortune to those people.

I returned the next day and tried tracking the NVA. We picked up their trail a few times, but they got away. I wanted those fucking NVA badly, but I never could find them. I wanted to do to them what they had done to other living human beings. For the next week or two, we terrorized the VC and NVA in that area.

We took over the Iron Triangle from the Big Red One. The Big Red One had bulldozed a five-acre division patch in the jungle. We spent weeks trying to burn that son of a bitch down, but it was always still there. I got my first Silver Star in the Iron Triangle. An LOH was being flown by a new in-country transfer named Steve Ellis. We had a problem with Steve. When he got in contact, he liked to stay down and duke it out with the enemy, and wouldn't move out of the way so we could put down some Cobra ordnance. Steve was a fighter. I was in the front seat of a Cobra and Danny "Rags" Rager was flying back seat when Steve's LOH took fire and went down. They stitched him up one side and down the other. The aircraft was shot on the front, the left side, right side, and bottom side. Steve was badly wounded, but somehow managed to land in a semi-dry rice field. Both of my noseguns jammed up. I told the pilot, "Let's land and get him!"

I climbed out of my seat, rode the skid in and jumped while the Cobra was still in the air. I was half-dragging and carrying Steve back to the Cobra when I realized we were under fire. I pushed him into the front seat and grabbed my Kar-15 from the ammo bay. The Cobra pulled pitch and left me standing in that field with a Kar-15, a shot-down airplane, and a high pucker factor. I ran to the LOH and found it at flight idle while the torque and observer were firing at Charlie. The torque was using an AK, and that seemed to be pissing Charlie off even more. We jumped in the LOH, and I started rocking it to get it out of the mud. The poor bird was grunting and groaning, but I got it up to fifty feet, as high as it would go, and managed to make it back to Phuoc Vinh. Steve made it okay, and helping him made me feel great, even though I was scared shitless the whole time. End of story.

It's hard to convey the fear and the apprehension we felt when we were flying under fire, or cringing in our bunkers as our helicopters or ammo dumps were being blown up. It's hard to find the words to describe the concerns we had to put aside when we pressed the starter buttons on our helicopters. The missions wore on us. I was hit on three different occasions, but the last time was different. It began like this.

I had been switching off flying Cobras for a while and then going back to LOHs. I would take fire or hits in a LOH, say, "Fuck it!" and go back to flying Cobras. I'd fly around over the scouts for a few days while I watched them shooting it up, dropping super bombs and having a good time, and then go back to LOHs for a while.

I was short and had decided to stay with Cobras for the rest of my tour, but things changed pretty quickly. The Big Red One had been chasing the 101st NVA Regiment around the Iron Triangle for years, but now they were gone and it was our AO. We had word that a battalion of the regiment was dug in inside the Triangle, but we couldn't find them. The place had been Rome-plowed from one end to the other, Arc Lighted and shot to shit by artillery, but when we went in, we lost more LOH crews. Echo Troop needed scout pilots, so I volunteered.

Two days later, we went out on missions. I was flying with a brand new private on his first mission as an observer. Covering me in the Cobra was Captain Dagnon in the back seat and Captain Ritterer in the front seat. Dagnon was the Red Platoon leader and Ritterer was the troop commander. On the second mission of the day, I found some activity on a river—clothes, bunkers and a sampan. We put in a squad of Koreans and I sank the sampan. Then we got the call for a downed bird. A new lieutenant had taken hits and gone down in his LOH.

We flew to his location and found him out counting bullet holes in his chopper. He signaled a count of 31, all in the engine compartment. This immediately told me that it wasn't VC who had done this. They were NVA. It also told me that they were trying to get him down in one piece for a capture. I tried to signal him to get on his radio. He was so excited about getting his cherry busted that he wasn't concerned that what shot him down wasn't very far away. I needed to find out what we were dealing with and how close they were to him. It was one of the few times when the hair actually stood up on the back of my neck.

We went into the area where he took the fire, low-level, dragging the bamboo at eighty knots. All I could say to Captain Dagnon was, "It's just like Cambodia. There's shit everywhere. I've got campfires burning. I've got fatigues hanging out to dry. I've got weapons stacked, bunkers, clear areas, trails. We are into some heavy shit here."

Dagnon wanted to put down some rockets, but I had not taken any fire, so I told him we would work back into the area in a couple of passes, starting on the outside and moving into the center. On the first loop, I found bunkers, packs, canteens, rice cooking over fires, and two .51 caliber pits. I told him, "Call for everybody! Call for every available hunter-killer team in the squadron. Call for Blue Max. Lay on a couple of howitzer batteries. We need to blow this shit away. Contact the Air Force and get us some air strikes on here. This is good."

I was into my second 360-degree turn when we saw six NVA, packing AK-47s, jump out of the bushes and start running. Here we were doing sixty to eighty knots and they were running. I forgot everything we had learned in Cambodia. A decoy would stand up in the middle of a rice field and act like he was surrendering, then the LOH would come to a hover and some chump fifty meters away would zip it with an RPG. It had gotten to the point where we stood off and killed those guys with a minigun before they had the chance to lure us in to a trap. These guys were decoys. The NVA would never run from a God-damned LOH, but I forgot that for an instant. I stood that LOH up on its tail, came to a hover and told the torque, "Kill everything moving."

I was flying sideways to the right to keep the aircraft on track as he hosed them down. Just as the last one fell and I was getting ready to nose over and get out of there, I heard the rocket go off. Everything in the world turned to slow motion. I heard the rocket coming toward me, then, *"Bang!"* It hit my tail rotor and blew off the tail boom. Captain Dagnon saw a big puff of grey and white smoke from the explosion and watched the tail boom twirling through the air. My helicopter did a complete flip and was flying upside down. Then the AKs and .51s opened up on us. The first bullet that hit me entered on the top of my hand as I was holding the cyclic. It had passed through the rotor blade and the top doghouse of the LOH while we were upside down. It went sideways through my hand and exited at my ring finger joint, blowing off the ring finger.

The aircraft continued over until it was right side up and I entered auto-rotation. I looked through the chin bubble, and the ground and the bamboo were coming up at me as I got ready to pull pitch while bleeding off the engine. Plexiglas and pieces of glass from my instrument panel flew everywhere from bullet hits. At about 25 feet, my left leg fell over and the aircraft jerked all around. A .51 cal round had come through the floor, hit my leg between the ankle and the knee, broke the bone and took out 40 percent of my calf muscle. Pieces of meat and bone hit my face.

The last thing I saw was a .51 cal pit with some gooks working the big machine gun, then starting to run as we headed down at them. I intentionally rolled the airplane as we hit. I didn't want to land on the heel of the skids. The LOH left its skids in the machine gun pit, rolled two or three times and stopped on its left side. It shed all its rotor blades except one, and that came down through the cockpit and whacked me on the side of the helmet.

I looked down and told the observer, "My leg's blown in half. I need to get out of the aircraft. I'm going to drag myself out of the aircraft and you help by pushing." I told the torque to grab his weapons and get out. The thing might blow at any minute. I popped my seat belt, fell on my observer and looked down at my left leg lying on him. It looked like someone had taken a bucket of blood and dumped it all over him.

I stuck my head out of the greenhouse and saw the rotor head was still turning, minus its rotor blades. I had to reach around down to the collective and turn that son of a bitch off, pull myself out of the aircraft and roll away. We took a bootlace and tied it around my knee, and I made a tourniquet with my survival knife. I looked down again and my foot was pointing the wrong way. I flopped my leg back over.

I knew that the only thing holding my leg to my body was my flight suit. My hand was folded up, but the thumb and little finger worked. My ring finger was still in my flight glove. I removed the glove and put the finger in my pocket.

Bullets were going off all around us. I had never been on the receiving end of a snake, but dirt and bamboo was dropping all around us from the rocket explosions. I heard Dagnon make his runs and listened to the gooks firing back at him. He made three runs with rockets, M-79s and miniguns while I laid there knowing that his LOH was shot down. He was low on fuel and needed help to help me.

I worked my way over to a bomb crater, to my torque and young observer. Some gooks came out of the bamboo, looked at the smashed up helicopter, saw us and just froze. You could tell from the looks on their faces that they didn't think that we could still be alive after that crash. The observer and I shot six or seven of them about twenty feet away from us. My torque was firing his M-79 so fast it sounded like a semiautomatic shotgun. All I knew was that we were dead, and this bomb crater was our grave.

I heard my Cobra make its fourth gun-run, then silence. About thirty seconds later, I heard the beautiful whine of a LOH. Another team was on station, putting fire down everywhere. The LOH made a couple of passes over me taking fire and hits, then the pilot said the hell with it and hovered back over the bomb crater. They got my crew and me and got out of there. We are talking about a LOH with half its fuel load, all that ammo and six people on board. The pilot's name was Dryer. Somehow he flew us back to Phuoc Vinh. Unbeknown to me, the wind had blown blood all over my face and neck.

The medics ran out to help, all hyper and everything, and I told them, "Hey, guys. Take it easy. My leg's blown in half." As they carried me away from the LOH, I looked back at it. The helicopter looked like Swiss cheese. It had taken a lot of hits. They put me on a stretcher on the sawhorses and a guy came over with his clipboard to get my personal information. Then a doctor came over and asked where I was hit.

I didn't know it, but I had two bullet holes in my flight helmet, a gash in the helmet from the rotor blade strike, and pieces of Plexiglas in my face. The windblown blood made it look like all this shit was running out from under my helmet. There were also two hits in my Cav "target" yellow chicken plate. I didn't know all this, so I told the doctor I was hit in the hand and that my leg had been blown in half. He asked if they could remove my helmet. I reached up with my left hand and pulled the helmet off as they stood back and gasped. Next they removed my chicken plate and found no holes in my chest.

A guy started taking off my right hand boot, then reached over and grabbed my left foot. "God-damn! That hurts!"

The doctor asked me, "Have you got a shot yet?"

"Not that I know of." A medic hit my leg with a morphine styrette.

When the guy touched my foot and it hurt, I heard someone say, "Hey, guy. How are ya?" It was Red, Captain Dagnon. He was holding a bloody chicken plate over his left shoulder. His flight suit was all bloody and he had glass in his face. I asked what had happened to him. The Cobra had taken hits while covering us on the ground, and he had taken a bullet through the shoulder. What I didn't know at the time was that he hadn't been wearing his chicken plate at the time he was hit, and it was an Article 15 offense not to wear it in the AO. After they managed to set down the shot-up Cobra, he had grabbed his armor plate and smeared it with blood to make it look like the bullet had just missed it. Right, obey all the regulations! I told him not to worry about me.

A medic touched my left foot again and it still hurt. He hit me with another styrette of morphine. About that time, I looked over and saw Captain Ritterer, the new troop commander. He had cuts on him from the flying glass, and he said that he was fine, but you should have seen the look on his face. He had just had two LOHs and his Cobra shot down. Two other ships had gone down after I had been rescued. They had stitched the nose of his Cobra from front to rear. Forty percent of the new commander's best pilots and airplanes were gone. He had lost his Red Platoon leader, his Number Two scout pilot and acting Scout Platoon leader (me), and he looked like he had just lost the world. I knew that he would later get pissed off and fuck over the VC in the Iron Triangle for days.

They hit me with a third styette and I woke up down at Long Binh in intensive care three days later. The nurse standing beside me said that I had already been in surgery twice, and they were waiting for me to stabilize before evacuating me to Japan. Guys from the unit came to see me over the next few days. My new observer came by and I asked if he was going to keep flying scouts. He told me that most guys got it in their first week, and he had just made it through his, so he was going back to the LOHs. I told him, "Good for you." Can you imagine that? After being fucked on his first mission, he wanted to go out and pay back Charlie.

I was evacuated to Japan on a C-141 and ended up at Camp Zama. We were on a twenty-bed ward with forty-two beds in it and three more pushed out in the hall. The guy next to me was a double amputee from a land mine. The guy on the other side of me had lost a leg above the knee and had shrapnel all down one side.

These guys were from all walks of life and all units. They were

Rangers, officers, privates, everybody who got hit in Vietnam. What impressed me was the way we helped each other. Those who could get around helped those who could not. I'll never forget the smell on that ward. They named it right when they called it the "Butcher House," although that wasn't the fault of the doctors, nurses and orderlies. They worked hard with the facilities that were available to them, and did what they could. Some of the surgery was right in the beds, because they didn't have space in the operating room.

They pinned my hand together. There was one artery pumping blood to my left foot, so it stayed on. They told me it could be taken off later in the States if necessary. One day an orderly reminded me that I had signed a statement saying not to notify my next of kin if I was wounded. They had not done so. That was when I realized it had already been six weeks. I wanted to get the foot fixed and go back to Nam. When they told me that I faced six months to a year in the hospital, I called home. My dad accepted the collect call from Camp Zama. I told him about my leg and my hand, and he told me that he would set the wheels rolling to get me back to Fort Wolters. By then I knew that I had been hit three times in the leg and once in the hand. My whole chest area was black and blue and felt like Jell-o. The bullets in my chicken plate had busted some ribs.

Vietnam fucked up a lot of people other than the soldiers—wives, daughters, sons, fathers, mothers, etc., etc. All of them paid a price for this "conflict." I call it a war, where real guns and real bullets were used, where real people died and were wounded. I spent two years in the hospital and went through thirteen surgeries.

My Georgia Peach and I had a beautiful daughter, Celena, during this period, and we traveled to Germany for my first back-to-active-duty assignment since being wounded. We were divorced several years later. She ended up hating me and not caring. I was a workaholic, and was intent on showing the army that I was physically competent to go back to the aviation branch. Meanwhile, I was stuck in the club field, a favorite dumping ground for wounded aviators who didn't want to get out of the army after their hospital stays.

My narrow-mindedness was only part of the reason for the divorce. I truly believe we would never have made it anyway. But one mistake I did make was promising my "ex" that I wouldn't interfere with her new life or her new husband (an Army NCO of top quality). I haven't been allowed to see my daughter in fourteen years, nor is my "ex" willing to let me see her now. Once she turns eighteen, legal, adult age in March 1990, hell won't be able to keep me from seeing her!

I stayed in the army for over twelve years, first as a club officer while waiting to get back on flight status, and later as a maintenance officer. In 1981, I basically got tired of the volunteer peacetime army. It had major problems. Some of the mechanics couldn't fix shit. My last assignment was to a medevac unit where the aircraft were supposed to be flyable twenty-four hours a day, and we had "zeros" working on them. I can imagine what it was like in less critical units. I retired as a CW-3 in April of that year. I knew that I would miss army aviation, but the all-volunteer army sucked.

No one has ever truthfully explained what Vietnam really was or what we were doing there. I thought the war was a pretty good idea at the time, but now I see Vietnam as the war that defeated itself. Nobody wanted to go. Everybody wanted to come home. You know how our own American people treated us vets for many years after we came back. The men in uniform were blamed by civilians for what our civilian leaders sent us to do. I despise 98 percent of politicians to this day for what they did to my age group.

Most of us were teenagers. The story needs to be told someday about what this country did to an army of teenagers, the youngest soldiers it ever sent to fight a war, who were brought home in disgrace and pushed under the carpet like they were dirt. We were exposed to too much hardship and brutality at too young an age, so we tried to make a game out of our miseries. We played it hard, tried to stay sane and then came home and went on with life, if we could. We water-skiied behind helicopters on the Song Be River. We had dogfights with geese and shot them down with Cobra miniguns, like dogfights in the movies. We skipped 2.75-inch rockets off the water, like a child skips stones on a lake. We made plastic explosive bombs instead of making love.

My experience was with two Air Cavalry troops whose members took care of each other and did the best job that they could do. I saw too many high officers decorate themselves for actions that didn't happen. On the other hand, the medals our pilots won over there don't mean anything, except to the individual. I came home with fifty-seven of them, including two Silver Stars, but what I think about when I look at them are not the citations, but the people and events and what they meant to me. The medals represent moments in time and life.

I wanted to stay in Vietnam until the war was finished, then come back to the States as a test pilot for Hughes Aircraft. A lot of that went out the window when I got hit. I eventually ended up with a total of twenty-three surgeries and a plastic foot by 1988, but I have no regrets. I am proud of the 9th Cav and the job we did as ordered by civilian leaders.

Words cannot describe how proud I am to have served with such a unit. The war hasn't ended for me yet, but I know when it will end. When I go to the Wall in Washington and read the names of one of my scout crews that was killed by a dumb-ass, glory-seeking, RLO lieutenant; once I see that Wall and touch those names and so many others, that will be the end of it for me. For you who are reading this and weren't there, Nam will never end.

I think that no one who served in Vietnam could tell the story of that war as well as members of 1/9th hunter-killer units. We worked with all branches of the armed forces, and with every known type of military equipment. I have told the story of one such unit in the vernacular we used at the time. My words are less harsh today, and I don't curse every other word, but the flavor is important to the time and the events.

For those of us who have fought for it, freedom has a flavor the protected will never know. I pray that God holds a special place in heaven for all those who died fighting for their countries and their beliefs, for those from all armed forces and from *both* sides of all conflicts. I dedicate my story to the young men of the 1/9th Cav Headhunters, and those on the Wall. May we never have to tell stories like this again.

28. ECHO RECON

(Scout Section Leader, Delta and Echo Troops, 1970)
*Sergeant **Richard Jenkins** spent a year in Vietnam before volunteering for a job where he could ride instead of walk. He ended up fighting some memorable actions with the 9th Cav's newest Air Cavalry troop.*

I had been a straight leg grunt for thirteen months in Vietnam when I reported for duty with Delta Troop at Phuoc Vinh in early August 1970. That same afternoon, the first sergeant introduced me to my men. I only wanted to ride for a change, instead of walking everywhere, but they put me in charge of a whole damned scout section of five gun jeeps and fifteen soldiers. At first, I didn't like the responsibility of leadership, but when I asked to be relieved and allowed to lead the infantry section or become a gun jeep commander, I was told that I couldn't be spared.

The other two sections in my 2nd Platoon consisted of two recoilless rifle jeeps with four-man crews, and an eight-man infantry section that rode in a three-quarter-ton truck. The 1st Platoon was composed exactly like us, but the 3rd Platoon was made up entirely of amphibious armored cars that we called "Ducks." Each platoon usually operated independently of the others, patrolling roads, making medcaps (medical assistance calls in the villages) and setting up ambushes. We sometimes ran two or three different missions in a single day. I especially liked convoy duty, because it gave me the chance to see towns and cities that I had only heard about before.

Shortly after I arrived, they flew us into a clearing in the middle of the jungle in Chinooks. The idea was to patrol the boonies in our jeeps.

We slogged through the undergrowth and trees for two or three days, and stayed stuck in the mud most of the time. They finally aborted the mission and chalked it up as a bad idea. It took considerable effort to get back to the Chinooks and get the jeeps loaded, but this time we were happy to put our backs into it. Every mission was a new and exciting experience for me.

By early September, the troop had lost five men killed, including the entire crew of a 106mm recoilless rifle jeep. We were barely able to keep both jeep platoons operational by then. Replacement parts were almost impossible to find, because the South Vietnamese Army now had top priority on everything, and we had to skeletonize the damaged vehicles to keep the rest of them running.

It was then that Echo Troop was formed at Lai Khe, and the jeep platoons were "volunteered" to become Blue platoons. The Cav was conducting a phased withdrawal from the Cambodian border toward the sea, and it was a confusing situation for us. We had to provide road security for all these big moves, but were also mounting ambushes along infiltration routes and making insertions as a Blue platoon.

While 1st Platoon began training in rappelling and squad tactics, my platoon escorted a convoy of empty trucks to Quan Loi to evacuate the base. When we arrived at Quan Loi, we set up at the old French mansion, which was close to where the heaviest fighting had occurred during the big battle on 12 August 1969. The upstairs window overlooked the bunker line. It took a couple of days to assemble the convoy, so we spent the time patrolling down roads through the rubber plantations. The last convoy rolled out of Quan Loi, this time escorted by the tanks and APCs of the 11th Armored Cav Regiment, and we were the last to leave.

There had been looting and vandalism in the area as we pulled out, including shooting by Vietnamese civilians and ARVN soldiers, but we were ordered not to fire unless fired upon. I made one last spin around the empty base in my jeep and then joined the rest of the platoon at the front gate, knowing that none of us would ever see the place again.

It took two days to get to Phuoc Vinh, then we refueled and repaired and headed for LZ Mace, located just north of the Mekong Delta. On the second night at Mace, we were hit by a typhoon. The rain came down in sheets of water driven by ninety mile per hour winds. We lost all but one of our tents, and it took teams of men, working in relays, to hold that one down.

We were ordered to another firebase the morning after the typhoon ended, before the roads were even dry. A half-day trip took us two days through more rain and mud. We picked up an armored escort and provided security as a company of infantry and an artillery battery abandoned the base. Our jeeps became so hopelessly bogged down that tanks and APCs had to tow us along behind them in strings, like a half-dozen sleds. The column was outside of artillery range, the sky was so heavily overcast that helicopters couldn't fly, and the region around us had turned into an impenetrable swamp, but the gooks let us escape.

The withdrawal took two days, and we arrived outside of LZ Jeannie with the armored vehicles towing the jeeps behind them like dogs on leashes. The jeeps couldn't climb the last hill up to the LZ, so we sat outside the base and baked in the sun for another day while the roads dried. The trip back to Mace was much quicker, but it was the end of 2nd Platoon. Our jeeps were worn out and replacement parts were almost all gone. The platoon chugged back to Phuoc Vinh by way of Saigon, Long Binh and Binh Hoa, then we began rappelling training. We began making short road patrols one day and Blue landings the next, alternating with the 1st Platoon as Echo Blues.

The first action was on September 17th. We had been at the new routine for a week when the aero-scouts spotted enemy activity in a bunker complex about thirty miles from Bien Hoa. It was a hot and sunny day as we lifted off with seventeen men in three slicks. Gunships made rocket runs on the bunkers and LOHs hovered overhead as we jumped from the slicks. In a grunt unit, you would put out flank security after the lift birds took off, but we had to move quickly and there were too few of us to do that. We entered the jungle and immediately took fire. We fired and advanced, fired and advanced, until the gooks broke contact and ran deeper into the woods. I sent a team to check the first bunkers, and called in a situation report on the radio.

A machine gun opened up and pinned us down. My section laid down a base of fire to keep the enemy soldiers' heads down, while Ed Wagner took a fire team and moved up to flank the gun. Wagner knocked out the crew with his M-16, then a gook threw a grenade and Wagner dived for cover. The blast wounded him in the arm and shoulder and put a couple of fragments through the stock of his rifle. The North

Vietnamese seized the opportunity and manned the machine gun a second time. One NVA had taken over the firing, and another one had just run up to load for the gunner. Dave Bezjesky killed the new crew with his rifle. Dave was later shot three times in October. The fire team grabbed the RPD and pulled back to my position.

I reported four enemy KIAs and one friendly WIA to the high bird, and called for the QRF (Quick Reaction Force). The foliage was thick, and we had more movement to our left. We talked about it among ourselves and decided to try to flank the new movement. One team moved into the woods in a column and took the enemy under fire from the side. The rest of us got on line and moved forward, firing as we walked. The NVA broke and ran a second time, and the gunships and LOHs drove off an enemy squad that was trying to get behind us. We were in continuous contact for four hours, and ended up killing seventeen members of the Dong Ngai Regiment and capturing five more, in addition to 13 rifles and the machine gun. Our casualties in the action were only three men wounded.

A platoon-sized reaction force got there after it was all over. The lieutenant reported to me and assumed overall command, and I asked him for permission to take a team to the LZ to escort my wounded Vietnamese Kit Carson Scout. He had been shot through the arm. The lieutenant refused, so I volunteered to escort him alone. The two of us cautiously moved back to the clearing and ran out to meet a resupply chopper. The clearing was about 100 meters wide, and solid elephant grass from treeline to treeline. I was running toward the chopper when I disappeared from sight and had the wind knocked out of me. I had fallen into a spider hole that was hidden in the tall grass. I crawled out as fast as possible and hoped that no one had seen what happened, but they had. My "disappearing act" became a popular joke in the troop for weeks afterwards.

I was shocked to learn that we had discovered the base camp, hospital and supply depot for the Dong Ngai Regiment, but had been fighting new replacements and rear echelon troops. The combat troops were out in the field somewhere else. That explains their sloppy and disorganized defense. The division commander was happy enough with what we did to give us all Arcoms (Army Commendation Medals) for valor, but I managed to find an excuse to miss the awards ceremony. Public displays like that always scared the hell out of me.

The rest of September, October and into November was a busy time.

We were strictly Blues by then, and they kept us busy securing downed choppers, reconning bunker complexes and running day and night ambush patrols. On Thanksgiving day, we were at Phuoc Vinh when Staff Sergeant Miller gave us the good news that Charlie Troop scouts had spotted gooks in another bunker complex. Sergeant Miller was in command this time, and I was one of his team leaders. It had rained for days, and it looked like we were going to get wet again.

We were able to jump off the slicks this time, instead of rappelling, but it was an eight- to ten-foot drop to what appeared to be solid ground. I landed in soupy mud up to my knees. It took us half an hour of slogging through that swamp to get to the bunkers. A lone sniper potted at us with an SKS rifle until we managed to flank him. A Blue killed him with a hand grenade. His black pajamas indicated that he was a Viet Cong who had been left behind as a rear guard.

A QRF was sent out to join us in that miserable place. We spent the night trying to sleep in water up to our necks as the wind howled and the rain came down in torrents. It was an awful night. Blues traveled light, so we had no food or bedding with us. We were mighty hungry by the time we got back to a late Thanksgiving dinner that evening.

I went on my last mission on 29 November 1970. I was short by then and didn't have to go to the field. I had quit school in the seventh grade and was studying for my high school GED (Graduate Equivalent Diploma), but the platoon was short-handed, and I asked the lieutenant to let me postpone the last exam and hump a radio for him on the mission.

We landed on a sunny morning to conduct a recon of a bunker complex on the edge of the Song Be River, about forty miles from Bien Hoa. It was empty. We were using inflatable rubber boats, and the scouts reported activity downriver in another complex. The lieutenant left Sergeant Miller with a team to guard the boats and a detachment of engineers, and took fourteen of us on our second air assault of the day.

We jumped into a 500-pound bomb crater on the edge of the river, and set up a tight perimeter around it, then they hit us from the jungle with B-40 rockets. We had gooks on three sides of us and the river to our backs, and already, two of us were wounded. We pulled back to the water, and gunships made minigun and rocket runs along our front. The NVA stopped shooting for a while, but we still had to get the wounded men out, so the lieutenant decided to follow a trail along the river. He planned to evacuate the wounded from the trail, go back to the bomb crater where we could be extracted, pound the place with air strikes and artillery, and then go back in and rout out whoever was left. It didn't happen that way. The gooks opened up again, and now we crawled along the trail. We set up a line with our backs to the water and fired back at them with everything we had.

The lieutenant wanted to make a report to the high bird, and I had to raise up and reach over John Hamm to hand him the radio handset. I emptied my magazine at a muzzle flash and reached out with the handset just as a gook came out of nowhere with an RPG. I couldn't reload in time and knew that I was a dead man.

The rocket exploded against a tree right in front of us. It felt like a giant hand picked me up and threw me clean over John Hamm and into the bushes next to the lieutenant. I was hit in twelve places. Two other men were wounded by the rocket, but the lieutenant didn't get a scratch. Eleven men out of fifteen were wounded out there, and we got only one confirmed NVA kill. It was not a good day for Echo Recon.

I was treated and returned to duty, then left the troop for good on 16 December. I was discharged seven days later, and arrived home at two o'clock on Christmas morning, finally a civilian. I received a letter from John Hamm dated 31 March 1971. It stated, ''As of today, Delta Troop is no more! The Cav is going home. Only the 3rd Brigade is staying, but the other two brigades have been disbanded and only a small color guard will take the colors back to Fort Hood. The lieutenant says, 'Hi!' I guess we'll go have another beer.'' I got to take my last GED test a month later. I got a Good Conduct Medal seventeen years later, in April 1988.

29. LAST FLIGHTS OVER CAMBODIA

(Scout Gunner, Alpha Troop, 1970–71)

*Specialist **Mike Williams** tells the story of the 9th Cav's later operations in Cambodia while the ARVN advanced into Laos farther north. As has so often been said, the air crews maintained their morale and fought aggressive actions until the last days of the Second Indochina War. This story is an example.*

In February 1971, while many divisions in Vietnam were winding down, the ARVN forces were preparing for major pushes into Laos and Cambodia with U.S. air support. The Laotian operation was widely covered, and overshadowed the actions going on in Cambodia, but there were some exciting times going down in that "neutral" country, and the scouts were in the middle of it.

A Troop, 1/9th Cav, was assigned with other air cav troops to support the ARVN 5th Infantry Division, and we were placed under their operational control. All well and good, except for one small item. Because of the political nature of the war, no American ground combat forces could be utilized in Cambodia.

I still have a cartoon in one of my scrapbooks depicting a general telling a senator, "Oh, those aren't combat troops, Senator. They're only fliers." The general is pointing to a flight of aircraft in battle over the jungles. For the men in helicopters in our troop, this meant that we couldn't rely on the Blues to save our young asses if we got shot down over the Red Line. The scout crews were not overjoyed at the prospect of trusting their lives to the assigned ARVN reaction forces. The Blues weren't exactly thrilled about the situation either, for it effectively took them out of the action, and relegated them to the more mundane tasks of base security and details.

At any rate, we were committed, and we hit Cambodia to do what scouts were supposed to do—find the enemy. We found the enemy. In fact, they made it pretty easy for us. The units we went up against were NVA regulars in up to regimental strength, and they weren't at all bashful about shooting up our scouts, and then dueling it out with the Cobra gunships that covered us.

I had been flying with the scout platoon full time for only a few weeks when we started losing ships on a regular basis. One was shot down northeast of Snoul, Cambodia, by a .51 caliber on 7 March. All three crew members were wounded. Another Loach was shot down over a bunker complex northeast of Snoul on 10 March, this time with one KIA and two MIAs. One of the MIAs, Warrant Officer-1 Houser, made it to an ARVN firebase after walking east through the jungle for three days, past NVA camps and rice caches. Then came my turn.

We lifted off from our forward staging area at Loc Ninh and headed almost due north across the border, accompanied by three Cobra gunships. Three seemed like a good number to try to keep the little people off of us in case anything happened. Our search area was northeast of Snoul, in the general direction of the 10 March shootdown. One of our missing had returned, and there was still a slim hope for the other man. Of course, the whole area was crawling with little people.

Piloting our ship was Warrant Officer-2 Long, an experienced pilot who had been shot down several times before. Crazy as could be, but a hell of a great pilot. The gunner, or "torque" in scout jargon, was Michael Anderson, a relative old-timer in the scout platoon. I was flying in the Oscar, or observer slot, left front seat, next to the pilot. My job was to cover the left side of the ship with my rifle and toss a red smoke grenade if we made contact, thus giving the Cobras a general target. I was also trained to fly the ship if the pilot was hit.

Knowing that our chances of contact were about 100 percent, I had elected to carry two rifles—my assigned M-16 and my nonregulation AK-47, the folding stock variety. At the time, my idea was to be able to empty one magazine, drop the gun in my lap, pick up the other one and empty it—fifty rounds without changing magazines. It sounded fine in theory, but proved to be embarrassing in its consequences.

Upon reaching our search area, we dropped down to treetop level and began our sweep with the three guardian angels taking their orbit several thousand feet above us. After fifteen minutes of low and slow cruising, we skirted the edge of a large clearing where all hell suddenly broke loose. Heavy machine-gun bullets and small arms fire ripped through the ship from more positions than I had time to count. The noise was incredible, even above the engine racket, and it was unrelenting. I knew that we were in deep stuff.

Mr. Long tried to give us a burst of speed to clear the area, but the engine got shot to hell, and the radios were blasted out before he could squeeze out a "Taking fire!" message. The gunships didn't need a radio call, anyway. The fuel cells were ruptured in the first few seconds and the entire aft section of the ship turned into an inferno. One of the Cobra pilots told us later that when he saw the ship fireball in the air, he figured we were all dead. My thoughts at the time were running along similar lines. I was not a particularly religious person, but as Father Cummings had said at Bataan, "There are no atheists in foxholes." I remember saying to myself, "Oh, God, don't let us go down here."

I thought that those were my last seconds of life. Anderson was standing out on the skids, as far forward as he could get, screaming and still shooting his M-60 with one hand for the few seconds before he lost his grip on it. His flame-retardent Nomex flight uniform was burning, melting onto his body, the flames fanned by the rushing air. Mr. Long was struggling with the ship, trying to convert our forward motion into a little lift to get us over a narrow band of trees and into the next clearing.

I had dropped my red smoke as soon as the shooting started, emptied my M-16, and was already in the process of expending the magazine in the AK when the instrument panel between the pilot and myself was riddled by bullets from soldiers almost directly beneath us. Neither of us was even scratched. At this point, probably only five or six seconds had passed since the shooting had started, but it seemed like we were suspended in the air forever. Too much time to think.

I thought that I was going to take a bullet; I thought we were going to explode in mid-air, or even worse, be roasted alive before the ship could make it to the ground. Even now, eighteen years later, I get a rush from reliving this.

Everything seemed to be rolling in slow motion, exaggerated time, as the ship just cleared the stand of trees and I finished the thirty-rounder in the AK. Gunfire continued to follow us, but I suspect that most of it had been diverted to engage the Cobras as they rolled in. One of the Loach pilots from an earlier shootdown had been injured on impact, because his Oscar forgot to lock down his seat belt. That item had impressed me. I reached across, locked down Mr. Long's seat belt, then locked my own belt and braced for the crash.

I can't remember the impact. One moment we were falling, and the next we were on the ground. The skids had buckled, the ship was sitting on its belly, burning fiercely, blades still staggering around. I was on the ground. Anderson had rolled away from the ship while trying to smother his flaming uniform. Mr. Long was struggling to get out of his seat, and didn't seem to realize that I had locked him in. I got up far enough to unlock him, and he got the hell out of the ship. He made sure that Anderson was okay, and they both took off for a treeline that was the farthest away from where we had just come.

I dropped back down on the ground for a moment, laid my hand on a rifle, felt for a magazine with the other hand, found a heavy one, presumably full, and started one of the fastest sprints of my life. Halfway to the treeline, I tripped on something and went sprawling face first into the ground, hoping that I hadn't been shot in the back and just couldn't feel it yet.

Anderson, burned and bleeding, must have heard me go down, because he turned around to come back and get me. That still impresses me. I waved him off, and at that moment, lying there in the middle of the clearing, I realized something. In one hand I held my M-16, and in the other hand was an AK-47 magazine.

I can see some vet reading this right now and saying something like, "How could anyone, even by touch, mistake a heavy thirty-round AK magazine for an M-16 twenty-rounder?" Beats the hell out of me. I wasn't exactly a rookie—twenty-one months in Nam at that point. Maybe it was blind fear. At any rate, I realized that no amount of determination was going to make that M-16 shoot AK ammunition. I glanced back at the helicopter with the idea of running back to salvage some ammunition, but that thought was short-lived. As I watched, a series of explosions went off, walking across the clearing and right into what was left of the burning ship.

I scrambled up and followed my companions who were disappearing into the edge of the treeline. We stumbled into a collection of old fighting positions. Mr. Long got me under control, and we took a quick inventory of our resources. Long was delighted to see that I still had my rifle, but not so happy when, with much embarrassment, I showed him the AK clip. Fortunately, it only cost me a little pride, and not any of our lives. We had our various handguns, a couple of knives, one red smoke grenade, two flight helmets, and one M-16A1 club. This was not real encouraging, since we knew that there was a large force of enemy soldiers less than a few hundred meters from us. And they had bullets for their guns.

Anderson had to be in a lot of pain, but he didn't show it. Mr. Long was uninjured, and my most serious wound of the war was a skinned knee from when I had tripped. I stood guard in one of the old fighting positions while Mr. Long took care of Anderson's wounds as best he could. Our gunner was severely burned on the legs and back, and there was a sizable chunk of flesh missing from one of his upper arms. When the medical care was done, we just sat there—watching, listening, waiting.

The Cobras were still working out over the first clearing, and believe me, that was a comforting sight. Having those three gunships there probably saved our lives by keeping the NVA too busy to get to us. I don't know what thoughts were going through the other men's heads, but I still wasn't sure that we were going to make it. I just knew that there had to be hundreds of NVA slipping toward us, and I was wrestling with the idea of saving that last bullet for myself. It sounds rather melodramatic now, but it didn't back then. The idea of getting captured and tortured to death was a very definite and unpleasant possibility.

It seemed like we were on the ground forever, but it was actually less than ten minutes before we heard the sound of a C&C (Command and Control) chopper dropping in. What a sight! For reasons I have never heard, the command ship zipped in and sat down out near the middle of the clearing, giving us an opportunity to practice our Olympic sprinting once again. All the way to the rescue ship, my biggest fear was that some little guy was going to step out of the treeline and back-shoot me before I could get there. That did happen to one of our Cobra pilots in the same area three days later.

We launched ourselves into the ship, and I swear that I have never been on a slower moving helicopter in my life. I could still hear enemy gunfire as we gained altitude, and I was yelling at the crew chief to fire, but he didn't. When we finally touched ground again at Loc Ninh, our crew made the rounds, gratefully thanking the pilots and crew that had pulled us out of that small spot in Cambodia. We were reunited with the other members of the Scout Platoon, and the three of us posed for a picture before Anderson was hustled back to the rear. He was eventually medevaced out to a burn unit in Japan. I wish that I could find the guy that took the picture.

There were other casualties that day. I lost my AK, my movie camera, and my black Stetson, all gone up in flames.

Mr. Long was awarded the DFC for his actions. If I had been with a less experienced pilot, we probably all would have died that day. Michael Anderson, for his efforts, was awarded the Purple Heart, and I believe, the Silver Star. As for me . . . in a different war or a different army, I'd have probably been court-martialed or at least reprimanded for the rifle foul-up. But this was at the end of an unpopular war. The U.S. Army gave me a DFC for heroism. It was one crazy war.

When the 1st Cav went on stand-down in April 1971, the 1/9th was reassigned to the 1st Aviation Brigade to continue our operations in Cambodia. No disrespect is meant to the good men of the 1st Aviation Brigade, but none of us took very kindly to replacing our Cav patches, and we didn't do it for quite a while.

Alpha Troop continued operations in Cambodia until 19 May 1971. On that day, we flew our last combat missions of the Vietnam-Cambodia War. I was on a scout mission that last day, and it was a strange feeling, knowing that all you had to do was survive that flight, and your part in the war was over. The following day, we started getting our materials ready for turnover to the ARVNs.

I spent twenty-four months in Vietnam, but the months that I flew in Cambodia with the Apache Scouts were the most exciting time of my life. I experienced the highs of violence, pride, sorrow and rage, and I would not trade away those memories for anything else that I have yet experienced.

A FINAL WORD: DECISIONS

This book is filled with combat stories, but sometimes, combat is best avoided. Wise men know when the cavalry should not be sent. This short section tells about a few decisions not to commit the aero-rifle platoons. Most importantly, some of those judgments involved the two Bravo Troop commanders to whom this book is dedicated.

Matt Brennan

Some dangerous missions were avoided through a mixture of common sense and compassion. On one of the first recon missions along the coast north of Chu Lai in November 1967, a Pink Team (one OH-13 and one Huey gunship) spotted a column of NVA on the beach. The scout gunner killed thirteen of them. The troop commander, Major George Burrow, wanted to send the Blues to collect weapons and papers, but first he sent another Pink Team to investigate. The two Pink Teams passed each other in the air, one coming back to our base to refuel, and the other heading toward the coast. There was a period of about five minutes when the sky above the bodies was empty. When the second Pink Team arrived, there were only dark bloodstains in the sand and drag paths leading into the hedgerows and palm trees. The commander didn't send the Blues.

The Cav moved down to the area northwest of Saigon in late 1968. On one of the first recon missions in that area, a Pink Team (now one LOH and one Cobra) spotted a column of Viet Cong on a trail at the edge of a rubber plantation. The scout gunner killed eight VC in black pajamas, armed with US carbines. Again, a troop commander was ready to send the Blues to investigate. Again, another Pink Team was dispatched to check the area. The first Pink Team ran low on fuel, the sky above the bodies was left empty for a few minutes, and the two teams passed each other in mid-air. When the second Pink Team arrived, the bodies were gone. In another time, at another place, other men debated the same type of situation and reached the same conclusion. If bodies could disappear that quickly, there were a lot more than eight people around. The Blues were not sent there.

On another early recon flight northwest of Saigon, a Pink Team found a group of males, military age, trying to hide in a small village north of Loc Ninh. The Blues were scrambled for a mission. It was aborted in mid-air after it was decided that a larger force of armored personnel carriers and Cav grunts should sweep the area. Whoever made the decision probably kept Bravo Blues from being badly hurt. The larger force killed fifty-eight NVA and captured machine guns, recoilless rifles and a mortar. These last two incidents convinced the commanders that the aero-rifle platoon should be used with caution in the new AO. Landings over the next six months were restricted to short recons and rescue operations for downed aircraft crewmen.

I was young and stupid then, and wanted more action, but my commander through most of this time, Major Frank Stewart, undoubtedly saved a lot of lives because he cared enough to use us wisely.

Contributors to *Hunter-Killer Squadron*

Name	Home Town	Current Home
R. B. Alexander	Newport Beach, California	San Clemente, California
Ed Beal	Greensboro, North Carolina	Greensboro, North Carolina
David Bray	Ukiah, California	Sacramento, California
Lloyd J. Brockney	Willsboro, New York	Willsboro, New York
Larry G. Brown	Battle Ground, Washington	McMinnville, Oregon
George Burrow	Port Arthur, Texas	San Antonio, Texas
Ron Chapman	Columbus, Ohio	Fort Lauderdale, Florida
Rick Chesson	Pacifica, California	Louisville, Kentucky
Stephen E. Douglas	Long Beach, California	Richmond, Utah
Jack H. Fischer	Glenwood Springs, Colorado	Carbondale, Colorado
William C. (Bill) Frazer	Galveston, Texas	Weatherford, Texas
Robert Hillerby	Amarillo, Texas	Norman, Oklahoma
Charles Hooten	La Grange, Georgia	Jackson, Georgia
Richard Jenkins	Sebago Lake, Maine	Sebago Lake, Maine
Joseph R. Kelbus	Chicago, Illinois	Orland Park, Illinois
Mike Kelley	East Cambridge, Massachusetts	Wilmington, Massachusetts
Robert D. Lackey	Santa Monica, California	Santa Rosa, California
William R. Neuman	Tracy, California	Manteca, California
Bob Parker	Cottonwood, California	Elk Grove, California
Louis J. Rochat III	San Saba, Texas	San Antonio, Texas
Joe Salamone	Miami, Florida	New Smyrna Beach, Florida
Robert W. Sisk	East Peoria, Illinois	Emmett, Idaho
Daniel E. Wardzala	Chicago, Illinois	Chicago, Illinois
John F. Wiegert, Jr.	Kingston, New York	Monroe, New York
Michael G. Williams	Enid, Oklahoma	Pine, Arizona
Steve Yarnell	Loogootee, Indiana	Columbus, Georgia
Terry Young	Corning, New York	Leesburg, Virginia
Randy R. Zahn	Sunland, California	Kintore, Scotland